# Populism and Time

# Populism and Time

Temporalities of a Disruptive Politics

*Edited by*
Andy Knott

EDINBURGH
University Press

Edinburgh University Press is one of the leading university presses in the UK. We publish academic books and journals in our selected subject areas across the humanities and social sciences, combining cutting-edge scholarship with high editorial and production values to produce academic works of lasting importance. For more information visit our website: edinburghuniversitypress.com

© editorial matter and organisation Andy Knott, 2024
© the chapters their several authors, 2024

Edinburgh University Press Ltd
13 Infirmary Street
Edinburgh EH1 1LT

Typeset in 10.5/13pt Bembo
by Cheshire Typesetting Ltd, Cuddington, Cheshire, and
printed and bound in Great Britain

A CIP record for this book is available from the British Library

ISBN 978 1 3995 2772 9 (hardback)
ISBN 978 1 3995 2774 3 (webready PDF)
ISBN 978 1 3995 2775 0 (epub)

The right of Andy Knott to be identified as the editor of this work has been asserted in accordance with the Copyright, Designs and Patents Act 1988, and the Copyright and Related Rights Regulations 2003 (SI No. 2498).

# Contents

Notes on Contributors     vii
Acknowledgements     ix

1. Introduction: Populism, Metaphor, Temporality     1
   *Andy Knott*

## Part I Populism, Politics, History

2. On Populism's Beginnings     27
   *Andy Knott*

3. Populism, Impossible Time and Democracy's People Problem     52
   *Clare Woodford*

4. Politics and Time: The Nostalgic, the Opportunist and the Utopian. An Existential Analytic of Podemos' Ecstatic Times     75
   *Adrià Porta Caballé*

## Part II Populism and Technology

5. Populisation: Populism – Temporary Dysfunction or Modernity's Revenge?     107
   *Simon Tormey*

6. Populism and the Mirror of Technology     126
   *Michaelangelo Anastasiou*

7. Populism, Social Media and the Technospheric     148
   *Jamie Ranger*

## Part III Populism and Time in Latin America

8. Antagonism, Flexibility and the Surprising Resilience of
   Populism in Latin America      169
   *María Esperanza Casullo*

9. Rupture, Institutionalisation and Tension: About Populist
   Temporality in Latin America      188
   *Paula Biglieri and Gloria Perelló*

10. Populism and Constitutionalism in Brazil: An Enduring or
    Transitional Relationship in Time?      207
    *Eleonora Mesquita Ceia*

11. Conclusion: Time for More? Populism's Prospects      235
    *Andy Knott*

Index      249

# Notes on Contributors

**Michaelangelo Anastasiou** is a research associate at the Digital Transitions & Society research initiative, at the University of Nicosia, Cyprus. He specialises in studies of nationalism, democracy and technology, being principally interested in how sociopolitical configurations are implicated in the constitution of power relations, hegemonic regimes and processes of (de)democratisation. His recent book, *Nationalism and hegemony: The Consolidation of the Nation in Social and Political Life*, develops a post-foundational theory of nationalism, which examines the complex interplay between historical structures, modern technology and the hegemonic consolidation of 'the nation'.

**Paula Biglieri** holds a PhD degree from the National University of Mexico and has been a Fulbright scholar at Northwestern University. She is a researcher at the National Scientific and Technical Research Board in Argentina and is also in charge of the Cátedra Libre Ernesto Laclau, at the Faculty of Philosophy and Letters of the University of Buenos Aires.

**María Esperanza Casullo** is a researcher at CONICET and Professor at the National University of Rio Negro in Argentina, where she directs the Center for Studies on the Penal System and Human Rights. She studies the relationship between populism and democracy, Latin American parties, and the impact of women's leadership on political movements. Her most recent published article was 'The populist body in the age of social media: a comparative study of populist and non-populist representation' in *Thesis Eleven* (co-authored with Rodolfo Colalongo).

**Andy Knott** is Senior Lecturer at the Centre for Applied Philosophy Politics & Ethics (CAPPE) at the University of Brighton. He has edited several books and special issues of journals on populism and his current work includes rethinking left and right in contemporary politics (with Bristol University Press).

**Eleonora Mesquita Ceia** is Professor of State Theory at the Federal University of Rio de Janeiro, Brazil. She holds a PhD in Law from Saarland University, Germany and an LLM in European Integration from the Europa-Institut of Saarland University. Her research interests include populism, democracy, transitional justice and contemporary legal theories.

**Gloria Perelló** has a PhD in psychology from the University of Buenos Aires. She is a psychoanalyst and Professor-Researcher at the Instituto Interdisciplinario de Estudios e Investigaciones de América Latina (INDEAL), and Co-director of the Cátedra Libre Ernesto Laclau, Facultad de Filosofía y Letras, UBA. She is a professor within the Faculty of Psychology, UBA and the National University of Moreno (UNM).

**Adrià Porta Caballé** studied for a BA in Philosophy, Politics and Economics at the University of Essex, where he specialised in the theory of hegemony and populism in the School of Ideology and Discourse Analysis. He achieved a scholarship from La Caixa Foundation to study an MA in Philosophy with a focus in psychoanalysis at the New School for Social Research in New York. He also holds a postgraduate qualification in the 'Analysis of Capitalism and Transformative Policies' from the Universitat Autònoma de Barcelona, and he has carried out a research stay at the Université Paris 8 Vincennes – Saint-Denis. Currently, he works as a predoctoral researcher in the Faculty of Philosophy at the University of Barcelona, where he is a member of the research project on 'Post-foundational Contemporary Philosophy'. His most recent publication is 'The deconstructive effects of combining discourses. A case study: Marxism and psychoanalysis' in *Psychoanalysis, Culture and Society*, 28 (2003), pp. 411–429.

**Jamie Ranger** is a political theorist interested in radical democratic theory, political ontology, the philosophy of technology, and the politics of memory. He holds a DPhil in Politics (Political Theory) from the University of Oxford.

**Simon Tormey** is Professor of Politics at Deakin University Melbourne. He is the author of numerous books and articles including most recently *Populism: a beginners guide*, published with Oneworld in 2019.

**Clare Woodford** is Principal Lecturer in Philosophy and Politics in the Centre for Applied Philosophy, Politics, and Ethics (CAPPE) at the University of Brighton, UK.

# Acknowledgements

Thank you to *ProtoSociology* for allowing us to reprint an article that originally featured in that journal by Simon Tormey, entitled 'No going back? Late modernity and the populisation of politics', *ProtoSociology*, 37 (2020), pp. 77–98. The version included in this collection is slightly amended and goes by the title 'Populisation: populism – temporary dysfunction, or modernity's revenge?'.

    This edited collection has been long in the making. Most of all I'd like to thank the contributors to this collection, who have developed some absorbing ideas in connecting populism with time. They have also been patient with my time and suggestions which is what any editor wants of such a process. Publishers are key to considering, guiding, pulling together and, finally, publishing books, and Edinburgh University Press has been particularly helpful and patient in bringing this to collection, so thank you to Ersev Ersoy, Beatriz Lopez, Sam Johnson and Sarah Foyle for making this go smoothly and for the advice given.

    This collection emerged out of an idea for a workshop which eventually took place online during lockdown, in which the keynote speakers were María Esperanza Casullo and Simon Tormey – both of whom have contributed chapters to this collection. This was just one of many workshops I've had the pleasure to organise for the Populism Specialist Group of the Political Studies Association in the UK. Thanks especially to the co-founders Emmy Eklundh and Yannis Stavrakakis, and to the subsequent convenors that I've collaborated with: Giorgos Katsambekis, Marina Prentoulis, Giorgos Venizelos, Alen Toplisek, Thomás Zicman de Barros and Théo Aiolfi. Thomás and Théo have now taken over the reins, alongside Lone Sorensen, George Newth and Juan Roch Gonzalez. Thanks also for the myriad of other contributors who have made this Specialist Group such a buoyant, inspiring academic platform; it is the workshops of the Populism Specialist Group and the annual conferences of the Political Studies Association over the past seven years that have prompted the majority of the chapters in this collection.

Finally, and on a personal note, thanks to Jean whose time unfortunately came too quick, to Ken who is still going strong as I type, but especially to Jane and Elliott who lighten the load, provide welcome distractions, and help things along.

# 1

# Introduction: Populism, Metaphor, Temporality

*Andy Knott*

While talk about populism very much defines our political present, analyses that explore the connections between populism and time have been absent. This is in stark contrast to the prevalence of spatial considerations of populism. The prominence of spatiality in populism studies is driven by numerous factors, including the centrality of geographical comparison between different nations or even continents. The import of space to populism reflects, in turn, the way politics itself is studied, wherein international relations and – even more relevant on this topic – comparative politics are widely considered as two of the three branches of the discipline. A further factor has contributed to this focus on space, and that is the academic and wider political attention bestowed upon globalisation and other post-national developments in recent decades. This has prompted Moffitt (2016), for instance, to outline 'the global rise' of populism, and other contributors to invoke the globality of populism in the new millennium (Ostiguy, Panizza & Moffitt, 2021; De La Torre, 2015, 2019), while those who consider populism at the continental level are long established (De La Torre, 2010; De La Torre & Arnson, 2013; Mudde, 2007). A focus on space, in short, is firmly consolidated within the study of populism.

The same cannot be said for time, on the other hand.[1] And the purpose of this volume is to establish a foundation through which the relationship of populism and time can be considered. This is as much to lay out this ground such that a better understanding of populism can emerge – and 'what is populism?' remains one of the most heavily contested questions in politics. Bringing time into the equation can provide a different lens through which to consider populism, and its broader impact on politics. A wager behind this collection is that the encounter it stages between populism and time can yield consolidations, improvements and realignments in understandings on the thorny issue of populism. In laying out analyses that bring populism and time together, further critical frameworks can emerge, as understandings of the phenomenon shift or become clarified – which are better able to incorporate populist practice taking new and potentially unexpected turns.

When confronted with the question of how to connect populism to time, the first response would be to turn to history. While this collection features political history, the contributions to it are far more wide-ranging and interdisciplinary, bringing philosophies, theoretical frameworks and contemporary political approaches to the table, while by no means neglecting the discipline of history. Such an inter-, multi- and transdisciplinary frame can facilitate the interrogation of populism – and to probe deeply into what several commentators have characterised as its 'ontology'. An ontological analysis explores not only the 'what is' question, but also why it is that populism is such a prominent feature of our political lives in the early twenty-first century, while additionally enquiring how its emergence is generated. To speak of populism's *emergence* is already to position it within a temporal frame. It suggests that populism wasn't a feature of political life prior to its emergence, while also prompting speculation about its persistence: is it now a permanent feature of politics in the twenty-first century, something that we all are going to have to get used to?

In order to investigate the relationship between populism and time, this introductory chapter now proceeds in three parts. The first section surveys the metaphors that are linked to populism, in order to delve into the temporalities these metaphors suggest. This is an entry point into the populism-time relation, which also teases out the way these metaphors align with different geographies and histories of populism. The second section is denser, and explores three different configurations of the philosophy of time and their linkage to an understanding of politics that have been proposed at very different moments of 'modernity': Machiavelli's proposal for a modern approach to political temporality; the linkage offered between ontology and temporality by Heidegger that has provoked further critical enquiry into being and time; and, finally, the recent account offered by Jacques Rancière that disrupts the political-time continuity. These three different accounts are introduced with the aim of aligning their understandings to the theme of populism, and politics more generally. The third and final section outlines this collection, highlighting the manner in which the contributors have alighted on different component parts of temporality in order to address recent developments in populism and its analysis.

## 1. Populism and its Metaphors

During the second half of the twentieth century, analyses of populism – particularly of Latin American populism – were inserted into a rigid totalising framework, ultimately guided by teleology. This is most pronounced in those modernisation and developmental accounts (Di Tella, 1965; Germani, 1978) that viewed populism as a temporary aberration prompted by anomalies within these frameworks that would be overcome once the ineluctable processes associated with modernisation and developmentalism play out. Populism, in short, was a fleeting phenomenon and, due to its transience, would be swiftly superseded once the logic of the totality reaffirms itself and restores modernisation and development on its rightful track.

Over the past half-century, it is these totalising frames of modernisation and developmentalism, rather than populism itself, that have been increasingly sidelined. Populism's persistence, on the other hand, has prompted a multiplicity of metaphors to account for its appearances. These metaphors are invariably linked with the question of time so, accordingly, this section introduces and briefly examines the underlying assumptions and implications of the temporality of these metaphors – and analyses them in conjunction with examples of populism across several continents, using the twenty-first century experience as a primary guide, but also delving back further into the history of populism.

Populism's most widely deployed temporal metaphor is the tidal. It has been further qualified with a colour, as 'the pink tide' sought to capture a series of developments across the South American continent at the turn of the millennium. The pink blush was invoked to capture a new form of leftist politics, paler than its twentieth-century comparators, and the pink tide was used alongside 'left turn' and even 'socialism for the twenty-first century'. These developments were, and continue to be, aligned with populism, and the tidal metaphor sought to express a new configuration of populist politics, that differs from both its alternatives and its predecessors. Within the literature on populism, a growing practice has been to periodise Latin American populism into three phrases – or tides. The classical mid-century period of Perón, Vargas, et al. constitutes the first, whereas the century's closing decades ushered in the second tide of neoliberal populism or what became known as 'neopopulism' (Weyland, 1996). Military and other dictatorial regimes across the continent invariably separated these first two phrases. The interlude between neopopulism and the pink tide was far more truncated, as the latter was as much a response to the former. The Washington Consensus and its Structural Adjustment Programmes led to increased poverty, widening inequality and frustrated expectations in the longer term, which combined with more turn-of-the-millennium developments such as spiralling inflation, currency crashes and an economic downturn. These led to popular mobilisations and opened the space for new political projects and politicians to emerge. This manifested in multiple countries across the continent and this pink tide resulting in new left populists entering office, with many remaining for protracted periods.

The tidal metaphor in other words clearly conveys a transition from one mode of politics to another. Yet it symbolises further elements, most prominently those of cyclicality and repetition. The cyclicality implies peaks – high tides – and troughs which, when applied to populism, intimates an ebb and flow, its appearance and disappearance. It creates the impression of populism alternating with other political forms, and the metaphor itself points towards a repetition of this cycle such that populism becomes a permanent feature of politics. This illustrates a distinct contrast between the permanence, repetition and cyclicality of the tidal metaphor, on the one hand, and the earlier presentation of populism as an abrupt yet impermanent aberration within the totalising teleologically informed frame, on the other.

The final feature of the tidal metaphor worth highlighting is its placidity: this is an ongoing natural process that is manageable. The serenity of the tidal metaphor draws a helpful contrast with another nautical metaphor aligned with populism. A wave's disruptive power invokes unruly and damaging connotations, and the contrast recalls a distant echo of earlier debates between reform and revolution. The wave metaphor conveys both irregularity and impressive force, and its association with populism has been applied to developments in European politics over the past decade (Aslanidis, 2017; Bale & Rovira Kaltwasser, 2021), and even aligned with the impetuous politics of youth (Foa & Mounk, 2019). This application to Europe in recent decades is illustrative of the novelty or at least rarity of deployment of the signifier 'populism' to account for developments in European politics. While the notion of 'the populist hype' (Glynos & Mondon, 2016; De Cleen, Glynos & Mondon, 2018) was developed to account for the imprecision, hysteria and overuse of the signifier populism in contemporary Europe, the reverse is the case for twentieth-century Europe. Then, instead of hype, there was silence about populism, when numerous political phenomena warranted the signifier populism. The absence of an entry for Western Europe in the landmark collection from Ionescu and Gellner (1969) speaks volumes of this populist silence. After such a prolonged preclusion, the intensity of the hype surrounding the 'wave' of twenty-first-century European populism becomes that much more pronounced. The wave metaphor speaks of the unexpectedness, surprise, horror and novelty of the appearance of populism on the twenty-first-century political stage, alongside the disorientation it has generated. It engulfs in its untamed wildness, destroying and reshaping all that lies in its wake – and it is this frightening power that has provoked such a hostile response.

Similar imagery flows once we shift to the terrestrial metaphor of eruption. The eruption of populism conveys a terrifying natural power that is occasional, often unexpected, sudden, impactful, at once capable of reconfiguring the landscape and leaving enduring effects. Eruptions are conceived as highly irregular, such as once-in-a-century events that are sandwiched by protracted periods of calm and normality. It's somewhat surprising then that the eruption metaphor has been recently applied to describe populisms across multiple continents. As just indicated, Europe's experience of populism – or at least the talk or 'hype' about populism – is a recent one. While there is the impression that it exploded onto the European stage during the 2010s with Brexit as its exemplar, multiple analyses have tracked a slow-burn incremental rise of right-wing populism stretching back at least until the 1990s (Betz, 1994; Mudde, 2007; Taggart, 2000; Ford & Goodwin, 2014) if not further back to Jean-Marie Le Pen and the formation of the National Front in 1972. European populism's left variants have proved more impactful this millennium following on from 2008, particularly the movement of the squares that began with Occupy. The Greek and Spanish iterations led to left-populisms heading an administration through Syriza, while Podemos went on to enter government as a junior partner. The persistence of Latin American populism from the post-war period and intensifying during the twenty-first century, by contrast, problematises even the widely deployed tide metaphor. The ongoing persistence and resilience of populism on this continent call into question the recurrence and cyclicality intimated by the tide metaphor; instead, a permanent presence seems more apt. Such permanence jars more starkly with the irregularity invoked by the eruption metaphor. While the US experience with populism is more contested (Frank, 2020; Hofstadter, 1955, 2008; Judis, 2016; Kazin, 1998), Donald Trump's recent impact on its politics provoked scholars to deploy the eruption metaphor (Roberts, 2018; Lee, 2020).

The etymological root of volcano springs from Vulcan, the Roman god of fire, and volcanic is a frequent metaphor deployed to fiery characters but, perhaps more importantly, is also widely aligned with anger. Populism's association with emotions is well-established within the literature (Eklundh, 2019) and anger frequently features as its principal emotional trait. Populism emerges when such anger is widespread and deeply felt such that alternatives are sought. Anger and emotionality highlight the anthropomorphism of (most) populisms and, at the same time, underscore the metaphorical status of the terms under consideration: metaphors jar with literality, and their operation entails the transfer from one realm to another. Natural metaphors have been explored thus far, and we now train attention on those metaphors where human agency is more evident.

The metaphor of eruption shares many resemblances with that of explosion, save for the human element. It is sufficiently prominent for it to be deployed to analyses of populism as a phenomenon, but also to the literature on populism. Dynamite is deployed to detonate a kinetic explosion, which invites the question: If populism has exploded if not globally, at least across several continents, then what has served the role of dynamite? This is to invoke the causal question, but it also calls attention to a host of temporal questions: Why now? What is it about our conjuncture that has led to the populist explosion? What lasting effects will it leave behind? What happens after the populist explosion? And what impact does the explosion have on populism itself? Does it kill or sustain?

Suggestions of alchemy also feature in the final metaphor. Populism has not just risen here and there, its rise has been global (Moffitt, 2016). This metaphor suggests the transformational process prompted by the action of yeast on the combination of flour and water to produce a staple of widespread popularity. What is the active ingredient in politics to produce populism? Moffitt suggests that populism has two 'stages' that serve such a role: crisis and the media.

What unifies this array of metaphors is to suggest that populism is a dynamic, diachronic political phenomenon. This dynamism poses a challenge to, and is disruptive of, political stability. The instability and motion these metaphors align with populism are heavily suggestive of the distinctive backdrop within which populism operates. In terms of economics, issues such as growth, stability and security ward off the populist challenge, while their antonyms – recession, instability, insecurity – provide that alchemy for populism's rise. Profound shifts in the communicational landscape, in the operation and efficacy of political institutionality, and in the cultural spheres – all offer fertile ground for the populist challenge to assert itself.

## 2. Time, Politics, Philosophies, Theories

Analyses combining time and populism have been under-theorised, and the argument of this collection and chapter is that their connection can enrich and open up understandings of the contested notion of populism. The absence of this combination is all the more surprising given that the notion of time has increasingly been brought to bear on evaluations of politics and its trajectories.[2] This section accordingly engages with the way in which time has been conceptualised in continental philosophy and political theory, before linking these philosophies of time with populism. Focus here will turn to Martin Heidegger, Jacques Rancière and Niccolò Machiavelli.

One of the most influential books in twentieth-century philosophy is *Being and Time*, which has generated the 'ontological turn' while raising the profile of the question of temporality. Heidegger's core focus in this text is a deep enquiry into the notion of being, something he regarded to have been neglected by the Western philosophical tradition. As the title suggests, however, any enquiry into being inevitably leads on to the question of time. Heidegger's meditation involves the interrogation of being and, in doing so, generates multiple distinctions. Arguably the most important is the distinction between *Sein* and *Dasein* – Being in general (*Sein*) as an abstract concept enveloping all living things, and the being-there (*Da-sein*), the being in front of us, that being that we can identify, point at and intone: 'you there!' It is *Dasein* as opposed to *Sein* that is Heidegger's overriding concern and, within this, the focus hones down not on any *Dasein* but more specifically, a *Dasein* that is both individual and human. When a human individual reflects on their being, according to Heidegger, at some point a whole life comes into view: 'the constitution of Dasein … is primordially a whole' (Heidegger, 2007, p. 236).[3] He also writes that *Dasein* at any moment in time is always 'beyond itself' and therefore due to the potentiality inherent in a/ny life, once this is alighted upon, each *Dasein* is a 'Being-ahead-of-itself'.

This is one of a plethora of hyphenated terms that Heidegger connects to Being, where the punctuation is doing a lot of heavy lifting. Due to its being-ahead-of-itself, *Dasein* is also a being-towards-death, a feature that also follows from any consideration involving the whole of life. All three of these elements – a whole life, being-ahead-of-itself and beings-towards-death – lead Heidegger to present readers with a choice between authentic and inauthentic existence. Authentic *Daseins* confront the whole of their very being, and adopt a temporality to accommodate this. An authentic temporality requires shunning the 'now-time' (p. 474) that the inauthentic majority inhabit, and this is so because they haven't given their being the requisite attention. In Heidegger's terms, they haven't 'reckoned with time' (p. 456) and are immersed in an understanding of temporality as a succession of nows, as 'now and now and now […]' (p. 470) – we might say of them that they know nothing of time but to live in the moment. Heidegger deems time conceived as a sequence of nows as 'the ordinary understanding' in which time flows constantly, successively through 'the course of time' (p. 474). A profound implication of this ordinary understanding of now-time for Heidegger is that there is no place for significance; as each now is undifferentiated from one another, it becomes impossible to ascertain whether one is more significant than the other.

The ordinary conception covers up significance: 'the significance of the "now" … gets *levelled off*' (p. 474).

How is Heidegger's understanding of the ordinary now-time and significance relevant for thinking about populism? When translated from the level of the individual granted by Heidegger to the realm of politics, populism entails the announcement of the end of a political now-time, and the entry of reflections on significance by growing sectors of the public. Let's unpack this claim, and begin with one account of what populism is. Margaret Canovan argues: 'populism in modern democratic societies is best seen as an appeal to "the people" against both the established structure of power and the dominant ideas and values of the society' (1999, p. 3). Prior to an/y appeal to them, the people are within political now-time: they accept the established structure of power and the dominant ideas and values of their society. At this point, power is stable or, using different language, a hegemonic formation is consolidated – the political context is one of hegemonic calm. Populism does not emerge within a vacuum but, rather, within a very specific context: the context of crisis. To designate a context as a crisis involves the insertion of significance into politics. Another way of saying this is that a growing number of the public begin to critically evaluate their lives, their futures, and this critical evaluation rejects the way in which power is – and has been – exercised and the effects it produces – and has produced. This growing number feel, or have been made to feel, insignificant, and this insignificance can only be addressed by opposing the established structure of power and the dominant ideas and values of their society. These ideas and values no longer generate calm but, rather, antagonism: the hegemonic framework's calm disintegrates and, in its place, new actors, ideas and values vie for attention in their quest to become dominant.

The appearance of populism, in short, is as much a sign of crisis as its enunciation. Its appearance injects increasing salience – significance – to different actors, ideas and values, and constitutes the rejection of the continuity of a political now-time in which 'what is' will be, whereby one 'now' closely (if not exactly) resembles its predecessor. With populism, the prevailing now of politics is rejected alongside its predecessors, and is cast as a failed project. Instead, another and different now is proposed and demanded. The succession of nows that constitute now-time and lead to the repetition of the same give way to the call for something different, a new now projected into the future. The shift is that significance has been granted to the question of the now, and a struggle emerges as to which 'now' should predominate.

Heidegger insists that the principal thesis of the ordinary way of interpreting time conceives of it as infinite. Every now is either a 'just-now' or a 'forthwith', cast within a sequence that has no beginning or end. With no beginning and end, time is a continuum stretching to infinity. This serves as a useful entry-point into more recent theoretical analyses of time and its linkage to politics (and sometimes populism). Heidegger's accusation of the ordinary understanding of time as infinite devoid of beginning evokes a distinction introduced by Edmund Husserl, who taught Heidegger and to whom *Being & Time* was dedicated. Husserl distinguished between sedimentation and reactivation and, in order to address the issue of new and forgotten beginnings, Ernesto Laclau applies these to politics. Ideas, institutions and beyond become sedimented in politics, such that they are naturalised and viewed as normal. Such naturality and normality effectively wards off wider questions and debates such that Laclau insists 'the political' gives way to administration – which is akin to Heidegger's 'now-time'. Laclau aligns the political with populism which emerges when grand questions are reactivated, increasingly bringing those sedimented practices of the administration into doubt. Rather than having a monopoly on what constitutes the 'right' practices, politics reveals the administration's beginnings and, through this, the availability of alternatives offering different trajectories and practices. There is an opening of the field of possibility and, once the beginnings of an administration are reactivated, its existence likewise becomes a leading question. The appearance of populism on the political stage constitutes the reactivation of sedimented practices.

The debt to Heidegger's account of time is well consolidated within twenty-first-century political theory. Here, a more recent account will be briefly introduced, and then linked to populism.

A starting-point for Jacques Rancière is that there is no such thing as a modern time, or time of modernity in the singular. There is instead a plurality of modern times, in which experiences of time differ socially and sometimes even contradict. This produces an interlacing and clashes of temporalities, such that modern times ultimately entails 'a conflict over the distribution of life forms' (Rancière, 2022, p. x). This pluralisation of time in modernity builds on a long-standing hierarchy of time stretching back at least as far as the ancient Greeks, whereby the social is split in two, between those that have time and those that don't. The former, for instance, do politics, whereas the latter are precluded from that realm. Alongside these broader chrono-historical features, Rancière identifies a more recent and continuing temporality emanating from the late twentieth century. The collapse of the Berlin Wall and the Soviet Union ushered in the dominance of a crude positivistic notion of time. One way of characterising this is as 'presentism', but it replicates the 'now-time' introduced by Heidegger. This is reinforced by the announcement of 'end of history' which itself followed hot on the heels of the 'end of ideology' and indeed declarations of the demise of politics (Fukuyama, 1992; Bell, 1960;

Mouffe, 1993, 2000, 2005). Presentism and now-time, as Rancière conceives it, announces the 'end of grand narratives'. Presentism is the dominant (new? grand?) narrative of time but, due to the pluralisation of modern temporalities, not the only one. This fits into the most widely recognised aspect of Rancière's theory, the police-politics distinction (Rancière, 1999). The dominant presentism aligns with the police account of time, whereas politics constitutes the rupturing of, the disruption and challenge to that ordering of time and its hierarchical distribution of forms of life. New temporal possibilities emerge, alongside visions of a revised distribution of forms of life in which its hierarchies are dismantled. Rancière characterises this as a transformation from that of repetition or 'this succession of hours' imposed on those 'who do not have time', to 'a time characterized by a multitude of events' (Rancière, 2022, p. 19). Such eventual ruptures are aligned with working-class and intellectual emancipations, although they are by no means limited to that. The plurality of starting points or subjects of these emancipations echoes the manner in which a heterogeneity of demands combine in populism's challenge to the establishment. Similarly, the interruption of the sequence, of presentism, of now-time mimics the manner in which populism appears on the stage. It interrupts the erstwhile calm temporal continuity of the establishment, posing a challenge to its ideas and values, while simultaneously developing its own alternative political project.

Machiavelli is the second philosopher who provides a theoretical resource to situate the encounter between populism and time. While this early modern philosopher is *of* modernity, he pre-dates it, so cannot be considered to be living *in* it. This means that Machiavelli provides a vastly different understanding of temporality to both the predominant accounts of the premodern and modern worlds. The dominant modern version was generated by Hegel, developed by Marx and impacted through the prevalence of Marxists and Marxism as the nineteenth century passed into the twentieth.[4] Hegel offers an account of time that is complete, idealised, abstract and universal. Hegel forwards an understanding of time wherein only the present exists. It has being, as opposed to the past and the future which (currently) have non-being, the opposite of the present's being. This is not all, as this present that has being is also seamlessly integrated into what comes before, and what emerges out of it. While the past and the future don't exist as they lack present being, the former has existed and the latter's existence will subsequently be confirmed. Hegel writes:

> Thus in a positive sense one can say of time that only the Present is; the 'before' and 'after' are not; but the concrete Present is the result of the past and is pregnant with the future. Thus the true Present is infinity. (Hegel, 1970, p. 235)

It is this integration of time within a metaphysical whole that subsequently gets picked up by Marx, whereby there is an integrated whole in which the past leads into the present, and from which the future results. This account of time and history that is historical materialism plays out on the world stage as Marxism becomes a dominant force across the globe as the nineteenth century moves into the twentieth, the century in which it has its greatest impact. In its most basic outlines, historical materialism regards history as an integrated whole but, as with the Hegelian system, this is not a static whole as dynamism is injected into it by class conflict – whereby class struggle is viewed as the motor of history, and this motor will only be erased once class consciousness is achieved by the proletariat, conscious of and fulfilling its universal role in this integrated whole that is history.

For Machiavelli, by contrast, time is less accessible to thought for the very reason that it is incomplete. This means that the future has multiple potential pathways: there is no future in the singular, only plural futures that are at the same time possible yet very different from one another. The Machiavellian account of time is relayed through the conceptual framework highlighted by Quentin Skinner (2019), who identifies the notions of *necessità*, *fortuna* and *virtù* as key to understanding Machiavelli. While we're at the mercy of the first two of these, they are very different from one another. *Necessità* evokes what many currently view as necessity, akin to natural laws, whereas *fortuna* is closer to what is now known as contingency. Necessity and contingency are usually presented as dichotomous, mutually exclusive metaphysical concepts but, against this understanding, Machiavelli presents them in tandem. That is, contingency operates within necessity, compromising the solidity of necessity and redirecting it. Due to the operation of contingency within necessity, necessity is necessarily incomplete and open – alive to various possibilities.

It is here that *virtù* enters the equation. While *virtù* will never be able to master necessity and contingency, it can act on them and channel them in new directions. In Machiavelli, *virtù* is less like the virtue of virtue ethics, and more like the collective agency of social groups, their ability to act politically, akin to the manner in which Hannah Arendt theorises action, power and politics and, in so doing, confirming a debt to Machiavelli's account. To complicate this picture, Mikko Lahtinen (2009) adds a further element into Skinner's tripartite schema in interpreting Machiavelli. Alongside Skinner's trio of *necessità*, *fortuna* and *virtù*, Lahtinen also identifies *occasione* as integral to Machiavelli's system. Translated into contemporary English, *occasione* is best rendered as context. So, in Lahtinen's reading of Machiavelli, we have the complex interplay between four elements that collectively enrich understanding of politics and its operation within time. Necessity, contingency, action and context all interact within politics, with none proving ultimately decisive – wherein their non-hierarchical combination and interaction provides a complex picture of how politics proceeds through time.

Now that this philosophical framework has been laid out, we can begin to apply its concepts to populism. Taking the quartet Lahtinen offers, we could say that *necessità* and *fortuna* combine as the backdrop to *occasione* or, translated into contemporary philosophical terminology, that the operation of contingency within necessity provides the context within which populism emerges. There are enduring contexts in which contingency appears to be absent, as necessity holds sway. Within British politics over recent decades two phrases stand out as illustrating or, better, consolidating necessity's sway. The first is TINA, Margaret Thatcher's announcement that 'there is no alternative' (Thatcher, 1980); whereas the second is Tony Blair's speech to the Labour Conference in which he asserted that 'I hear people say we have to stop and debate globalisation. You might as well debate whether autumn should follow summer' (Blair, 2005). These were declarations of necessity, and contingency has returned to demonstrate what they always were: contingent assertions appearing as necessity, which were also accepted by significant sectors of the population to (con)temporarily validate that appearance of necessity. Necessity, then, appears to prevail for enduring periods of politics while contingency sleeps. Populism is absent from such contexts, but its return is facilitated by contingency's awakening and operation on necessity.

Due to contingency's action on necessity, populism's contextual background is one of movement, one in which necessity has been opened up to challenge such that the illusion of a stable background that necessity provides (and formerly provided prior to the challenge to it) no longer holds. The context is both spatial and temporal. In terms of spatiality, and in keeping with the dominant approach to the study of politics, the context is usually conceived at the national level. That said, both the political practice and academic analyses of populism have exceeded that level to the continental, especially since the rise of South American populisms in the aftermath of the Second World War and, more recently, this extension has been further such that commentators take into account the globality of populism (Moffitt, 2016).

It is the temporal aspect of the context, however, that plays a more substantial role in the politics of populism. If we go back to the overview of populism introduced earlier by Canovan, the stress is on how populism constitutes a challenge to the established structure of power, alongside the dominant ideas and values the society held which are reinforced by the establishment. As populism challenges these, the established power, its ideas and its values no longer have their hold over the population at large. While this hold was firm and gripped across suitably wide sectors for a preceding period, this sway no longer holds. Its control loosens, as increasing groups, sectors and demands begin to question and reject it, and seek an alternative power informed by different ideas and values. Put differently, the hegemonic framework that cast its spell over society begins to break down, as it moves from a stable period of calm and into one of crisis. So the appearance of populism on the political stage announces that a hegemonic framework has entered into crisis. Although the emergence and consolidation of populist politics may well heighten and reinforce that hegemonic breakdown, the widespread practice of populism is a sign of that entry into hegemonic crisis. With the increasing rejection of those ideas and values that previously predominated, the search opens up for alternatives capable of forging a new hegemonic framework.

The struggle to consolidate and implement a different set of ideas and values such that they become a new established hegemonic frame is where *virtù* comes in. It is not enough for a populist actor to appear and announce these new ideas and values. In order for populism to take hold, growing sectors of the population not only need to reject those ideas and values erstwhile dominant, they also need to accept a proposed new set of ideas and values. This combination of what Cas Mudde and Cristóbal Rovira Kaltwasser (2013) refer to as the supply of and demand for populism symbolises a new collective project. Such an arrival of collective agency is the political appearance of a new *virtù* acting to forge a new consensus, and seeking to become the new hegemonic framework. This new *virtù* is equivalent to a coalition of forces or what Gramsci refers to as a 'historic bloc' (1971).

The content that the collective agency of each populist project attempts to implement – its ideas and values – will vary according to the context within which they operate. This again illustrates populism's difference from Marxism which is integrated into, and necessarily informed by, historical materialism and its account of time. The context for Marxism does not have a life of its own, whereas contexts are pivotal for populism. The ideas and values of the People's Party of the late nineteenth-century United States differs from those proposed by more recent iterations of US populism, such as Occupy, Bernie Sanders or Alexandria Ocasio-Cortez. Yet other populist projects can be articulated by the latter's contemporaries – witness the Tea Party and Donald Trump, for instance. This is another way of saying that populism is a form and not a content – and, hence, distances populism from any ideological content, as is argued by Mudde (2004) whose approach to populism insists that it is an ideology. It also illustrates the importance of qualifying populist projects, with left and right being the most obvious qualifier.

The articulation and appeal of these differing populist projects follows from the different understanding of the future the populist holds. This populist understanding differs from both the Marxist or Hegelian account, and that associated with the established hegemonic framework that populism subjects to challenge. In contrast to the open future of populism or, better, the futures populism offers, their futures are constrained. The Marxist and Hegelian account is constrained through its integration into a philosophical or metaphysical whole. For any extant hegemonic framework, by contrast, centrality is bestowed upon continuity of the establishment frame – whereby their project revolves around carrying forward the ideas, values and structures of power from the past through the present and into the future. Populism constitutes a challenge not only to the establishment, but also to its settled understanding of time and its continuity which, all of a sudden, are thrown into doubt through the populist challenge. This explains how the appearance of populism disorients those associated with the establishment, but also so frequently induces them to mimic the antagonistic style aligned with populism. Here, their ire is directed not towards the establishment as is the case with populism, but towards populism and its adherents. Through this adoption of antagonistic politics against populism, they become practitioners of anti-populism.

The accounts of time aligned with Machiavelli and Hegel have influenced subsequent accounts of politics. Laclau's account of time, politics and populism show a closer debt to the former. In the following lengthy passage, Laclau relays several of the themes developed in this section which can, in turn, be directly contrasted with Hegelian time: incompletion versus a future that is completed; contingency operating within necessity via the notion of grounding; an open account of time versus a closed future determined by the past and present, and integrated within a metaphysical whole; and, subsequently, the presentation not of the future in the singular but of multiple futures, which is explicitly aligned with democratisation. Laclau develops these themes through an engagement with Derrida's *Spectres of Marx* (2006), and its focus on Hamlet's statement that 'the time is out of joint':

> It is because of this constitutive incompletion that decisions have to be taken, but because we are faced with incompletion and not with total dispossession, the problem of a *total* ethical grounding … never arises. 'The time is out of joint' but, because of that, there is never a beginning – or an end – of time. Democracy does not need to be – and cannot be – radically grounded. We can move to a more democratic society only through a plurality of acts of democratization. The consummation of time – as Derrida knows well – never arrives.

Immediately, following this, Laclau reflects on the implication of this theoretical account of time for politics in the wake of the rejection of Marxism's eschatology:

> This leaves us, however, with a problem: how to conceive of emancipation within this framework. What kind of collective reaggregation is open to us once we have moved away from the eschatological dimension of the classic emancipatory model? (Laclau, 1996, p.79)

The conditions Laclau outlines in these quotations – the absence of both a radical grounding (post-foundationalism) and a classic emancipatory totalising model, pluralisation, contingency, and so on – are exactly the same conditions within which populist actors operate and impel their equivalentialising logics.

## 3. Outline of Collection

This introduction concludes by providing a brief outline of the collection, its three parts, and component chapters. Part I begins with a chapter analysing the question of populism's origins. Chapter 2 identifies three different responses within the literature, and outlines the theoretical assumptions, requirements and methodologies associated with those responses. This identification provides the framework from which to critically reflect on the three responses, and offer a more sustained analysis on the broader question of populism's beginnings which, in turn, opens up suggestions for further research into populism and its history.

In Chapter 3, Clare Woodford delves deep into democratic theory to interrogate understandings at democracy's core. Modern democracy, in short, introduces elements that are at one and the same time logical impossibilities yet necessary in order for democracy to function. The impossible register applies both to the people – the central actor of democracy – and to its temporality. The people is not one, and can never be, yet this generates the dynamism of both the people and of democracy itself. As with democracy, the people is decisive for populism too, and populism's distinctive contribution is that it reveals something that is otherwise only latent. This is that there are (at least) two conceptions of the people that operate in politics, and populism uncovers the second of these, thereby making manifest the rivalry between these differing conceptions. While 'Populism, Impossible Time and Democracy's People Problem' draws on the work of Jacques Rancière, one of the most fertile features Woodford highlights is the different 'moments' of the political to which Rancière is drawn. These are then compared with the work of Laclau and Mouffe. Whereas with Rancière attention is focused on the aesthetic moment of perception change that launches the people against the establishment, for Laclau and Mouffe the focus is on what follows: the process of coalition-building and negotiation that facilitates the populist challenge to the establishment.

Chapter 4 points towards the final part through an extended focus on a case study. While the terrain of Part III is Latin America, attention here is trained on Spain, and the manner in which Podemos combined three of its distinctive leftist traditions. In contrast to the analyses that have offered one of ideology, class or politics to frame these three traditions, Adrià Porta Caballé identifies time as the mode through which to investigate the travails of Podemos and its component parts. This is achieved through staging a philosophical encounter between Nietzsche and Heidegger, to produce a comprehensive temporal framework to account for the key moments, decisions and departures that have beset this new political party as it moved from its origins in the streets through its formation and rapid breakthrough and onto entry into government. This temporal frame that Caballé constructs offers a heuristic for other case studies of left populism as new or reformed political parties – and their component parts from which they emerge – confront the disparate challenges thrown up by the contexts within which they operate.

Part II has a sharper focus, through its engagement with the relationship between populism and technology, situating this relationship within a wider analysis of modernity and the political modes it generates. The theses in this part broadly identify an association between technological developments in modernity and the (re)appearance of populisms. Chapter 5 adopts a wider synoptic lens to identify crises affecting liberal democracy, advanced capitalism and their enforcement mechanisms in 'late modernity'. It is the broader ground of crisis and these specific contemporary crises that Simon Tormey imputes for the growing prevalence of populism in recent politics. Late modernity displays a range of trends and tendencies that are inducing the ongoing crisis – one that is morbid and chronic, rather than acute – experienced by liberal democracy and advanced capitalism. These tendencies are so complex, multifarious, protracted and pervasive that populism is no longer an aberration. This is the view held by populism's critics: that populism is a temporary interruption, a deviation from the norm, destined to dissipate once its supporters return to their senses. Tormey's analysis makes uncomfortable reading for those critics of populism, as he speculates that populism has become, is becoming, and will remain 'the new normal', a persistent even banal feature of our politics. This inference is drawn due to the endemic character of the tendencies – globalisation, decline in the role of authority, the new media ecology, and so on – of late modernity. As these are the causes behind the rise and consolidation of populism, and that

INTRODUCTION: POPULISM, METAPHOR, TEMPORALITY    17

these tendencies are endemic, *ergo* populism is not going away in a hurry. This amalgamation of factors prompts the coinage of the neologism 'populisation' in order to account for the prominence of the consolidation of populism on the contemporary political stage. It is this claim about populism and our current political times, alongside the causal analysis aligning populisation with the five broad, endemic tendencies of late modernity, that makes this chapter so original, stimulating and provocative.

In Chapter 6, Michaelangelo Anastasiou surveys the literature on populism within which synchronic analyses constitute the predominant temporal frame. As a critique of this predominating position, Anastasiou elaborates a compelling argument that synchronic analyses neglect both the historical and political dimensions of populism and, instead, proposes that a diachronic temporality offers a more robust frame for understanding populist practice. Diachrony in politics is facilitated by the expansion and scope of modern technology which facilitates dislocations and disruptions that interrupt the synchronicity that is associated with both the notion of spatialisation, but also the predominant methodological frame adopted within populism studies. Anastasiou in short insists that technology, alongside its scope and scale in modernity, facilitates diachrony in politics and, within that, the populist political form. This means that, to quote Anastasiou, 'creative disruption, to play on words, inheres in the populist operation' and that creative disruption emerges out of the twin themes of temporality – or diachrony – and technology.

In Chapter 7, Jamie Ranger encourages a fuller engagement with the 'technospheric' in order to understand populism's popularity in the twenty-first century. 'Populism, Social Media and the Technospheric' carefully elucidates the notion of the technospheric, drawing on the work of Bernard Steigler and Hartmut Rosa. Ranger insists we are living in and through the technospheric condition which shapes our sense of temporality. This technical milieu received a decisive jolt with the Industrial Revolution, and has continued to accelerate thereafter. The Internet and social media are its most recent developments. Ranger argues that the technospheric condition distorts what is properly political and democratically contestable and, instead, makes it appear technical. Such technicity prompts the deferral to experts which, in turn, helps explain the resonance of the populist appeal to the people against elites and their attempt to distort democratic contestability and 'the political' proper.

Part III has an exclusive focus on Latin American populism. This region has experienced the most extensive time with populism and this experiential depth has generated arguably the most important theoretical, critical, analytical and historical accounts on populism. Put simply, familiarity with Latin American politics during this millennium and stretching back a century is essential for any serious engagement with populism. The three chapters comprising this part exemplify the imagination and indispensability of accounts written by Latin Americans on populism. The four contributors are all female, have Latin American provenance, and focus on distinctive elements of Latin American populist politics.

In Chapter 8, María Esperanza Casullo surveys the multiple incarnations of populist politics across the region during this century. Focusing on 'the pink tide' that enveloped numerous countries in the early years of the millennium, Casullo effectively demolishes the popular view widely held across the Global North that populism is a temporary phenomenon. As the title of the chapter indicates, at least in Latin America, populism is far from a brief political interlude and, instead, is marked by 'surprising resilience'. 'Antagonism, Flexibility and the Surprising Resilience of Populism in Latin America' presents a robust analysis of Latin American twenty-first-century politics, focusing on five countries – four of which had populist presidencies exceeding a decade – to illustrate the central thesis of populist resilience. Such resilience is built not only on the flexibility of the antagonisms deployed by populist leaders, but also by the sustained levels of popularity amongst their people – as evidenced by the popular mobilisations that protected and prolonged these administrations when under threat. Alongside the two ensuing chapters, the broader portrayal this 'surprising resilience' depicts is of a region and its people determined to carve its own distinctive political future. Those alive to decolonial theory and its practitioners, for instance, will recognise the history, passion and determination to diverge from a politics devised elsewhere and imposed on the region (Mignolo, 2011; Mignolo & Walsh, 2018; Dussel, 2008; Escobar, 2017) – not to mention the continuing role of Bolivarianism (Brown, 2009).

In Chapter 9, Paula Biglieri and Gloria Perelló mine the Latin American experience with populism to provide a novel theoretical thesis on time and space. In, 'Rupture, Institutionalisation and Tension: About Populist Temporality in Latin America', they point to the inexorable temporality of populist politics highlighting the roles of tension and rupture within its practice. This is not a one-sided analysis, however, as they also align populism with spatialisation. The focus on time and space is at the same time a focus on the politics of opposition and proposition or, in other terms, institutions and institutionalisation. While populism rises with crises and constitutes a temporal rupture, populism has by no means been restricted to oppositional politics. Populisms in power, in office, in administration, as governments – all have equally been the Latin American experience. This chapter highlights the interplay between time and space within this history, focusing on how populist institutionalisation adopts new spatial political configurations, bringing the theme of populist spatialisation to the fore.

These issues are taken further in Chapter 10, where focus shifts from institutions to the constitution itself. In 'Populism and Constitutionalism in Brazil: An Enduring or Transitional Relationship in Time?', Eleonora Mesquita Ceia restricts attention to Brazil in order to hone in on the country's history and, within that, the relationship between its constitutionalism and its politics – and, focusing further still, the diverse forms of populisms across the previous century. Again, this extended investigation calls into question a widely held truism in the Global North that insists that populism attacks or seeks to capture the constitution and, more specifically, undermines its core features such as the rule of law and the separation of powers. Ceia converges on five different populist presidents stretching back to the 1930s and, in this informed, rich survey, finds a variety of different engagements with the constitution and its institutional components. Far from identifying a simple relationship between populism and constitutionalism, Ceia outlines a complex, variegated history that suggests a far more ambiguous interaction that militates against any distinctive 'populist constitutionalism'. This outcome of the investigation, moreover, calls into question the widely held binary pitting liberal-democratic constitutionalism against populist constitutionalism. Such a binary is problematised, in turn, due to the vastly different histories of both liberalism and democracy in Brazil – indeed, in Latin America more broadly – which have rendered their compatibility and connection less tenuous than other regions and continents with their own distinctive events, histories and trajectories.

Rather than attempting to unify the rich and disparate accounts within the collection, the concluding chapter considers populism's prospects. An orientation towards the future, after all, fits snugly with the narrative structure that continues to capture our imaginaries. Rather than offering a vision, programme, moral or even prediction about the future, however, in the Conclusion I pose an unanswered question. This is unanswered because it is unanswerable, given the openness of the future – or, much better, the multiple openings to the many possible futures in front of 'an us' that similarly lacks fixity. The question posed relates to how populism will fare in the future – how much of it, how and when will it re/appear, and so on. This question regarding populism's prospects delves into populism's ontology, and enquires into the context and/or conditions in which this form of politics appears and thrives. Two speculative responses are offered in response to the dominant (anti-populist) presentation of populism as a temporary aberration destined to be consigned to history. These two speculations ultimately probe into related questions of how and why populism appears and endures, and what are the components that comprise the conditions in order for it to do so.

The contributions herein illuminate our understanding of populism. Collectively they vividly demonstrate two overriding points. In the first place, the diversity of factors that an encounter between populism and time generate. The themes developed in this collection invite connections between populism and various disciplinary practices – these include a welcome and under-investigated engagement with philosophy while also utilising history, political science, political theory, technology studies, sociology and media theory. These are grounded in the European, US and especially Latin American experiences and episodes with populism. These facilitate interactions with numerous temporal themes, including resilience, rupture, beginnings, nostalgia, opportunism, utopia, alongside disruptions prompted by technology, the experience of democracy itself, and the 'late modern' condition of contemporary politics. This rich yet eclectic range of themes nod towards the second point, which is the wager of this collection: that the prior neglect of an encounter between populism and time warrants a reckoning with, and the hope is that the reckoning conducted herein prompts further productive engagements on populism and its temporalities.

## Notes

1. The connection between populism and time has been considered – to different degrees – in the following texts, Bødker and Anderson (2019), Laclau (2008), Lazar (2019), Lazar (2022), Palestrino (2022) and Taş (2022).
2. The following list is necessarily selective, but includes Arendt (2006), Auge (2014), Baraitser (2017), Bloch (1988), Cazdyn (2012), Derrida (2001), Jameson (2007), Lazar (2019), Negri (2003), Ochoa Espejo (2011), Osborne (1995), Rancière (2022), Shapiro (2016).
3. Subsequent citations from *Being and Time* in the following paragraph feature solely the page number.
4. The contrast in the understanding of time between Heidegger on the one hand, and Hegel, Marx and Marxists on the other hand is based upon the reading of time offered in *Being and Time*. This presents a simple contrast between the two understandings, which has been adopted for the sake of brevity and analytical focus. The contrast Heidegger presents has been subjected to withering criticism, see, for instance: Ikäheimo (2012).

## References

Arendt, H. (2006) *Between past and future*. London: Penguin.

Aslanidis, P. (2017) 'Avoiding bias in the study of populism', *Chinese Political Science Review*, 2, pp. 266–287.

Auge, M. (2014) *The future*. London: Verso.
Bale, T. and Rovira Kaltwasser, C. (2021) *Riding the populist wave: Europe's mainstream right in crisis*. Cambridge: Cambridge University Press.
Baraitser, L. (2017) *Enduring time*. London: Bloomsbury.
Bell, D. (1960) *The end of ideology: on the exhaustion of political ideas in the fifties*. New York: The Free Press.
Betz, H. (1994) *Radical right-wing populism in Western Europe*. London: Palgrave Macmillan.
Blair, T. (2005) 'Labour Party Conference Speech', retrieved from https://www.theguardian.com/uk/2005/sep/27/labourconference.speeches.
Bloch, E. (1988) 'On the present in literature', in *The utopian function of art and literature*. Cambridge: Cambridge University Press, pp. 206–222.
Bødker, H. and Anderson, C. (2019) 'Populist time: mediating immediacy and delay in liberal democracy', *International Journal of Communication*, 13, pp. 5948–5966.
Brown, S. (ed.) (2009) *Hugo Chávez presents Simón Bolívar: The Bolivarian Revolution*. London: Verso.
Canovan, M. (1999) 'Trust the people! Populism and the two faces of democracy', *Political Studies*, 47 (1), pp. 2–16.
Cazdyn, E. (2012) *The already dead: the new time of politics, culture, and illness*. Durham, NC: Duke University Press.
De Cleen, B., Glynos, J. and Mondon, A. (2018) 'Critical research on populism: nine rules of engagement', *Organization*, 25 (5), pp. 649–661.
De la Torre, C. (2010) *Populist seduction in Latin America*. Athens: Ohio University Press.
De la Torre, C. (ed.) (2015) *The promise and perils of populism: global perspectives*. Lexington: University of Kentucky Press.
De la Torre, C. (ed.) (2019) *Routledge handbook of global populism*. London: Routledge.
De la Torre, C. and Arnson, C. (eds) (2013) *Latin American populism in the twenty-first century*. Baltimore, MD: John Hopkins University Press.
Derrida, J. (2001) *Writing and difference*. Abingdon: Routledge.
Derrida, J. (2006) *Spectres of Marx*. Abingdon: Routledge.
Di Tella, T. (1965) 'Populism and reform in Latin America', in Veliz, C. (ed.) *Obstacles to change in Latin America*. London: Oxford University Press.
Dussel, E. (2008) *Twenty theses on politics*. London: Duke University Press.
Eklundh, E. (2019) *Emotions, protest, democracy: collective identities in contemporary Spain*. Abingdon: Routledge.
Escobar, A. (2017) *Designs for the pluriverse: radical independence, autonomy, and the making of worlds*. Durham, NC: Duke University Press.

Foa, S. and Mounk, Y. (2019) 'Youth and the populist wave', *Philosophy & Social Criticism*, 45 (9–10), pp. 1013–1024.

Ford, R. and Goodwin, M. (2014) *Revolt on the right: explaining support for the radical right in Britain.* Abingdon: Routledge.

Frank, T. (2020) *People without power: the war on populism and the fight for democracy.* London: Scribe.

Fukuyama, F. (1992) *The end of history and the last man.* New York: Free Press.

Germani, G. (1978) *Authoritarianism, fascism and national populism.* London: Routledge.

Glynos, J. and Mondon, A. (2016) 'The political logic of populist hype: the case of right-wing populism's "meteoric rise" and its relation to the status quo', *Populismus* Working Papers No. 4.

Gramsci, A. (1971) *Selections from the Prison Notebooks.* London: Lawrence & Wishart.

Hegel, G. (1970) *Hegel's Philosophy of Nature*, M. J. Petry (ed and trans), 3 volumes. London: Allen and Unwin.

Heidegger, M. (2007) *Being and time.* Oxford: Blackwell Publishing.

Hofstadter, R. (1955) *The age of reform: from Bryan to F.D.R.* New York: Vintage.

Hofstadter, R (2008) *The paranoid style in American politics and other essays.* New York: Vintage.

Hom, A. (2018) 'Timing is everything: toward a better understanding of time and international politics', *International Studies Quarterly*, 62, pp 69–79.

Ikäheimo, H. (2012) 'The times of desire, hope and fear: on the temporality of concrete subjectivity in Hegel's Encyclopaedia', *Critical Horizons*, 13 (2), pp. 197–219.

Ionescu, G. and Gellner, E. (1969) *Populism: its meaning and national characteristics.* London: Macmillan.

Jameson, F. (2007) *Archaeologies of the future: the desire called utopia and other science fictions.* London: Verso.

Judis, J. (2016) *The populist explosion: how the Great Recession transformed American and European politics.* New York: Columbia Global Reports.

Kazin, M. (1998) *The populist persuasion: an American history.* Ithaca, NY and London: Cornell University Press.

Laclau, E. (1996) *Emancipation(s).* London: Verso.

Laclau, E. (2008) 'Is radical atheism a good name for deconstruction?', *Diacritics*, 38 (1–2), pp. 180–189.

Lahtinen, M. (2009) *Politics and philosophy. Niccolo Machiavelli and Louis Althusser's aleatory materialism.* Leiden: Brill.

Lazar, N. C. (2019) *Out of joint: power, crisis, and the rhetoric of time*. New Haven, CT: Yale University Press.

Lazar, N. C. (2022) 'Populism and time', in Manucci, L. (ed.) *The populism interviews*. Abingdon: Routledge, pp. 159–163.

Lee, S. P. (2020) 'Democracy and populism', in Navin, M. C. and Nunan, R. (eds) *Democracy, populism, and truth*. Cham: Springer, pp. 35–46.

Mignolo, W. (2011) *The darker side of western modernity: global futures, decolonial options*. Durham, NC: Duke University Press.

Mignolo, W. and Walsh, C. (2018) *On decoloniality: concepts, analytics, praxis*. London: Duke University Press.

Moffitt, B. (2016) *The global rise of populism*. Stanford, CA: Stanford University Press.

Mouffe, C. (1993) *The return of the political*. London: Verso.

Mouffe, C. (2000) *The democratic paradox*. London: Verso.

Mouffe, C. (2005) *On the political*. London: Verso.

Mudde, C. (2004) 'The populist zeitgeist', *Government and Opposition*, 39 (4), pp. 541–563.

Mudde, C. (2007) *Populist radical right parties in Europe*. Cambridge: Cambridge University Press.

Mudde, C. and Rovira Kaltwasser, C. (2013) 'Exclusionary vs. inclusionary populism: comparing contemporary Europe and Latin America', *Government & Opposition*, 48 (2), pp. 147–174.

Negri, A. (2003) *Time for revolution*. London: Continuum.

Ochoa Espejo, P. (2011) *The time of popular sovereignty: process and the democratic state*. Philadelphia, PA: Penn State Press.

Osborne, P. (1995) *The politics of time: modernity and avant-garde*. London: Verso.

Ostiguy, P., Panizza, F. and Moffitt, B. (eds) (2021) *Populism in global perspective: a performative and discursive approach*. London: Routledge.

Palestrino, M. (2022) 'Neglected times: Laclau, affect and temporality', *Journal of Political Ideologies*, 27 (2), pp. 226–245.

Rancière, J. (1999) *Disagreement: politics and philosophy*. Minneapolis: University of Minnesota Press.

Rancière, J. (2022) *Modern times: temporality in art and politics*. London: Verso.

Roberts, K. (2018) 'Populism, democracy, and resistance: the United States in comparative perspective', in Meyer, D. S. and Tarrow, S. (eds) *The resistance: the dawn of the anti-Trump opposition movement*. New York: Oxford University Press.

Shapiro, M. (2016) *Politics and time*. Cambridge: Polity.

Skinner, Q. (2019) *Machiavelli: a very short introduction*. Oxford: Oxford University Press.

Solomon, T. (2014) 'Time and subjectivity in world politics', *International Studies Quarterly*, 58 (4), pp. 671–681.
Taggart, P. (2000) *Populism*. Buckingham: Open University Press.
Taş, H. (2022) 'The chronopolitics of national populism', *Identities: Global Studies in Culture and Power*, 29 (2), pp. 127–145.
Thatcher, M. (1980) 'Speech to Conservative Women's Conference', retrieved from https://www.margaretthatcher.org/document/104368.
Weyland, K. (1996) 'Neopopulism and neoliberalism in Latin America: unexpected affinities', *Studies in Comparative International Development*, 31, pp. 3–31.

# Part I
# Populism, Politics, History

# 2

# On Populism's Beginnings

*Andy Knott*

## 1. Introduction

Accounts of populism have proliferated in the twenty-first century, but a comprehensive survey of its historiography is yet to emerge. This chapter takes the first steps down this path. It focuses on the question of populism's origins, and identifies three different approaches in the literature. These approaches hail from diverse disciplines within the humanities and social sciences, reflecting their distinct methodological concerns and features, while the authors and their approaches display vastly divergent normative, theoretical and strategic registers. As this is a preliminary survey bringing together accounts from historians, political scientists and theorists utilising diverse methodological frameworks, the core aim of the chapter is to map out the key features of these three accounts, isolating their distinctive concerns and the implications they generate for the dynamic between populism and politics – whether that be temporal, spatial, ontological or methodological. The mapping of these three approaches affords the additional opportunity to critically engage with each approach, and to offer some initial reflections on populism's origins and practice. These critical reflections are offered to encourage further engagement with populism's history, origins and, especially, historiography – with the aspiration that such an engagement can contribute to a fuller understanding of the phenomenon, amidst the 'hype' (Glynos & Mondon, 2016; De Cleen, Glynos & Mondon, 2018) that has accompanied its analyses in recent decades.

Federico Finchelstein offers an original approach to the question of populism's beginnings in the recent *From Fascism to Populism in History*. Its novelty emanates from the scale and prominence this historian grants to populism. Alongside liberal democracy, fascism and communism, Finchelstein elevates populism as the final of the four regimes to impact upon twentieth-century global history. The global scale afforded to populism here clearly differentiates Finchelstein from the approach that has predominated amongst historians. Specific case studies, bound to a particular historical period and within national borders, constitute the predominant way in which historians have engaged with populism. By isolating distinct case studies from history and not delving back further into the political past, implicit within this approach is that populism has its origins in the case study furthest into the past. Here, the late nineteenth century serves as populism's launch pad, with attention trained on the People's Party's emergence in 1890s United States, and the experience of Russia's *narodniki* in the decades following the Emancipation Act of 1861. Such a point of origin aligns populism with particular historical developments, including industrialisation, urbanisation and the modern project more broadly. Populism's foundation within such a particular set of economic and social historical circumstances is rejected by the third approach, which isolates its practice across a longer historical trajectory, even aligning its logic with the political itself. This imbrication between populism and the political hails from the centrality afforded to the notion of the people – the most important subject throughout the history of politics.

## 2. Populism as a Global Regime

'Our theories of populism lack history' (Finchelstein, 2017, p. 21).[1] This observation guides Federico Finchelstein's analysis in *From Fascism to Populism in History*, an intervention into the barren field of the historiography on populism that is so bold, that it holds out the promise for further audacious innovations to this field. Two elements highlight the import of Finchelstein's intervention. In the first place, it insists that populism is first and foremost a transnational phenomenon, and should be understood as such. This claim sets Finchelstein apart from preceding historians, who have treated populism as a series of discrete and isolated phenomena restricted to distinct national trajectories which appeared at particular moments in their historical development. Populism, in short, transcends national boundaries for Finchelstein and, as a consequence, deserves insertion within a global – rather than national – historical framework. The spatial extension Finchelstein grants to populism echoes the global scope contemporary political scientists and theorists offer to it (Moffitt, 2016; De La Torre, 2019; Ostiguy, Panizza & Moffitt, 2021) yet Finchelstein's novelty is to trace populism further into the past – to the mid-twentieth century, as opposed to the current millennium. The second novel element differentiates between populist projects or forms. Finchelstein distinguishes between 'pre-populism' and 'proto-populism' on the one hand, and 'populism proper' on the other. Such a 'proper' or 'regime' status elevates populism up the hierarchy of political phenomena warranting historical interest for Finchelstein. This section first fleshes out Finchelstein's analysis, and then critically interrogates its core features and underlying assumptions.

It is in the immediate aftermath of the Second World War that populism 'proper' first emerges for Finchelstein, and becomes a significant 'regime actor' on the world stage. The point of eruption occurs in Argentina with the election to office of Juan Perón in 1946, before rapidly spreading to several other countries across the South American continent, in the ensuing years and into the next decade. This rapid continental spread assured populism proper as a newcomer regime, alongside earlier transnational regimes. Prior to the Second World War, Finchelstein identifies three 'ideological' regimes available to twentieth-century citizen-subjects: liberal democracy, communism and fascism. The emergence of populism as a regime coincided with the defeat and discrediting of fascism, leading to its withdrawal as a viable 'ideological regime choice'. Into that void stepped 'populism proper' which Finchelstein views as offering a 'third way' between the two remaining regime alternatives: 'populism first emerged as an antileftist democratic solution and an attempt to overcome the Cold War dichotomy between liberalism and communism' (p. 165). In this account of twentieth-century regimes, there is an echo of the work of both the Marxist historian Eric Hobsbawm and the political theorist Michael Freeden. Hobsbawm regards the 'short' twentieth century as a three-sided struggle between liberal capitalism, fascism and 'really-existing socialism' (Hobsbawm, 1995), while Freeden integrates history and ideas to investigate ideologies, which produces three 'thick-centred' versions, namely conservatism, liberalism and socialism (Freeden, 1996). Finchelstein adds a further 'regime' impacting on the world stage, extending these two triplets into a quartet.

Finchelstein emphasises the democratic origins of this new transnational regime, as Perón initiates populist democracy – 'if democracy begins in Athens, modern democratic populism begins in Buenos Aires' (p. 81) – thereby offering itself as a democratic rival to liberalism, in contrast to the authoritarian regime types of fascism and communism. Populism is a deceptive form of politics for Finchelstein, however, as although it originates and dresses itself in democracy, this origin and external face becomes compromised when(ever) a populist regime solidifies, as it starts to merge with authoritarianism. Populist authoritarian democracy 'undermines tolerance and democracy' (p. x) and 'downplays the separation of powers, the independence of a free press, and the rule of law' (p. xix). It also makes 'nonelectoral claims' for democracy, whilst sidelining and subjugating minorities as the clamour for the will of a singular, pure people is pursued (p. 163) – 'populism is the opposite of diversity, tolerance and plurality in politics' (p. 173). The introductory remarks confirm that 'this book describes the dictatorial genealogies of modern populism' (p. 1), and the trajectory and ideology of the regime of populism is clear.

The gradual uncovering of these ideological authoritarian underpinnings situate populism within the dynamic interplay of Finchelstein's four twentieth-century regimes. It is not just that populism supplants fascism, it is its outgrowth which 'reformulates the legacies of "anti-Enlightenment" for the Cold War era' (p. xiii). This Enlightenment hostility is reinforced by its truth-relation: 'populism relates directly to fascism's refusal to determine the truth empirically' (p. xvii). Such intellectual affinities invite historical connectivity: 'we can better understand populism if we think of it as an original historical formulation of fascism that came to power after 1945' (p. xix). The overall analysis Finchelstein offers on populism and its relationships with both democracy and fascism is proposed *in nuce* by:

> Populism is both genetically and historically linked to fascism. One might argue that it is an heir to fascism – a postfascism for democratic times, which combines a more narrow commitment to democracy with authoritarian, antidemocratic impulses. (p. 251)

With this account laid out, attention now turns to its examination. Arguably its most significant feature is the prominence it invests in populism, through situating it as one of just four regime types that dominated the twentieth-century stage. With both fascism and communism compromised, populism's profile as a regime continues into the new millennium. Such a position jars acutely with the treatment it had received by other historians who have restricted analysis within national borders and, more usually, to case studies. Finchelstein's placement of populism as one of the primary modes of politics of global and continental import is an inducement to take populism seriously, and for an enrichment of its historical analyses.

While isolating instances to regimes highlights populism's global prominence and offers analytic clarity, such an approach is not without its problems. The contrast between police and politics recently introduced by Jacques Rancière (1999) has facilitated understanding of the operations and practices of politics. Police in Rancière has affinities with regime in Finchelstein, and Rancière's politics-police distinction most starkly illustrates any account that considers populism as a regime. Finchelstein's distinction between 'populism proper' and 'proto-populism' invites consideration of whether investigation should be oriented towards 'populisms in power', or towards populism as an oppositional force. It also invites enquiry into whether analysis should focus on one more than, or instead of, the other. An exclusive focus on the former would restrict contemporary political observers and future historians to the study of Trump, Erdoğan, Duterte, Orbán, Chávez, Syriza and Podemos as a few examples, and to neglect Brexit, UKIP and Farage, Le Pen and *Rassemblement National*, Pauline Hanson and even movements such as Occupy. The approach of restricting populism to a regime precludes analysis of the *influence* populism can exert on a political scene that is stale and ossifying. The impact that the People's Party had on US politics is noteworthy here, shaking up a complacent duopoly, injecting untapped political questions and novel solutions, and the longer-run effect the policies advocated by this third party had on subsequent historical developments, particularly the New Deal (Frank, 2020; Goodwyn, 1976, 1978; Grattan, 2016; Hicks, 1931; Judis, 2016; Kazin, 1998; Lowndes, 2017; Pollack, 1962; Postel, 2009). Recent developments in UK politics also illustrate the impact of oppositional populisms. Brexit constitutes a major shift in the political, constitutional and economic relations that the United Kingdom has with its European neighbours. It was implemented by the party of the establishment, the Conservative Party, a political party with a history exceeding three centuries, and holding office for the majority of that period. Despite this, Brexit is frequently associated with populism, and here the charismatic figure of Nigel Farage looms large. The long-time leader of UKIP and ex-MEP adopted a basic strategy of pitting the British people against a European (or EU) elite – whereby the latter was aided and abetted by 'political elites' from the UK's own party duopoly of Labour and the Conservatives. UKIP was light years away from forming a populist regime – at their high point, they only had two MPs, both with brief tenures – yet their impact on the single largest policy of this millennium was enormous. Their presence, articulation and electoral breakthroughs proved vital in securing the Brexit referendum, but also in transforming the Conservative Party. UKIP's influence as an oppositional force shook up British politics, reinforcing John Judis' proposal of populists as catalysts (2016, pp. 20–21). An exclusive focus on populism as a regime also neglects enquiry into how populists move from opposition to office – a scenario well captured by the cases of Syriza and Podemos.

The account of the history of both Argentina and populism that Finchelstein offers is questionable and lacking in nuance at best, as is the characterisation of Perón's first regime. While the history of populism offered can be explained by the analytic focus on populism as a regime, the history of Argentina Finchelstein provides is extremely selective, and selected in order to reinforce the narrative of anti-populism the book elaborates. Argentina provides the primary national focus for Finchelstein, but there is little on what preceded and succeeded Perón. A widely accepted account of Argentina's entry into the twentieth century depicts both liberalism and capitalism as central features, but not representative democracy, leading to charges of oligarchy. When overturned, oligarchical regimes were not replaced by elections and representation but, rather, by military dictatorship. Perón was a member of the military coup in 1943, for instance, which hints at the genetic and historical link Finchelstein draws between fascism and populism. What happened after 1943, on the other hand, severs that linkage. During this military dictatorship, Perón served as head of the Secretariat of Labour and Social Security, and it was his stewardship of this organisation that swelled his popular reputation enormously. This popularity reached such intensity that a chasm emerged between Perón and the military regime and, by October 1945, in an attempt to dampen this enthusiasm, the regime imprisoned Perón. Perón had amassed further ministries by this stage – Minister of War, head of the Post-War Council and the vice-presidency – but he inaugurated a truly radical wave of reforms at Labour and Social Security which were transforming Argentina's economy and society. The scale and depth of this reform programme is acknowledged by Finchelstein as 'improving working conditions, enforcing labor laws, giving more rights to farm and urban workers, fully funding state retirement, significantly expanding the power of unions, restricting the conditions under which workers could be fired, enacting paid holidays and vacations' (p. 111).

This social and economic transformation was intensified when Perón became president, and his 1946–1955 regime was marked by extending and deepening the reform programme Finchelstein outlines directly above, with profound effects on the reduction in social and economic inequalities, and a rapid spike in living standards for the majority of citizens (James, 1988). This began in February 1946, following elections that he and his followers insisted upon. The introduction of electoral democracy, following the popular mobilisations that secured the release of Perón and, ultimately, the downfall of the military dictatorship constituted a concomitant transformation of Argentina's politics. Electoral democracy was secured with Perón's elevation to presidency, and even deepened thereafter, with the franchise extended to women in 1947. It was only with the president's ousting by another coup in 1955 that the electoral process was abandoned, and for decades. This illustrates that electoral democracy was something of an anomaly in Argentina, and it wasn't for decades that the Perónist democratic experimentation was revived. In short, democracy was an outlier in Argentina's history, both before and after Perón.

These radical social, economic and political transformations hardly seem in keeping with Finchelstein's characterisation of Perón as 'antileftist', and this is further called into question when the issue of minorities is addressed. The impulse of populism and Perón to unify the people into a single will left few spaces for such minorities to express themselves and accusations of treachery when they did, according to Finchelstein. Yet the regime's popularity was in no small part due to its inclusivity – the inclusion of previously marginalised groups and minorities. The groups that were welcomed by Perón's inclusionary policies included the *cabecita negra* – 'the little blackheads', rural migrants to Buenos Aires that had previously attracted the scorn of its middle classes – and the 'shirtless' labourers known as *decamisados*. The extension of suffrage to women is indicative of further inclusion and through Eva, for the first time in its history, Argentina had a female role model at the heart of its government. All of this points to one 'regime' that is conspicuous by its absence in Finchelstein's quartet, namely social democracy, which experienced its heyday across multiple continents in the post-war decades, coinciding with Perónism. While there were clear departures from social democracy in Perónism, they resemble one another far more than Finchelstein's three other regime types.

In sum, Finchelstein's account is novel and bold in its elevation of populism to a regime of twentieth-century importance. The details Finchelstein offers of the history of Argentina, Perónism and populism are wanting and constitute revisionism of three phenomena that were far more complex than he allows (see James, 1988; Karush & Chamosa, 2010). It also jars noticeably with the Argentinian and broader Latin American experience with populism in the twenty-first century (Casullo, 2024; Biglieri & Perelló, 2024). Such incongruity warrants exploration into the theoretical presuppositions informing Finchelstein. The argument is founded in Enlightenment philosophy, yet the book's depiction of authoritarianism versus democracy alongside their revisionist deployment in the histories of Argentina, Perónism and populism, and the associations of populism with antileftism, antipluralism and ultimately fascism, all of these are suggestive of a more situated register than Kantian universalistic rationality. The prologue begins with the juxtaposition of a visit to the Anne Frank Museum in Amsterdam and a Pegida demonstration in Dresden, and it is the deep concern about fascism's revival and populism's complicity in this that informs the analysis. Of the four twentieth-century regimes Finchelstein identifies, both fascism and communism (or, more precisely, Soviet-style command socialism) remain sidelined globally.[2] That leaves populism as liberalism's threat. The democratic credentials of both have been widely debated (Bobbio, 1990; Mouffe, 1993, 2000, 2005, 2013, 2018; Brown, 2015; Rancière, 2014; Mounk, 2018; Müller, 2016; Rosanvallon, 2008, 2015;

Urbinati, 2014). Finchelstein aligns liberalism with democracy, and populism with authoritarianism. While this populism-authoritarianism link is nuanced by acknowledging populism's origins and dressing in democracy, its direction of travel is clear. Such a telos is difficult to reconcile, however, with multiple historical and recent iterations of left populisms that Finchelstein raises in his analysis – including the People's Party, Perónism, Vargas, Gaitan, Ibarra, Syriza, Podemos, the Kirchners and Morales – alongside plenty of others that aren't identified. The novelty and ambition of Finchelstein is clear, yet the execution, presuppositions and motives of defending a liberal democracy perceived to be under threat from populism have all provided a simplistic, one-way account of the beginnings, ontology and teleology of populism. Yet, the scale, novelty, ambition of the project offers a frame for other transnational and historical research agendas of populism which can cast further light on its beginnings.

## 3. National Case Studies

The predominant approach to the question of populism's origins has been forged and consolidated by historians who restrict their analysis to a specific time and place. Within this, two case studies have featured prominently as populism's pioneers, both from the late nineteenth century. The first is the *narodniki* of 1870s Russia, while the second is the People's Party which shook up politics in the United States in the 1890s. Historians analysing each of these two national case studies in isolation have deemed these political phenomena as populist. The same applies to those more general surveys of populism that cover its history that consider both as examples of populism (Canovan, 1981; Ionescu & Gellner, 1969; Taggart, 2000). This section, in contrast, develops a distinctive approach in highlighting radical differences between the two case studies. It builds on the recent contribution from Ely (2022, pp. 215–216) which raises profound differences between the two cases studies, but goes further still and poses the question as to whether the *narodniki* can be considered as an example of populism at all. Their distinctive aspects and divergences raise the question of their combination under the same conceptual heading or, put differently, their radically different attributes cast doubt on their sharing the same signifier. These radical differences point to markedly different understandings of the ontology of populism.

### *3.1 Narodniki*

The Bolshevik revolution generated historical investigation into its ideological origins, and such enquiry was given an additional boost during the Cold War when an Anglophone partner emerged to supplement Soviet historiography. Broadly, this literature identified two strands of leftism – or revolutionary tradition, socialism, and so forth – in late nineteenth-century Russia. Marxism was one which emerged in the century's final decades, while the other was a distinctly indigenous variant that ebbed and flowed throughout that century, and proved inspirational to, even the forerunner of, the Socialist Revolutionaries of the early twentieth century.

The *narodniki* are situated within the latter in the literature, and analyses more often than not begin with its theoretical origins (Ely, 2022; Mudde & Kaltwasser, 2017; Taggart, 2000; Ulam, 1977, 1981; Walicki, 1969; Wortman, 1967). Here, Alexander Herzen looms large and, in particular, the impact of the journal *The Bell*. Written in London and exported to Russian cities during its heyday between 1857 and 1863, the ideas Herzen promulgated prompted others to advocate for a politics based on the *narodniki*, with Nicholas Chernyshevsky the most prominent, both through the journal *The Contemporary* and his influential essay 'What is to be Done?' In tracing the *narodniki* back to theoretical origins, the methodology replicated those of the other ideologies to emerge in modernity. So, just as considerations of the ideology of socialism were traced back to the philosophical, sociological and economic underpinnings laid by Marx and Engels or their utopian predecessors, and the *Two Treatises of Government* is deemed to originate liberalism, the *narodniki* and, as a consequence, Russian populism find their origins in theory. To inaugurate and situate the *narodniki* and ergo populism in theory is, at the same time, to locate it in the realm of ideology. Such ideological beginnings align these methodologies with a particular approach to the study of populism – what is now known as the 'ideational' approach associated with Cas Mudde, which regards populism as a thin-centred ideology (Mudde, 2004, 2007, 2017; Mudde & Kaltwasser, 2017).

The emergence of the *narodniki* followed on from the most profound political development in nineteenth-century Russia, the Emancipation of the Serfs, or Great Reform of 1861. This signalled the end of feudalism and, for Russian intellectuals, promised further reforming developments, even revolutionary ones. Intellectuals were a prominent social group in Russian society by this stage, a feature of its distinctive trajectory, with a large student community based in Moscow and especially St Petersburg. Inspired by recent peasant uprisings and the writings of Herzen, Chernyshevky, et al., a new political party was formed, Land and Freedom. As Russia was still devoid of a representative parliament, Land and Freedom directed their activity outwards, towards society. And society at that moment meant the peasantry, who comprised some 85 per cent of the population. While the Great Reform signalled the long-run demise of this social category, peasant identities remained stable in the decades immediately following their act of emancipation, when they remained in their rural settings, continued to farm, and the differentiations within their ranks were yet to become stark. It was towards the peasantry that Land and Freedom went in 1874, largely from their St Petersburg base. This 'Pilgrimage to the People' flowed from the injunction Herzen made in 1861 to 'go to the people':

> From all parts of our enormous country … one hears groans, one hears the growing murmur. This is just the beginning of the tidal wave which after that oppressive period of calm, boils up, pregnant with storm. *To the people, to the people* – there is your place, you exiles from seats of learning. Show that you will become fighters for the Russian people. (Herzen, *The Bell*, 1861, in Ulam, 1981, p. 102)

This pilgrimage campaign emerged out of the restrictions any movement seeking social transformation encountered in Russia. Autocracy sidelined any expression through parliament, and the secret police became more prominent after an assassination attempt on the tsar in 1866, clamping down on radical groups assembling even in private, and preventing the production and publication of newspapers, journals and other literatures.

With such channels of expression and assembly denied, the *narodniki* adopted the strategy of descending on the countryside to merge with the peasantry and to proselytise their revolutionary cause. Herzen and other intellectuals were convinced of the peasants' egalitarianism and that their communal institutions provided the route to a Russian form of socialism. Land and Freedom had confidence in the pilgrimage unlocking that potential.

The practice of 'going to the people' frustrated these expectations. The *narodniki* found conditions tough with many unable to match the long hours and hard work of the peasantry, who were malnourished and unhealthy. The peasants were unreceptive to the ideas the *narodniki* brought with them, disappointing their supposed revolutionary potential. This was exacerbated by their experience of communalism, which transpired to be adopted not out of egalitarian commitment but out of expedience, and solidarity amongst the peasantry was found to be singularly lacking. As the medical specialist, Vera Figner, wrote, 'I felt alone, weak and powerless in the peasant sea' (cited in Ely, 2022, p. 110). The pilgrimage of summer 1874 was unsuccessful and short-lived. Many of its practitioners were shopped into the authorities by the peasants and, on regrouping in St Petersburg, some members of Land and Freedom tweaked their approach, rejecting the earlier hopes of winning the peasants round through direct and immediate means. Instead, they sought to extend their stay, bring practical skills such as teaching and medicine to the countryside, and play the longer game to bring the peasantry round to their revolutionary proposals. This tweaked approach petered out without success and, by the late 1870s, they turned to terrorism as a strategy.

This shift to terrorism highlights an overriding feature of the *narodniki*: the distance between them and the people. This distance can be teased out by focusing on the two related issues of their social provenance and ideological orientation. Nineteenth-century Russia was starkly divided between two main social groups: the *narod*, usually translated as 'ordinary people' which in practice meant the peasantry – rural, largely illiterate, manual labourers – comprising about 85 percent of society; and 'educated society' or 'polite society', comprising nobility augmented by growing numbers of educated urbanites as the century developed. It was from the ranks of the latter that the *narodniki* hailed. These were, in short, two cultures, and the pronounced cultural differences between the rural, labouring, illiterate, agrarian peasantry – that is, the *narod* or even *muzhik*, another name used to describe the peasantry which translates as 'small man' – and *obshchestvo*, the urban, cosmopolitan, Western-oriented Europhiles resting on their intellects and education. That social chasm problematises any association of the *narodniki* or indeed late nineteenth-century Russia with populism, which should be understood as the emergence, consolidation and repeated practice of the people as an actor on the political stage. For this to happen, the *narodniki* would have achieved success in their goal of 'merging' with the people, whereby the *obshchestvo* and *narod* became one. Instead, as a recent overview of Russian populism insists, 'while Russian populism focuses its interest on the *narod*, it was entirely a product and practice of *obshchestvo*' (Ely, 2022, p. 3).

This social and cultural chasm is reinforced by the role and import commentators attribute to ideology within Russian populism. As already indicated, it is with theory that analysis of Russian populism begins. That theory was as much informed by the hope, imaginary and expectations of the *obshchestvo* and, within that, the *narodniki* than it was with personal acquaintance with or scientific understanding of the *muzhik*. Nor did this theory develop out of any range of demands that emerged from the countryside. At its core, this theory insisted on respect for and devotion towards the peasantry. To this was added the revolutionary instinct and route to socialism. These core features were unified into a distinctive Russian understanding of a transition to socialism – via the peasantry and, within that, its purported traditions of solidarity and the egalitarianism of its communal forms of organisation. Within the *narodniki*, nuances emerged about how this transformation would occur, with one position opining that the role of the *narodniki* was to catalyse the peasants' revolutionary instincts which would usher in a new socialist order, while others viewed that the *obshchestvo* needed to merge into the *narod*, and that process of unification would prompt the utopian transformation of Russia. Again, this highlights the ideological distance between Russia's two broad social groups, a distance that was manifested by the indifferent even hostile reaction of the *muzhik* to the 'going to the people' campaign. It is also illustrative of the trouble with associating populism with ideology or, more broadly, a theoretical starting-point – which has been the approach of most commentators considering Russian populism. The ultimate chasm between the *narodniki* and the *narod* indicate a further chasm: between populism and its association with ideology. Rather than an ideology – or seeking its beginnings in theoretical texts and underpinnings – populism should be viewed as a practice, as a form, as a logic or as a phenomenon that emerges under certain conditions that enables the construction of the people as an actor on the political stage, one that is capable of articulating an antagonistic relationship to the establishment. This populist construction of the people is as much done from within the people and its component parts, and never occurs purely from without, as was the case with the *narodniki*. We now turn to the other example historians have deemed a pioneering case study of populism, which emerged from within and not without, and through practice and not in theory.

### 3.2 The People's Party

Since the Civil War, the People's Party remains the largest and most prominent third party in American politics. The challenge it posed to the party duopoly ensured it garnered (and generated) widespread attention in the late nineteenth century, and historians have retained a sustained and keen interest subsequently.[3] While dovetailing temporally, the context within which the People's Party emerged contrasted markedly with its purported late nineteenth-century populist Russian counterpart. It's worth highlighting a few of these contextual factors because they illustrate how and why US populism materialised, and the extent to which it differs from the *narodniki*. The most obvious difference is the representative political system, and the liberal freedoms – of speech, the press, association – accorded to the majority of the population springing from its formation. The United States' economy in the reconstruction era and, more broadly, in the latter half of the nineteenth century underwent gradual yet profound transformation, building on technological developments in transportation and communication which, in turn, facilitated spatial extensions to trading patterns. At the same time, banking and finance carved a more prominent role within the economy, and the combination of these developments led to an increasing role for monopoly players in the economy – heavy industries such as steel, banking, railroads, and so on. On the flipside, monopolisations of wealth, industry and technologies posed challenges to the producing classes – farmers were squeezed as concentrations of scale developed in agriculture, whereas the size of transport and heavy industries required mass labour through which employers could exercise control over working conditions and wages.

The economy, in short, moved towards a monopoly variant of capitalism, with its concentrations of wealth in a few hands amidst widespread impoverishment, diminished hopes and opportunities (see especially Pollack, 1962). Such economic monopolisation was reinforced by the party political duopoly, as the Republicans and Democrats became entrenched. The role of the increasingly influential press consolidated this political economy further still, through its articulation of the interests of the big players and advocacy of the status quo. This combination generated the impression of an establishment operating in unison, and against the wider public interest. In Laclau's terms, a frontier had been established, and the hegemonic framework of the establishment entered into crisis, as increasing sectors of the public became hostile towards the social, political and economic direction of travel.

This establishment convergence went hand in hand with a counter-development, namely the proliferation of numerous organisations seeking to represent the demands of multiple sectoral interests, emerging from different localities. These organisations formed the basis of the People's Party but also retained their own autonomy and interests – which had more often than not been decades-long in cultivation, and required careful nurturing and protection. The People's Party was, in short, a balancing act between the twin requirements of party organisation and electoral breakthrough on the one hand, and the myriad forms of demands, organisations, subjectivities and strategies that fed into it. It's worth quoting two lengthy passages from Laura Grattan's survey of populism, also known as 'American radical grassroots democracy', to illustrate the wide array of groupings that fed into the People's Party's formation in the early 1890s. Grattan enumerates the practices that fed into it:

> the public work of cooperative farming; the insurgent rituals of boycotts and strikes; the political education carried out in rural lecture circuits, immigrant social halls, and union reading rooms; the revivalism of prohibition; the cross-cutting fabric of women's social networks; the disruptive energies of suffrage; and the resilient efforts of black communities to build schools, promote economic independence, and secure civil and political rights. These were the spaces in which, for decades prior to the People's

Party, grassroots Populists experimented with parallel institutions and practices of political economy and democracy. In doing so, they cultivated dispositions toward horizontal cooperation and spirited rebellion. (Grattan, 2016, p. 50)

This list illustrates the range of subjectivities flowing into the People's Party:

> the insurgent activities of white and black agrarian rebels, urban immigrant laborers, agitators for women's rights, prohibitionists, greenbackers, single-tax advocates, saloon utopianists, Marxist and Christian socialists, armies of the unemployed, and other 'cranks, tramps, and vagabonds' ... the original 'Populism' was really many populisms at once. (Grattan, 2016, p. 49)

The People's Party was not only a negotiation between the organisations and subjectivities that coalesced into it, these organisations also required regular concessions between local, state and national levels.

The pluralities behind its formation meant that the People's Party emerged out of practice – in stark contrast to the theoretical underpinnings of the *narodniki*. It's striking that whereas historians of the latter turn to Herzen, Chernyshevsky, and so on to begin their accounts, when we turn to American nineteenth-century populism, theoreticians are conspicuous through their absence. Instead, and as Grattan's approach exemplifies, it is towards the rich myriad of practice that attention is turned. Grattan reinforces this process of diversity coalescing into third-party formation by resorting to the notion of 'peopling', which highlights the dynamism of the movement – and generates the welcome contrast with those ontological projections onto a static, unchanging and 'pure' *narod* and *muzhik* undertaken by the *narodniki*, which Grattan terms 'peoplehood'. Peopling aligns with those approaches to populism that highlight the construction of the people, and is also suggestive of the import of language. New languages emanate from the range of practices that flow into the populist construction of the people, which is why the celebrated historians of American populism and the People's Party emphasise the role of language. For Kazin, the language of populism is its 'most basic and telling definition' (1998, p. 1) which explains the resort to (its powers of) persuasion per as the text's title. Kazin insists populism is more an impulse – that is a practice, a persuasion – than an ideology grounded in theory, whose practitioners use 'a flexible mode of persuasion. They used traditional kinds of expressions, tropes, themes, and images to convince large numbers of Americans to join their side' (1998, p. 3). Similarly, Goodwyn speaks of the centrality of the invention of new languages in forging the multiple organisations into a new subjectivity (1976, xi; 1978, pp. 174–212).

This new subjectivity was not only multiple but explicitly collective. Against the consolidating monopoly capital credo of Lockean individualism and social Darwinism that reinforced the establishment, emergent identities and actors emphasised their subjectivities as collective. This incorporated farmers in alliance, the manual working class, women and black communities – all of whom developed collective understandings not only within their own subjectivities, but also the importance of constructing the people through their combination and against the identity the establishment attempted to bestow upon them. Such a collective subjectivity would have its replication in the demand for a combinatory and coordinating – or 'activist' – state that abandoned the logic of laissez-faire and began acting in the interests of the radical, democratic, populist people while at the same time activating a mobilised citizen body participating in the state.

### *3.3 Concluding Comments*

This section has isolated the two candidates that historians have designated as populism's progenitors. In highlighting the stark differences between the *narodniki* and the People's Party, the question as to whether they both can or should be considered under the banner of populism has been raised. While these two political organisations are frequently characterised as populism's originators, the accounts of historians complexify the question of populism's origins. In terms of the *narodniki*, their practice was traced back to theoretical origins (Ely, 2022; Ulam, 1977; Wortman, 1967). Historians of American populism have cast their net more widely in identifying forerunners to the People's Party, whether that be the Jacksonian inheritance (Hofstadter, 1969) or the myriad of 'Populist' organisations that fed into the formation of the third-party challenger itself (Grattan, 2016).

In the approach of isolating case studies to identify populism's beginnings, there is always the potential for a more distant case study to appear as the logic is that each of these are discrete from one another. Yet in insisting on populism prior to the People's Party and locating it in the practice of the decades-long organisations that eventually formed this third party, Grattan intimates towards the third response within the literature as to populism's origins.

### 4. Populism and Politics, or as the Political

The third and final position on populism's beginnings is outlined by two of the most important contributors to populism studies: Margaret Canovan and Ernesto Laclau. Both trace populism or at least its people versus elite logic further back than either of the first two positions do. Both, moreover, even align populism with politics and the political. They hail from a different academic field to the historians of the first two positions, in identifying as political theorists. Yet both are alive enough to developments in the history of politics to track the populist logic or the logic of a particular understanding of the people at least as far as the Roman republic. They arrive at this point through somewhat different means which, in turn, explains the different trajectories that point onwards. Although there are other political theorists – such as Pierre Rosanvallon (2008, pp. 265–274; 2021, pp. 59–69) or Jacques Rancière (2013, 2017) – who locate populism's beginnings to events, practices and movements prior to the late nineteenth century – the remainder of the section will restrict itself to outlining the nuanced accounts developed by Canovan and Laclau.

### *4.1 Canovan, 'the People' and Populism*

Margaret Canovan trod a lonely furrow when working on populism in the 1970s. Even by the new millennium, Canovan (2004) complained of its marginal status within the academy, and the benefit its wider study would bring to the discipline of politics. It was with the 'radical populist' G. K. Chesterton that Canovan (1978) focused on this neglected feature of politics, but it was in the simply titled *Populism* (1981) that a comprehensive survey was generated. While this monograph attracted critical feedback as to its ambiguities and paradoxes (Laclau, 2005a, pp. 4–8), a series of articles on populism written around the turn of the millennium (1999, 2002, 2004) have justifiably received more positive responses. The 1981 overview prompted scrutiny into the notion of the people, with Canovan recognising that this notion too was under-investigated, particularly when compared to those of class, the nation and the individual. Subsequent years entailed addressing this lack (1982, 1984), eventually culminating in the 2005 survey *The People*.

While the 1981 overview began with the case studies of the *narodniki* and the People's Party, it is via Canovan's examination of the notion of the people that a theorisation emerged. Three distinctive understandings are proposed in the varying accounts of this pivotal, long-running and ongoing political subject, whereby Canovan designates the people as: nation; underdog; and everyman (1984, p. 315). By the 2005 monograph, Canovan retains the tripartite classification but shifts terminology somewhat to the people as nation, as the common people, and as sovereign (2005, p. 2). It is the second understanding within both of these typologies that is most pertinent to populism, but before analysing this, some brief remarks on the other two are in order.

There are certain crossovers between the first – the people as nation – and third – the people as everyman, or as sovereign – understandings. These different understandings and their crossovers reveal the ambiguity and elasticity at the heart of this pivotal notion of politics. Canovan is surely right to highlight in line with Gallie (1956) that, whereas all core political concepts are contested, levels of contestation are rarely as elevated as with the people. When considering the 'myth' of the people, Canovan uses the following terms to describe the first understanding, the people as nation: all, collective, abstract, entity and continuous. This is in contrast with the 'people as everyman' who are viewed as individual members of a community, so as concrete and identifiable, yet also as discontinuous as they enter into that category analogous to a conveyor belt – in other words, individuals are born (or come of age) while others die. We might respectively characterise these two as the symbolic and aggregative models of the people, which echoes the distinction Rousseau carves between 'the general will' and 'the will of all' (2012). This explains the overriding difference between the two, whereas an absence – or, at the very least, limitation – of agency constitutes their similarity. Hobbes' portrayal of a national people governed by a Leviathan (1996) or sovereign explains the non-agency of the people: via the social contract, agency has been invested in the Leviathan, and this endorses the conservatism Canovan aligns with this understanding. The lack of agency of the 'people as everyman' follows from the opposite cause: its incongruence, its disunity – it is not that agency has been relinquished, but there is an inability to exercise it.

The second understanding of the people – as underdogs, or the common people – possesses the possibility to exercise agency, by contrast. And Canovan traces this iteration all the way back to the Roman *populus*, 'from which the language of "people" is descended' (2005, p. 10). This *populus* or *populares* was also known as the plebeians who posed a challenge to the unified understanding of the people articulated by the senators or patrician class. Rome's republican phase aligned with the reconfiguration forged by this challenge – whereby the ruling Senate had to grapple with a new institution representing the *populares*, the Tribune of the Plebs. It was not only the agency the people-as-underdogs exerted in establishing this institution, its existence enabled the continuing exercise of this agency. Canovan also illustrates this via the part/whole analogy, whereby an excluded part – the majority that is the *populares* – rejects the extant whole (as represented by the patricians) and announces itself as the (majority) part that is the whole. There is a process of part-becoming-whole here: the majority no longer accept their lowly status and assume that their numerical strength deems them representative – and representatives – of the whole.

Canovan insists that this political practice originating at least as far back as the Roman republic remains an obdurate if not continuous feature of subsequent politics: '[t]he stubborn ambiguity between part and whole has persisted through many political conflicts in which the people-as-excluded-part have claimed power as the largest section of the people-as-sovereign-whole'. Immediately afterwards, Canovan aligns this mode of politics with populist movements which 'still seek to mobilize the people as excluded part in the name of the people as sovereign whole, and their demand is still that power must be taken from the elite and given to the people' (2005, pp. 65–66). To capture this mobilisation, the narrative arc Canovan depicts is a familiar Western one: from Rome to Italian city-states and, more emphatically, the English Civil War, the French and American Revolutions, into Chartism and then beyond. The people-as-underdog practice of announcing and asserting itself which begins in Rome and ramps up in the modern world, in other words, has been a persistent if occasional feature of the history of politics. This very same people-as-underdog practice is synonymous with Canovan's later definition of populism, whereby 'populism in modern societies is best seen as an appeal to "the people" against both the established structure of power and dominant ideas and values of the society' (1999, p. 3).[4]

While multiple readings of Canovan's trajectory are available, one valid one is that via an investigation of both the people and populism, Canovan insinuates populist practice – or its twin or close cousin, the people-as-underdog – can be traced all the way back to Rome, that this reappears subsequently and becomes more extensive with the modern turn. There is a similarity here with Laclau.

### *4.2 Laclau: Populist Logic as the Political*

Laclau provides a more rigorous theoretical or ontological account in order to explain populism and its operation. Commentators point to its formalism (Stavrakakis, 2004) or characterise it as a logical approach to populism (Moffitt, 2016) in explicating its theoretical orientation. As with Canovan, Laclau traces the populist logic back to the Roman republic and the ambiguous status of the people situated between the *plebs* and the *populus*, and the paradox entailed by the necessity of the whole that is the people and the impossibility of representing that whole. The *populus* here is conceived as the whole body of citizens, whereas the *plebs* constitute the underdogs or underprivileged, that is, those other than the patricians.

While the account provided is multi-faceted, Laclau deems populism as the moment in which the *plebs* abandons the seamless unity between them and the patricians and, instead, announce and claim that they themselves represent the whole. Descriptively the claim that the *plebs* constitute the whole is evidently erroneous, for the very reason that the whole also includes the patricians. Laclau writes, 'the "people", as operating in populist discourses, is never a primary datum but a construct – populist discourse does not simply *express* some kind of populist identity; it actually *constitutes* the latter' (2005b, p. 48). This means that for Laclau the political exceeds description, and the political act *par excellence* is for the part to act as if they are the whole. Or as Laclau puts it, 'a partial object … can have a non-partitive meaning, not a part *of* the whole, but a part that *is* the whole' (2005a, p. 225). And again:

> In order to have the 'people' of populism, we need something more: we need a *plebs* who claims to be the only legitimate *populus* – that is, a partiality which wants to function as the totality of the community. (2005a, p. 81)

The republican turn in Rome when the *plebs* refused the existing state of affairs, formed and announced themselves as a political actor, and established the Tribune of the Plebs thus constitutes an early iteration of populist logic for Laclau.

Both Laclau's account of the political, and its association with populism are contentious aspects of his thought even for sympathetic commentators (Panizza, 2005, p. 28; Arditi, 2010; Borriello & Jäger, 2021). Laclau's ontological reading insists the notion of antagonism is pivotal to the political. He contrasts the political with administration, echoing Saint-Simon's frictionless formula 'from the government of men to the administration of things'. Laclau further aligns populism with the political when he states that his attempt in *On Populist Reason* is to prove 'that populism is the royal road to understanding something about the construction of the political as such' (2005a, p. 67). Yet, from its purported starting point in republican Rome, no further examples are offered in *On Populist Reason* until the French Revolution – and this despite comments such as, 'distinctive always present possibility of structuration of political life' (2005a, p. 13). One explanation for this extensive historical gap would be Laclau's formalism, in contrast to Canovan's case study-based 'phenomenological' method of 'presuppositionless description' (1982, p. 555). This does prompt the question as to whether a period approaching two millennia really was devoid of 'the political' – and as Laclau doesn't answer this question, the need for interpretation heightens. One helpful response has been offered by Borriello and Jäger (2021) in their proposal of a 'post-Laclauian approach', which distinguishes between populism and an older 'plebeian politics' of which populism is the modern update. This would align populism with modernity and, more particularly, certain of its most prominent features – including the overriding roles of electoral representation, capitalism and the broader themes of democracy, equality, inclusivity and freedom. These themes are in line with 'the democratic revolution' that Laclau and Mouffe develop in their collaborative work (1985, pp. 149–194; 1990, pp. 127–130, see also Laclau, 1990, pp. 78–84).

A modern starting point for populism that begins with the French Revolution then seems a plausible reading – or, at the very least, a reworking of Laclau, narrowing its scope. Such a modern origin would be in keeping with the contrast Laclau draws between the success of the French Revolution itself, when compared to the isolation and lack of coordination between various riots in the preceding decades, such as the Corn Riots of 1775 Paris (Laclau, 2005a, pp. 74–76, 79–80). Laclau insists that the success of the French Revolution flowed from the construction of a radical frontier, with the *ancien régime* on one side, and a plurality of demands and constituencies coalescing into a cohesive force on the other. The same process leads to the upsurge of the Chartist movement in the 1830s, while Laclau also brings Boulangism that swept through France in the 1880s into consideration (2005a, pp. 89–93, pp. 178–182). Chartism and Boulangism are nineteenth-century political episodes other – and, in Chartism's case, much earlier – than the case studies of the *narodniki* and the People's Party considered in the previous section that are the more broadly recognised pioneers of populism amongst historians.

The identification of earlier beginnings in all probability results from Laclau's formalism within which it is the populist *logic* that is crucial, rather than the case study approach favoured as an historiography. Yet one notable feature of Laclau's theory is its systematicity, and its ability to incorporate a wider range of disciplinary elements within itself – even if a resounding clarity is lacking. It is the focus on the logic of populism and its connection with the political that has enabled Laclau to track further back to earlier iterations of populism and, in doing so, both Laclau and Canovan open up important questions about populism's beginnings.

## 5. Concluding Remarks

This chapter has sought to begin a conversation on the question of populism's origins. The heightened level of interest in populism is a justification for such a conversation, and the initial plea is that this is conducted with at least a keen awareness of the way in which different methodologies and disciplines can contribute to interrogating this question – even if a transdisciplinary approach is not explicitly adopted. This early attempt at addressing populism's beginnings isolates three different responses to the question, emphasising the different disciplinary, methodological and motivational concerns along the way.

Further responses can be alive to a number of core considerations and contrasts in how populism itself is approached, and what precisely is under investigation. In this chapter, certain issues have been raised. While these issues cannot exhaust the potential angles through which to investigate the question of populism's origins, recognition of them will introduce some welcome clarity into the research agenda. We will finish by listing a few of the issues raised in this chapter, and aligning them with the authors considered within this chapter: while Finchelstein concentrates on history and Moffitt (2016) on contemporary practice, both authors focus on populism as a global phenomenon; how can the different 'levels' – of the nation, continental or regional, and global – be understood?; Finchelstein's insistence on populism as a regime or what is usually known as 'populisms in power', which can be contrasted to the far more prominent study of populisms in opposition; given its widespread exclusion from the register of populisms, the example of Chartism raises the issue of renaming it as populism – and the renaming of other case studies; does a different 'register' of populist case studies impact upon the 'ontology' or – more modestly – understanding of populism?; similarly, what effect does the identification of a new, alternative origin do to this understanding?

**Notes**

1. All subsequent references to this book are simply presented as page numbers in parentheses in this section.
2. While this section has questioned the fit of Perónism into Finchelstein's fourfold regime typology, equally contemporary China offers its own set of problems.
3. The literature on the People's Party is vast and growing. The following is a necessarily selective list of the most celebrated historical works on the People's Party and US populism more broadly over the past century: Hicks (1931); Hofstadter (1955, 1965); Pollack (1962), Goodwyn (1978); Kazin (1998); Postel (2009); Grattan (2016); Judis (2016); Lowndes (2017); Frank (2020).
4. This is to highlight a distinction between the 'early' and 'later' accounts of populism offered by Canovan, and to accept the latter and not the former. These early accounts of populism (1981, 1982, 1984) follow a methodology Canovan nominates as 'phenomenological' which is 'not intended in a strictly Husserlian sense, but refers simply to the ideal of presuppositionless description' (1982, p.555). Canovan presents this as one of 'Two

strategies for the study of populism', to draw on the article's title, and the other strategy is named as 'the theoretical approach'. Laclau (2005a, pp.5-8) has explained the shortcomings of the early Canovan, while at the same time endorsing the later Canovan (Laclau, 2005a, p.222): both of Laclau's assessments here are persuasive.

**Bibliography**

Arditi, B. (2010) 'Populism is hegemony is politics? Ernesto Laclau's *On Populist Reason*', *Constellations*, 17 (3), pp. 488–497.

Biglieri, P. and Perelló, G. (2024) 'Rupture, institutionalisation and tension: about populist temporality in Latin America', in Knott (2024), pp. 188–206.

Bobbio, N. (1990) *Liberalism and democracy*. London: Verso.

Borriello, A. and Jäger, A. (2021) 'The antinomies of Ernesto Laclau: a reassessment', *Journal of Political Ideologies*, 26 (3), pp. 298–316.

Brown, W. (2015) *Undoing the demos: neoliberalism's stealth revolution*. New York: Zone Books.

Canovan, M. (1978) *G.K. Chesterton: radical populist*. New York: Harcourt Brace Jovanovich.

Canovan, M. (1981) *Populism*. New York: Harcourt Brace Jovanovich.

Canovan, M. (1982) 'Two strategies for the study of populism', *Political Studies*, 30 (4), pp. 544–552.

Canovan, M. (1984) '"People", politicians and populism', *Government & Opposition*, 19 (3), pp. 312–327.

Canovan, M. (1999) 'Trust the people! Populism and the two faces of democracy', *Political Studies*, 47 (1), pp. 2–16.

Canovan, M. (2004) 'Populism for political theorists?', *Journal of Political Ideologies*, 9 (3), pp. 241–252.

Canovan, M. (2002) 'Taking politics to the people: populism as the ideology of democracy', in Mény, Y. and Surel, Y. (eds) *Democracies and the populist challenge*. London: Palgrave Macmillan, pp. 25–44.

Canovan, M. (2005) *The people*. Cambridge: Polity.

Casullo, M. (2024) 'Antagonism, flexibility and the surprising resilience of populism', in Knott (2024), pp. 169–87.

De Cleen, B., Glynos, J. and Mondon, A. (2018) 'Critical research on populism: nine rules of engagement', *Organization*, 25 (5), pp. 649–661.

De la Torre, C. (ed.) (2019) *Routledge handbook of global populism*. London: Routledge.

Ely, C. (2022) *Russian populism: a history*. London: Bloomsbury.

Finchelstein, F. (2017) *From fascism to populism in history*. Oakland: University of California Press.

Frank, T. (2020) *People without power: the war on populism and the fight for democracy*. London: Scribe.

Freeden, M. (1996) *Ideologies and political theory: a conceptual approach*. Oxford: Oxford University Press.

Gallie, W. (1956) 'Essentially contested concepts', *Proceedings of the Aristotelian Society*, 56, pp. 167–198.

Glynos, J. and Mondon, A. (2016) 'The political logic of populist hype: the case of right-wing populism's "meteoric rise" and its relation to the status quo', *Populismus* Working Papers No. 4.

Goodwyn, L. (1976) *Democratic promise: the populist moment in America*. Oxford: Oxford University Press.

Goodwyn, L. (1978) *The populist moment; a short history of the agrarian revolt in America*. Oxford: Oxford University Press.

Grattan, L. (2016) *Populism's power: radical grassroots democracy in America*. Oxford: Oxford University Press.

Hicks, J. (1931) *Populist revolt: a history of the Farmers Alliance and the People's Party*. Minneapolis: University of Minnesota Press.

Hobbes, T. (1996) *Leviathan*. Oxford: Oxford University Press.

Hobsbawm, E. (1995) *The age of extremes: the short twentieth century, 1914–1991*. London: Abacus.

Hofstadter, R. (1955) *The age of reform*. New York: Vintage.

Hofstadter, R. (1965) *The paranoid style in American politics and other essays*. New York: Vintage.

Hofstadter, R. (1969) 'North America', in Ionescu, G. and Gellner, E. (eds) *Populism: its meaning and national characteristics*. London: The Macmillan Company, pp. 9–27.

Ionescu, G. and Gellner, E. (eds) (1969) *Populism: its meaning and national characteristics*. London: The Macmillan Company.

James, D. (1988) *Resistance and integration: Peronism and the Argentine working class, 1946–1976*. Cambridge: Cambridge University Press.

Judis, J. (2016) *The populist explosion: how the Great Recession transformed American and European politics*. New York: Columbia Global Reports.

Karush, M. and Chamosa, O. (eds) (2010) *The new cultural history of Peronism: power and identity in mid-twentieth-century Argentina*. Durham, NC: Duke University Press.

Kazin, M. (1998) *The populist persuasion: an American history*. Ithaca, NY: Cornell University Press.

Knott, A. (ed.) (2024) *Populism and time: temporalities of a disruptive politics*. Edinburgh: Edinburgh University Press.

Laclau, E. (1990) *New reflections on the revolution of our time*. London: Verso.

Laclau, E. (2005a) *On populist reason*. London: Verso.

Laclau, E. (2005b) 'Populism: what's in a name?', in Panizza, F. (ed.) *Populism and the mirror of democracy*. London: Verso, pp. 32–49.

Laclau E. and Mouffe, C. (1985) *Hegemony and socialist strategy: towards a radical democratic politics*. London: Verso.

Laclau, E. and Mouffe, C. (1987) 'Post-Marxism without apologies', *New Left Review*, 166 (1), pp. 79–106.

Laclau, E. and Mouffe, C. (1990) 'Post-Marxism without apologies', in Laclau, E., *New reflections on the revolution of our time*. London: Verso, pp. 97–132.

Lowndes, J. (2017) 'Populism in the United States', in Rovira Kaltwasser, C., Taggart, P., Ochoa Espejo, P. and Ostiguy, P. (eds) *The Oxford handbook of populism*. Oxford: Oxford University Press, pp. 232–247.

Moffitt, B. (2016) *The global rise of populism: performance, political style, and representation*. Stanford, CA: Stanford University Press.

Mouffe, C. (1993) *The return of the political*. London: Verso.

Mouffe, C. (2000) *The democratic paradox*. London: Verso.

Mouffe, C. (2005) *On the political*. London: Verso.

Mouffe, C, (2013) *Agonistics: thinking the world politically*. London: Verso.

Mouffe, C. (2018) *For a left populism*. London: Verso.

Mounk, Y. (2018) *The people vs. democracy: why our freedom is in danger and how to save it*. Cambridge, MA: Harvard University Press.

Mudde, C. (2004) 'The populist zeitgeist', *Government and Opposition*, 39 (4), pp. 541–563.

Mudde, C. (2007) *Populist radical right parties in Europe*. Cambridge: Cambridge University Press.

Mudde, C. (2017) 'Populism: an ideational approach', in Rovira Kaltwasser, C., Taggart, P., Ochoa Espejo, P. and Ostiguy, P. (eds) *The Oxford handbook of populism*. Oxford: Oxford University Press, pp. 27–47.

Mudde, C. and Kaltwasser, C. (2017) *Populism: a very short introduction*. Oxford: Oxford University Press.

Müller, J.-W. (2016) *What is populism?* Philadelphia: University of Pennsylvania Press.

Ostiguy, P., Panizza, F. and Moffitt, B. (eds) (2021) *Populism in global perspective: a performative and discursive approach*. Oxon: Routledge.

Panizza, F. (2005) 'Introduction: populism and the mirror of democracy', in Panizza, F. (ed.) *Populism and the mirror of democracy*. London: Verso, pp. 1–31.

Pollack, N. (1962) *The populist response to industrial America*. Cambridge, MA: Harvard University Press.

Postel, C. (2009) *The populist vision*. Oxford: Oxford University Press.

Rancière, J. (1999) *Disagreement: Politics and Philosophy*. Minneapolis: University of Minnesota press.

Rancière, J. (2013) '"The people are not a brutal, ignorant mass", Jacques Rancière on Populism', retrieved from https://www.versobooks.com/blogs/1226-the-people-are-not-a-brutal-and-ignorant-mass-jacques-Rancière-on-populism.

Rancière, J. (2014) *Hatred of democracy*. London: Verso.

Rancière, J. (2017) 'Attacks on Populism seek to enshrine the idea that there is no alternative', https://www.versobooks.com/blogs/3193-attacks-on-populism-seek-to-enshrine-the-idea-that-there-is-no-alternative

Rosanvallon, P. (2008) *Counter-democracy: politics in an age of distrust*. Cambridge: Cambridge University Press.

Rosanvallon, P. (2015) *The society of equals*. Cambridge, MA: Harvard University Press.

Rosanvallon, P. (2021) *The populist century*. Cambridge: Polity.

Rousseau, J.-J. (2012) *Of the social contract and other writings*. London: Penguin.

Rovira Kaltwasser, C., Taggart, P., Ochoa Espejo, P. and Ostiguy, P. (eds) *The Oxford handbook of populism*. Oxford: Oxford University Press.

Stavrakakis, Y. (2004) 'Antinomies of formalism: Laclau's theory of populism and the lessons from religious populism in Greece', *Journal of Political Ideologies*, 9 (3), pp. 253–267.

Taggart, P. (2000) *Populism*. Buckingham: Open University Press.

Ulam, A. (1977) *In the name of the people: prophets and conspirators in prerevolutionary Russia*. New York: The Viking Press.

Ulam, A. (1981) *Russia's failed revolutions: from the Decembrists to the Dissidents*. London: Wiedenfeld and Nicolson.

Urbinati, N. (2014) *Democracy disfigured: opinion, truth and the people*. Cambridge, MA: Harvard University Press.

Walicki, A. (1969) 'Russia', in Ionescu, G. and Gellner, E. (eds) *Populism: its meaning and national characteristics*. London: The Macmillan Company, pp. 62–96.

Wortman, R. (1967) *The crisis of Russian populism*. London: Cambridge University Press.

# 3

# Populism, Impossible Time and Democracy's People Problem[1]

*Clare Woodford*

Recent right-wing electoral gains in Sweden, Italy, the Philippines, Nicaragua, and Israel; the storming of the Capitol in the US; Russia's ongoing war in Ukraine, and threats contributing to the resignation of New Zealand Prime Minister Jacinda Ardern are perhaps some of the most recent examples of a widespread trend identified as the growing threat of authoritarianism around the world (Freedom House, 2022, see also Economic Intelligence Unit/ Democracy Index, 2021; Pew Research Centre, 2021). This trend is seen by many to be, at least in part, caused by and manifested through the rise of populist politics over the last few decades (IDEA, 2021) leading to the widespread belief that we now live 'in populist times' (Moffit, 2016). In this chapter I question this claim that we are living through an era of populism, which is, furthermore, understood to be authoritarian and anti-democratic. Populism scholarship has been making this claim for at least the last fifty years (Mudde, 2004) and the concerns that form the basis of this claim have been around for as long as democracy itself. Given the historical association between populism scholarship and arguments that seek to limit and constrain democracy, I suggest we should be cautious of the familiar assumption that populist politics is anti-democratic. In contrast, I ask what might happen if we set out from the premise that populism need not be an exception to democracy nor necessarily anti-democratic. The alternative analysis provided by the latter approach indicates that the mainstream populism scholarship does not facilitate objective analysis but effects a distinct politics of its own. It has replaced the dominant political cleavage in democracy, that of a polar scale of gradations between left and right, with a binary model of politics as either populist or democratic. The result is a drastic narrowing of what is accepted as legitimate democratic politics, rendering unavailable the left-wing politics that would be most useful in opposing the popularity of growing right-wing authoritarian politics.

Inspired by the work of Chantal Mouffe, Ernesto Laclau and Jacques Rancière, I ask whether the transformation of the political landscape effected by populism studies might stem from a misconceputalisation of 'the people' as a problem, not just within populism scholarship but in the wider field of democratic theory. Conceptualising the people as problematic for democracy creates unnecessary apprehension regarding the aesthetic operation by which the people of democracy are constituted. In contrast with prevalent theories of democracy's founding, bounding and constituting, I argue that the people are constructed via an aesthetic operation which requires the simultaneous existence of competing definitions of the people at any one time. This is an operation that the dominant order will resist as 'impossible' since it will always pose a challenge to that order. However, it is not impossible, and is, instead, indispensable for democratic politics. Refusing to accept the premise that the people pose a problem for democracy, I argue that clarifying the temporal play that is so crucial for the relationship between the people and democracy helps identify a vital resource for developing anti-authoritarian political strategy. Yet, if we are to defend democracy against the rising threat of authoritarianism, any such strategy needs to be accompanied by theoretical work that first identifies how not only fascism but liberalism too can lead to authoritarianism; second, that it is necessary for progressive politics to cease criticising populism *qua* populism; and, third, against the false dichotomy of liberal minimal democracy on one side and the authoritarian right on the other, to articulate a left-wing, social democratic alternative.

## 1. The Populist Threat to Democracy

We apparently now live in 'populist times' (Moffitt, 2016). The first two decades of the twenty-first century have seen a populist 'resurgence' (Hawkins et al., 2019) across the globe. Recent phenomena treated under the topic of populism encompass politics as diverse as Corbynism and Trumpism; the Hong Kong pro-democracy protests and Brexit; recent electoral successes by Lula in Brazil, France's National Rally (previously National Front), Italy's 'Democratic party' and the 'Sweden Democrats'. Of particular concern to scholars is the realisation that this populism often emerges from within established (rather than new or underdeveloped) democracies. At work here is an assumption that populism has emerged from various crises (Moffitt, 2016, p. 1) which together contribute to a crisis of 'faith in democracy'. Populism is a reactionary exception to the norm of democratic politics as usual. It is the politics that emerges in response to crisis.

Yet it would seem that populism has been a rather long-standing exception to democracy. Cas Mudde claimed in 2004 that there was a 'rise' of populism dating from the 1960s leading him to name populism the 'zeitgeist' of modern representative democracy. Similarly, Jan-Werner Müller claims populism is 'something like the permanent shadow of modern representative democracy' (2017, p. 11). Indeed, in 1969, Ionescu and Gellner observed what they thought of as a post-war turn to populism across the world (1969). Further, although the name populism was not coined until the late nineteenth century, the concerns that scholars now raise about what they call populist politics (about a certain politics of the people undermining democracy) are as old as democracy itself, seen in the writings of Plato and Aristotle, and again in the political wrangling of the French revolutionaries. Thus, populism cannot just be a feature of modern representative democracy but is as old as democracy itself. It cannot be an exception in temporal terms to democratic politics as normal and yet it is still considered an exception. The desire to solve this riddle, according to which populism is an exception to democracy despite its perpetual presence in democracy, feeds endless debate concerning how best to explain populism's relationship to democracy.

It is evident that scholars are concerned about populism because they believe it is a threat to democracy. Although some claim their phenomenon of concern is not populism *per se* but right-wing populism (Abromeit, 2018, p. 18), the most cited populism theorists argue that all forms of populism – not just right-wing populism – have, at least in some respect, an authoritarian element (Müller, 2017, pp. 50, 56; Mudde & Kaltwasser, 2017, p. 18). With regards to what is meant by authoritarianism, it is important to note that the leading definition of authoritarianism still in use today dates from Juan Linz's 1964 work, which defined authoritarianism as simply the absence of democracy (Linz, 1964). Thus, these claims that populism is authoritarian mean no more than just the assertion that populism is somehow anti-democratic. Accordingly, populism is theorised as emerging from within democracy and thus somehow understood to be instigated by the people, but, nonetheless, functioning to undermine democracy. Thus, perhaps surprisingly, given their often significant differences, this means that the shared task of many populism scholars too often becomes one of identifying the key features of populism that enable it to operate within or masquerade as democracy, but which can be shown, under investigation, to not be properly democratic (Taggart, 2000; Rosanvallon, 2008; Urbinati, 2014; Müller, 2017; Mudde, 2004; Mudde & Kaltwasser, 2017; Moffitt, 2016; Arditi, 2003). This common endeavour has not led to agreement and has instead generated a proliferation of research disagreeing over how best to define populism, and how best to define democracy in the first place.

Although the lack of consensus may be frustrating from an analytic point of view, it is more worrying politically that this approach to the study of populism presents us with a paradox: scholars seek to defend democracy, understood as the politics of the people, by distinguishing proper democracy and the proper people, from its problematic version, populism, which is also a politics of the people, but a politics of the wrong people. Inasmuch as this involves experts seeking to direct the people in how they should do democracy, it undermines the people's ability to govern themselves. This is particularly perplexing because most populism scholars declare themselves to be supporters of democracy, adherents of progressive, liberal-left politics who exhibit concern for ever-deepening social inequalities (see for example Mudde, 2004, p. 555; Urbinati, 2014, p. 141). They thereby find themselves in an uncomfortable position for a democrat, distinguishing the proper people from the pseudo-people.

This anti-democratic perspective could be dismissed as an inconsequential by-product of populism studies. However anti-democracy is not new to populism scholarship. The first studies of populism adopted a hostile and suspicious attitude towards ordinary people (Rancière, 2013); identifying them with unruly, pathologised and criminal behaviours (Laclau, 2005a). Although the political outlook of many populism scholars today may not coincide with that of early populism scholars, it would appear that the very premise that there is such a thing as populism – understood as a form of politics that is not democracy, but that operates within democracy to its detriment – is intrinsically anti-democratic given that it starts from the premise that the people, the key constituent of democracy, will always comprise a threat to democracy. It locates democracy's key threat within its very structure – as a problem of democracy – rather than identifying potential threats according to their specific anti-democratic political content.

Given the lack of agreement concerning how best to define any of the key categories of populist politics, including populism itself, but also democracy and authoritarianism, I cannot help but ask why we are so determined that populism must be an exception to democracy or a problem for democracy, or, indeed, a category of political thought at all? Has political thought created, in the theory of populism, a self-fulfilling prophesy in the doomful rhetoric of the rise of populism and the decline of democracy, which itself has significant adverse effects on the stability of, and confidence in, democracy today?

A very real consequence of the confusion and damage that populism scholarship has generated is demonstrated by the startling claims found in Jon Henley's 2018 article in *The Guardian* which, rather too quickly paraphrasing Mudde, asserts that populism is defined as: 'the view that government must reflect "the will of the people" and that "the people" and "the elites" are two opposing groups' (Henley, 2018). This is concerning, since these two claims form the basis of all democratic politics, yet Henley goes on to argue that populism is undemocratic.[2] It is an indictment of populism scholarship that a purportedly left-wing and stridently pro-democracy UK newspaper has been led to assert that either of these two factors are, at face value, undemocratic. It leaves us wondering what definition of democracy *The Guardian* would prefer since the opposite situation, where governments would not reflect the will of the people, and the interests of the elites are taken to represent those of the people, would itself be decidedly undemocratic.

In the next section I seek to resist the anti-democratic stance of populism scholarship by asking what happens if we turn the above questions on their head and consider what would it mean for democratic theory if populism were neither an exception to democracy, nor necessarily a problem for democracy?

## 2. Populism, Democracy, Liberalism

A small number of scholars, associated principally with Ernesto Laclau and Chantal Mouffe, have already sought to redefine populism such that it is not assumed to be an exception to democracy or anti-democratic. I argue that their approach enables us to see that the dominant forms of populism scholarship discussed above, far from an objective method for political analysis, effect a particular politics which replaces political analysis of the left/right political cleavage with a simplistic populism or democracy binary, narrowing the scope of what is considered to be legitimate democratic politics.

Beginning with the theorisation by Laclau and Mouffe of the relationship between populism and democracy, it is often claimed that there is significant distance between the dominant populism literature and the account they develop because they articulate a particular form of 'left populism'. However, their assertion that populism, understood as the politics of the people, is a defining feature of any democratic politics, is a substantial challenge to nearly all other populism scholarship, including much on the left. A challenge because, if we start from this position, the question arises concerning what it would mean to imagine democracy without populism since this implies a democracy without the people. Such a democracy would no longer be democratic since it would imply a different and therefore non-democratic constituent unit (Stavrakakis, 2014, p. 506) such as the rich, the tyrannous, economic ratings agencies, the party, or the virtuous. From this perspective, critique of populism *qua* populism rather than specific so-called populist movements, seeks to constrain or eliminate the people from democracy in the name of protecting it. In contrast,

Laclau and Mouffe indicate that populism, if it really is populism, that is, of the people, must always, to some extent, be democratic, even if this can be further qualified as more or less democratic and could emerge from anywhere across the spectrum of left to right. Most challenging of all perhaps, since the measure of democracy concerns how much influence the people have in ruling themselves, this would imply that for Laclau and Mouffe the most populist forms of politics would be the most democratic – contra what is claimed by nearly every other theory of populism.

The work of Laclau and Mouffe is also distinctive due to their unique theorisation of the relationship between liberalism and democracy. Most populism scholars, rather confusingly, use liberalism as their measure of democratic political legitimacy, claiming that populism is opposed to liberalism. Emphasising that our democracies are not just democracies, but liberal democracies, these scholars assert that populism is to some extent undemocratic because it opposes the liberal element of our liberal democracies (Mudde & Kaltwasser, 2017; Müller, 2017; Urbinati, 2014; Mounk, 2019). Canovan identifies a 'two strand' model in many populism theories (2005, pp. 84–86) whereby populism is thought to occur when the strand comprising liberal values and rights is neglected in favour of direct popular (democratic) action such that, following Schmitt, liberalism and democracy are conceptualised in opposition: a move towards democracy leads away from liberalism and ultimately towards authoritarianism. Although advocates of this approach claim this ensures equilibrium or balance between liberalism and democracy, in the application of this theorisation it becomes clear that *any* curtailment of liberty by democracy is interpreted as a move towards authoritarianism, whilst they demonstrate little concern for limitations that liberty may effect on democracy.

Although some assume that Mouffe is an adherent of this dualist approach (Abts & Rummens, 2007) Mouffe's argument, although structured by an engagement with the work of Carl Schmitt, develops a distinct interpretation that results in a significantly different theorisation of the relationship between liberal values and democracy. Mouffe agrees that our overall regime type, which we may refer to in ordinary parlance as 'democratic', is more specifically liberal-democratic, and that this is made up of the two aforementioned separate traditions: liberal values on the one hand, and on the other, democracy as a form of rule (2000, p. 2). Yet Mouffe's critique of Schmitt asserts that the relationship between liberalism and democracy is neither a 'balanced compromise' (Abts & Rummens, 2007, p. 410) nor a 'harmonious equilibrium' (Mudde & Kaltwasser, 2017, p. 82) since this implies a binary (Mouffe, 2000, p. 10). Instead, for Mouffe, the relationship is more complex, better defined by the logic of contamination (2000, p. 10): the democratic principle of popular sovereignty is, within the liberal-democratic regime, always *in tension with* the liberal commitment that it is acceptable to 'limit popular sovereignty in the name of liberty' (2000, pp. 2–4). This implies not only that these two strands have developed alongside each other, but also (although this is rarely picked up by other commentators) that neither element can be curtailed without impacting and reshaping the other. Thus, although originating in two separate traditions, when united in the liberal-democratic regime type, these two traditions do not pull in opposite directions but are intimately connected in what Mouffe refers to as a 'gestaltic' relation where the possibility of pure liberty or pure equality have been renounced from the outset (2000, p. 10). Perhaps the nuance here is missed by many of Mouffe's readers because the detail is laid out in her earlier co-authored work with Laclau (Laclau & Mouffe, 2001), which offers a unique theorisation of the liberal-democratic regime type yet is rarely, if ever, commented on by their adherents. Nevertheless, it has considerable implications for how we conceptualise left-wing democratic politics.

## 3. Liberal Democracy and the Left

For Mouffe and Laclau, the liberal-democratic regime type, which coincides with what most of us might ordinarily just refer to as 'democracy', has endured with few interruptions since the French Revolution. This regime type is not an ideology, but a discursive formation of social practices that always *combine* liberalism with democracy in an ongoing democratic revolution (Laclau & Mouffe, 2001, p. 155; Mouffe, 2018, p. 42). This theorisation is novel since it emphasises the importance of liberal values in all forms of what we ordinarily recognise as democratic politics, whilst emphasising that liberal values alone are insufficient.

Mouffe clarifies that the precise combination of liberal values and democratic forms of rule will vary within socioeconomic institutions depending on the hegemonic articulation of politics at the time (2018, p. 44) which will likely be shaped by a particular ideology such as social-democratic, conservative, liberal or neoliberal. These ideologies are articulated *within* the liberal-democratic regime formation. This can lead to some terminological difficulties for those of us seeking to use their work to identify and analyse political formations. For example, what we might ordinarily refer to as liberal democracy to identify a liberal ideology operating in a democratic regime, would be, for Laclau and Mouffe, more precisely referred to as a liberal articulation of liberal democracy. Similarly social-democratic politics would be a social-democratic articulation of liberal democracy (although Laclau and Mouffe prefer to distinguish a new left-of-centre politics which they refer to as 'radical' democracy, to avoid the shortcomings of traditional social-democracy). In each articulation the practices of any liberal-democratic regime type will combine liberal values with democratic governance in quite different ways, but it will always combine the two in some way, even in the most conservative or social-democratic articulations. Also, the possibility will always remain of reorganising the combination, for example, opposing right-wing political articulations with left-wing. Far from seeking to overthrow the liberal-democratic regime type, Laclau and Mouffe's aim for the left is to 'deepen and expand' liberal democracy such that we can construct the most 'radical and plural democracy' within it (2001, p. 176). For Laclau and Mouffe, such a politics would be the epitome of populism. As such, it becomes evident that they are positioning what they would identify as the most populist form of politics left-of-centre on the political spectrum helping us to recognise that in their theorisation, and contra most populism scholarship, the more right-wing a politics is, the less populist it would be.

Additionally, to clarify the relationship between the political theory of Mouffe and Laclau and left-wing politics, if a politics moves too far left, rejecting the pluralising egalitarianism which they associate with populism, then this would also diminish its populist credentials. From *Hegemony and Socialist Strategy* onwards, Laclau and Mouffe reject classical left revolutionary politics in place of a radical reformation of liberal democracy (Mouffe, 2018, p. 49). This is widely misunderstood by commentators, as seen in Mudde and Kaltwasser's assertion that for Laclau and Mouffe 'liberal-democracy is the problem and radical democracy is the solution' (2017, p. 3). Instead, the aim is to counter the recent tendency to dismantle the relationship between liberal values and democracy by radically democratising existing liberal democracies, extending the libertarian and egalitarian elements of the liberal-democratic regime type. Laclau and Mouffe regard populism as the method to achieve this. They argue that their rejection of classical left revolutionary politics takes them to a position that is more deeply left-wing than classical revolutionary politics (Laclau & Mouffe, 2001, p. 152; Mouffe, 2018, pp. 40–41), albeit in their liberal-democratic sense, which means more radically egalitarian *and* libertarian.

Laclau and Mouffe thus force us to rethink the relationship between democracy and liberalism that is assumed by much populism literature, and which leads to the assertion that populism advocates a form of illiberal democracy (Zakaria, 2003; Mudde, 2004, p. 561). Müller too has argued that populism should not be identified as illiberal democracy because, arguing that populism opposes liberalism, he argues that this name fails to identify how populist politics also contorts the democratic part of liberal democratic politics (2017, pp. 49–60; see also Abts & Rummens, 2007). However, Müller does not question the assumed simple opposition between populism and the liberal tradition. In contrast, Mouffe and Laclau indicate that we must not assume that if a certain politics appears to constrain liberty to some extent in the name of democratic popular sovereignty then it must be illiberal (that is, oppose liberal values). This would be to confuse liberal ideology with the liberal-democratic regime type. A democratic politics that seems to constrain liberalism in a certain way may simply draw on a different articulation of the tension between democracy and liberal values in the liberal-democratic regime type. In any liberal-democratic articulation, Laclau and Mouffe contend that liberal values must always be present, whilst also always being limited in some way by democracy. If we simply aim to defend liberal democracy by rejecting every attempt to limit or constrain liberty for the sake of democracy, we risk increasingly eliminating what it is that makes our regimes liberal-democratic rather than simply liberal, and move instead towards the inequities and hierarchies of neoliberalism (as contemporary liberalism manifests itself) which purports to defend pure liberal rights against any curtailment by democracy (2001, pp. 172–175). As we have seen in contemporary examples, this type of politics antagonises the new right which responds by attacking the liberality of the resulting neoliberalism without seeking to rehabilitate the entwining of liberal values with democratic forms of rule.

The misplaced defence of liberalism at the expense of the liberal-democratic regime type de-legitimises any politics that does not accord economically and socially with liberal ideology whilst turning a blind eye to the erosion of liberal-democratic institutions. See for example Mudde, who emphasises that populism opposes the liberalism of liberal democracy and asserts the need to defend the democratic limitations of liberal democracy without acknowledging likewise the need to defend the concomitant liberal limitations too (2004, pp. 561–562). Whilst for progressives this has the short-term advantage of excluding fascists and conservatives from what is seen to be legitimate politics, in the longer term it limits economic and social policies to liberal policies and excludes left-wing political alternatives as illiberal, rather than recognising that they just utilise liberal values differently.

The theorisation of democracy and liberalism as a binary, rather than in tension, has caused populism scholarship to construct a model of politics where the principal cleavage is one of populism versus democracy. All non-centrist politics – that of both the left and the right – are grouped together under the name populism and identified as anti-democratic. Continued use of the term populism to refer to bad or poor-quality democratic politics contributes to the establishment of this new political cleavage in contemporary political thought. This is dangerous for three reasons. First, it disparages the role of the people in politics, too often associating the people's politics with anti-democracy, and thereby raising doubts about the viability of democracy as a political system. Second, it establishes the main task of political thought to be the study of populism and the defence of legitimate democracy from populism, which as we have seen, in some cases becomes the defence of democracy from the people. This closes down the question of how we might more precisely identify the particular threat posed to democracy by particular political movements and, by identifying them according to both their position on the left/right spectrum and whether they work within or against the liberal-democratic regime type, develop strategies to oppose them. Third, it has discredited left-wing politics by grouping it with right-wing politics under the name of populism, reducing the availability of theoretical alternatives to the right-wing and authoritarian politics that it claims to oppose. Altogether, these effects perform a sleight of hand whereby the anti-democratic impact of populism scholarship is concealed by presenting the anti-populist liberal articulations of liberal democracy as the only way to defend democracy, whilst discrediting alternative articulations, and failing to defend the democratic elements of liberal democracy from incursion. In this way, populism scholarship effects a grave attack on liberal democracy that is all but going unnoticed in democratic theory. By eliciting the narrative that populism is by default something that progressives should oppose, and if interpreted broadly along the lines of the quote from *The Guardian* above, then the prevalent populism scholarship undoes the link between progressive politics and three key democratic principles; namely: that the people are the constituency of democracy; that democracy should never be ruled by elite interests in opposition to the people; and that democracy should express the will of the people.

In contrast to this dangerous oversimplification of democratic politics, I will argue in the section below that Laclau and Mouffe help to discern whether a certain politics operates on the left, centre or right within the liberal-democratic regime type, or whether it falls outside of it. Furthermore, if a politics is identified as undemocratic this need not be equated simply with authoritarianism but can be further distinguished as either totalitarian or authoritarian (as defined by Sondrol, 2009; see further discussion in Woodford, 2022). Thus, Laclau and Mouffe provide not only a novel way to theorise the distinctions between left, centre and right-wing democratic politics but also how we distinguish these from different forms of non-democratic political extremism. Their work is a valuable resource if we are to, first, resist the reframing of the political debate into a populism/democracy binary, and, second, return political analysis to the task of understanding the relationship between different types of political movements, and that between these movements and democracy, so as to construct effective opposition to anti-democratic politics in its fascist but also liberal guises.

### 4. A Different Theory of Populism?

The novel theorisation of populism by Laclau and Mouffe as the way the people of democracy come together to form a political movement suggests that people are initially more likely to seek to collaborate, not, as usually suggested, due to a shared ideology, but due to a shared political demand – access to free healthcare for example. If this demand is met by those in power there is no need for a movement to form. If it is not, a set of demands, which may otherwise appear unrelated, such as access to free healthcare, racial equality, climate concerns, migrant rights, and better employment opportunities, might be grouped together into what Laclau and Mouffe refer to as a chain of equivalence. This does not mean that the demands are all the same (equivalent) in all ways, just that they are all part of a wider chain, which is comprised of demands that have something in common – they are part of the same coalition – despite their different content.

Laclau and Mouffe hypothesise that movements unite and grow in opposition to the government, who, in failing to listen to the people, have shown themselves to be comprised of the elites who do not have the people's best interests at heart. As a movement grows it will seek to link with other movements, building coalitions – for instance, feminists and food waste activists may join demands such as women's rights and affordable food, to the already existing chain of access to free healthcare, racial equality, climate concerns, migrant rights and employment opportunities.

To break up an opposition movement and reassert government authority or establish a rival opposition movement, it is necessary to fragment the coalition of demands associated with it. The linking of these demands into a chain occurs via a logic of equivalence so the process of breaking up the chain is said to occur via a logic of difference. The logic of difference could operate by making arguments to relocate certain demands with other political groups by, for example, suggesting that those who want access to jobs would be better off aligning with a group who opposes migration. Alternatively, if it is a government employing the logic of difference, they might insist that demands should be dealt with separately by various government departments. They might instigate a review of healthcare provision, promising that after the next election more people will have access to healthcare, and they may promise to invest in education. Members of the movement for whom health and education were the most important demands may no longer be motivated to support it, and it may diminish or dissolve.

Although it has not been widely acknowledged in the commentary on Laclau and Mouffe, it is essential to understand that the logic of difference is not the only way to weaken a populist movement. If the logic of equivalence starts to take priority over the logic of difference, the political movement may continue to exist but will become less populist and more homogeneous and hierarchical. This is because the function of the logic of equivalence is simply to link disparate demands, not to make demands the same. They must always retain an element of difference within them. Ideally, when a populist movement is at its most inclusive and pluralist, it will successfully hold together diverse demands without subjecting any particular set of interests to any other. Thus, contrary to theorists who assert that populism forces homogeneity (sameness) and social conformity upon a political group, Laclau and Mouffe argue that any attempt to collapse the differences between demands in a populist movement will weaken the populist character of that movement since it would allow a subset of the people and interests within the movement to dominate others. Hence the slide to totalitarian sameness, identified by so many other theorists as a key feature of populism (Urbinati, 2014, p. 201; Müller, 2017, p. 20; Mudde & Kaltwasser, 2017, p. 81) is, for Laclau and Mouffe, a threat to populism, who regard it to operate according to a pluralising logic.

At this point, it is possible to identify the relationship between populism as theorised by Laclau and Mouffe, and the traditional demarcation between left, right and centrist politics. I have argued elsewhere (Woodford, 2022) that populism for Laclau and Mouffe comprises six criteria: populist movements can be measured by the extent to which they begin from demands rather than ideology; and from the people rather than the party; can be named by a phrase or the name of a *primus inter pares* leader; build broad alliances; are pluralist rather than pure; and seek an ever-expanding and inclusive definition of the people rather than fall into the traditional binaries of nationalist or internationalist. These criteria align most closely with left-of-centre definitions of politics, and I would suggest here, accepting the concerns Laclau and Mouffe raise about its limitations, that they are perhaps most clearly aligned with the broad tradition of social democracy. It is important to emphasise, however, that this does not mean that all other articulations of liberal-democratic regimes are anti-democratic, or not populist (in Laclau and Mouffe's sense), just liberal-democratic and populist in different ways and to differing degrees. Elements of Laclau and Mouffe's populism (politics of the people) would exist within conservative articulations of liberal-democratic politics, and liberal articulations of liberal-democratic politics, but given the different ways that conservatives and liberals would apply these criteria it would seem that Laclau and Mouffe could be used to distinguish liberal and conservative articulations from more socialist versions. Furthermore, classical left revolutionary politics would be distinguishable from a social democratic articulation of liberal democracy. Consequently, by working through the criteria derived from Laclau and Mouffe, I posit that it would be possible to identify conservative, liberal and socialist positions within the liberal-democratic regime type, according to the interplay of the logics of equivalence and difference.

Furthermore, Laclau and Mouffe indicate that as either of the two logics, equivalence and difference, come to dominate a political movement, it moves more towards the extreme edges of the liberal-democratic regime type – with the logic of equivalence taking us towards totalitarianism and the logic of difference towards authoritarianism (Laclau & Mouffe, 2001, pp. 186, 188; Laclau, 2005b, p. 46; see also Woodford, 2022). According to their theory, I suggest that liberalism, if it continues to reject the interrelatedness of liberal democracy and seeks instead to oppose liberalism to democracy, would not long remain a liberal articulation within liberal-democratic regime but would begin to move outside of the liberal democracy regime type, employing a strong logic of difference that would tend towards authoritarianism. It is therefore all the more worrying that the dominant discourse of populism today has managed to identify all but the liberal articulations of liberal-democratic politics with authoritarianism or totalitarianism, thereby delegitimating a vast swathe of potential alternatives whilst obscuring its own authoritarian leanings. Although Mouffe and Laclau do not predict an end to the liberal-democratic regime type, it is incumbent on us to ask what it would take for politics to move beyond this regime type and usher in a new historical juncture. Surely the rejection of the gestaltic relation between liberal values and democracy, even when under the guise of a so-called defence of democracy, poses a serious threat to the continuation of the liberal-democratic regime type?

If we are to defend the liberal-democratic regime type and contribute to Laclau and Mouffe's project to deepen and radicalise it, it is helpful to re-evaluate how it emerged in the first place. Although it is naive to think we could identify a single cause for all this conceptual confusion, the problems we find in populism certainly cannot have been helped by the fact that democratic theory has always struggled to theorise the relationship between democracy and the people. In the final section, I will examine the mystique that has come to surround the key constituency of democracy, the people, to consider why the people of democracy cause such problems for democratic theory and ask how we might avoid this in future.

## 5. Populism, Democracy and Impossible Time

Rather than seek the cause of populism studies confusion in the disparate research on populism I suggest we need to evaluate the democratic theory that gave rise to populism scholarship, particularly with regards to how the relationship between democracy and the people is understood. As I have argued elsewhere (Woodford, 2024), democratic theory has often rather too quickly assumed that democracy is lacking compared to the apparently simpler prior regime of absolute monarchy. According to the widely influential theory developed by Claude Lefort (1981, pp. 16–17), the sovereign power of absolute monarchy was understood as incorporated in the physical person of the monarch. Consequently, representative democracy was thought to pose a problem right from the start. The emergence of representative democracy seemed to require sovereign power to pass from one body, that of the monarch, to many bodies, those of the people. Thus, the question emerged concerning where this power resides, since it is impossible to gather all the people together at all times to legislate. Hence the development of Lefort's formula 'the empty place of power' (1981, p. 17). Representative democracy is understood to operate by replacing the sovereign will of the monarch with an empty space, a gap (Lefort, 1981, p. 228) since the identity and community of the people in democracy remain 'indefinable' (Lefort, 1986, p. 232). This gap is both democracy's strength and its Achilles heel. It ensures democracy is always open and revisable, such that no group can be said to indefatigably represent democratic power forever. Yet, conversely, Lefort argued that democracy contains an impulse to fill the gap, to respond to what he refers to as its 'indeterminacy' (1981, p. 19). Particularly in times of insecurity or crisis, people will desire a 'substantial' political identity (1981, p. 20) which can be provided by totalitarianism with its aspiration to provide a simple full identity for the people 'the People-as-One' (1981, p. 20). Hence Lefort argues that democracy is particularly prone to totalitarianism since 'that which has been established never bears the seal of full legitimacy' (1981, p. 19).

Lefort's reading of the gap as a problem that always seeks resolution transforms this descriptive account into an ontological account. The people's indefinability is not just a feature of democracy. It is a problem. This reflects a view found throughout the history of democracy in the work of thinkers as diverse as Plato, John Stuart Mill and Maximillian Robespierre. Democracy is seen to comprise some mystery, some uncertainty, concerning how the people can be represented. It is as if the people are an embarrassment for democracy, one that democratic theorists are dedicated to overcoming. This was seen to be compounded by the emergence of representative democracy leading theorists to grapple with the challenges posed by the impossibility of the entire people ever being present to itself in any one time. Accordingly, theories proliferate concerning how the people can be represented by others (Pitkin, 1967), or how democracy is constituted, founded or bounded. But what if democracy does not have a problem after all?

Following Lefort to accept the symbolic assertion of monarchic rule that claims the absence of a blood line renders democracy lacking rather than just defines what democracy is, is not only unnecessary, but it wrongly asserts the primacy of the monarchic symbolic order. Instead, representation is a necessary part of all forms of human relations, including power relations. As history shows, despite the efforts of theologians and philosophers to prove the contrary, absolute monarchy was far from a simple affair, with the apparent representation of the monarch's body open to numerous forms of abuse and manipulation, by wily courtiers and advisors for example, such that the body of an absolute monarch would itself never coincide fully in simple terms with the location of sovereign power. Furthermore, the death of any monarch nearly always inaugurates power struggles despite the apparent clarity provided by the law of blood lines. There is no reason to assume that the way that the monarch's body represented sovereignty was particularly different from the way that a demonstration in the streets, an assembly of representatives, or the word of an elected legislator might represent the democratic sovereign will. Both forms of rule require elaborate forms of representation. Rather than assert democracy as lacking or inadequate in some way, leading us to ruminate on the mystery of how the ordinary people become a political collective and to fear the impulse by which we might seek to fill the gap once and for all by installing a totalitarian ruler, we can demystify this process and recognise that all forms of sovereign power operate through the process of representation in the realm of aesthetics which we access through our senses.

If the process of democratic sovereignty is less complex and mysterious than we have for so long assumed, perhaps we can worry a little less about the risk that it will 'go wrong', or at least the stakes of it going wrong appear diminished. Indeed, if the people's indefinability creates a gap that is just a gap, but not a lack, then the slide to totalitarianism is not an inevitable risk and can be averted through institutions and strategies, perhaps informed by Laclau and Mouffe's aforementioned work. If we know that the people are configured aesthetically then it is straightforward enough to devise strategies to oppose one configuration of the people with another. This is not to say that effecting these strategies will be simple, but that doing so becomes a question of power and access to resources rather than a mysterious, almost alchemic formula, concerning how to conjure a single body from multiple bodies.

This history of mystification concerning how the people of democracy might come to be, which has accompanied the modern democratic era for 250 years, has contributed to much confusion concerning the relationship between democracy and the people, which in turn has enabled the proliferation of much speculation concerning how we might distinguish the right people from the wrong. This has created the perfect environment in which the apparent paradox of populism – how do the wrong people come to rule in a democracy – can be seriously entertained as a worthy question of study. In the interest of helping to untangle this, I suggest we would benefit from attending to the role of time in the relationship between sovereign power and democracy.

In response to the populism debate, Jacques Rancière has recently asserted not just that the people cannot exist but that they simply 'do not exist' (2017). Rancière's polemical choice of language attempts to trigger a conceptual break with our ordinary assumptions. Such a break forces us to acknowledge that all the people, those who form the sovereign body in a democracy, can never be fully present to themselves in a simple sense of all being in the same place at the same time. Given Rancière's strident defence of democracy, it is evident that, for him, this inability of the people to be present to themselves is not the problem for democracy that others might assume it to be. Instead, democratic politics occurs when an individual or group, which can only ever be a subset of the people, seek to enact the whole people in various ways. The purpose of such a demonstration is to manifest their equality to the rest of the people, demonstrating that there is no sensible reason to treat them differently (Rancière, 1999, p. 8).

This is politics for Rancière because it goes against our general or everyday order. It occurs via the emergence of a group whose identity is not recognised as a legitimate grouping by the dominant political forces, and whose claim to be equal to everyone else – to be a part of the people on equal terms to the rest – cannot be accommodated without a change to that configuration (1999, p. 30). Politics in this sense is that which breaks with the fundamental assumptions of 'common sense' of the reigning order. It not only challenges the authority of that order, but the very sense of it – making it an aesthetic operation, since it makes visible what had no business being seen, and … a discourse where once there was only place for noise (1999, p. 30). Unlike many other definitions of politics, for Rancière politics is not about who has what and who does what – but about who matters. Who can be really seen, heard, acknowledged, rather than just dismissed, or ignored?

Although Rancière's politics is often misunderstood as a dispute about recognition, this is to miss the complexity of his argument. As Derrida reminds us in his critique of Levinas (2008, p. 109), for us to recognise someone or something it is required that they are already recognisable – somehow can fit into our sphere of recognition, our sensible order. In line with this understanding, Rancière's politics acts not within the sensible order but on its threshold – it is that which needs to happen to force us to realise that our current sphere of recognisability is lacking. Politics challenges our identification with that current regime by preventing it from continuing to function, making it nonsensical (Rancière, 1999, pp. 29–30; Woodford, 2017, pp. 152–153). Before we can even consider the responsibility or irresponsibility of how and to whom we respond (Derrida, 2008), something would need to 'annihilate' our current perspective (Cavell, 1991, p. 131), scrambling its meaning. It is not that our existing social relations no longer exist but that any reason for seeing them as necessary disappears, indicating that they are contingent and illogical. Such a disruption would have to operate on the terrain of perception, to open space for change to the ordering of the frame itself, not just reconfiguration within the order (Rancière, 1999, pp. 28, 30). From the confusion it would create, other possible relations may be constructed. This conceptualisation of rupture is aesthetic. It understands the disjuncture to go all the way down – to scramble meaning such that our usual relations fail. Furthermore, in Rancière's characterisation of such a moment as an interruption of the sensible (2010, p. 38), it can be seen to intervene in our affective experiences – our sensibilities. To scramble them, confuse them, render them nonsensical, just long enough for us to see that, although we may not yet have a solution, our normative frame is lacking.

So what is the role of the people in all this? For Rancière, all anyone can do when staging democracy is act *as if* they are the people (2009). In each of Rancière's examples people experience a moment of disjuncture when they realise there is no good reason why they are unequal in their current order. This prompts a staging of equality that could be said to be effective democratically if it succeeds in demonstrating that those enacting it are the people. But this is not necessarily the intention. Instead, the demonstration simply indicates that there is no good reason why they should be treated/allotted a place that is less equal than the rest. If this demonstration is accepted, then it is accepted that they are no different from the rest, from everybody else, from 'the people'.

This type of democratic enactment could involve an assembly of people, but it could be staged by just one person, or a small group of people. What makes it popular sovereignty is not the actual or symbolic presence of a crowd, or group, that is in any way substantively definable. Rather it is that it operates according to a principle of equality that is not substantive – not an equality according to identity or claims, but an equality based on the illegitimacy of any claim to treat a subsection of the people differently from 'the rest' (Rancière, 1999, p. 8). Furthermore, understood as an attempt to fill the gap, it will always need to interact with the institutions of a regime – since it is these institutions that enshrine and allot differences. However, democracy can never simply 'identify with' these institutions (Rancière, 1999, p. 101). Democratic politics can be found in struggles over state power, and state-based concerns such as rights and institutions (1999, p. 101) but this is merely one of many areas in which it operates.

Thus for Rancière, democratic politics is enacted by asserting a competing enaction of the people against the dominant status quo definition such that two competing definitions (in Lefort's terms) operate at the same time; impossibly we might say, from a logical point of view. It is this 'impossible' operation that is both an improbable enaction of equality and a never-reachable future horizon that enables the emergent staging of the people to rupture the prevailing definition of the people, to show that this prevailing view is no longer viable. This creates an opening for the existing configuration of democratic politics to change, to include those who are challenging it. Democracy's play of temporalities could be seen as a stretching of time, such that two opposing definitions of the people can exist simultaneously. Further, such an enaction of democracy will usually involve a challenge to the allocation of time in the dominant order. It requires the challengers to use time that is meant to be spent doing other things, differently to how they are expected to use it, so as to be somewhere or to do something that they are not supposed to be or do (Rancière, 1999). As Rancière's example of worker agitation in 1840s Paris demonstrates, for workers to be able to claim past-times and skills that were the preserve of the middle classes they had to practise them at the expense of other necessary activities, such as eating, sleeping or working. It was in part the requests for what we now might refer to as leisure time that marked the initial demands of workers. This, as Rancière realised when researching *Proletarian Nights*, is contrary to what we may have been led to expect according to Marxist theory which teaches that workers will struggle for rights and material betterment. This is not to say that the latter are not important, but that the importance of time to rest, enjoy oneself and engage in educational pursuits has too often been overlooked as a vital contributing factor in the process of political subjectification.

Following Rancière's polemical style, I refer in the title of this chapter to this play of time in the enactment of democracy as 'impossible time' which can only operate because the people of democracy do not exist in a substantive sense. It is only because democratic politics stages the people against dominant assertions of the people, because two competing definitions can, and must, operate at the same time, impossibly from a logical point of view, but entirely necessary from a democratic perspective, that it is able to enact politics and create an opening from which we can transform our world. Thus, in response to Lefort, the identity and community of democracy is not indefinable. It may be difficult to define, but the people can and must be enacted again and again against dominant definitions, if democracy is to continue to exist. It is not so much indefinable as only temporarily definable.

Consequently, populism's focus on how to best define the people of democracy in advance stems from a misconceputalisation of democracy found in the wider field of democratic theory which, as Lefort shows, asserts that because democracy exposes the contingency at its heart it is unstable and always in need of justification. Rancière's argument not only highlights that keeping open the question of who the people are is central to the democratic project, but also that if we are to avoid the people of democracy continuing to cause such trouble for the way we conceptualise democracy it would seem that we need to question our symbolic equation of contingency with instability or illegitimacy. To recognise the particular resilience that democracy gains by acknowledging its own limits, temporal and otherwise.

## 6. Conclusion

The prevalent premise of populism studies, that the people comprise a potential threat to democracy, has emerged from democratic theory's misconceputalisation of democracy as ontologically lacking in comparison with prior forms of rule. Given the difficulties concerning how the amorphous mass of the people can represent sovereign power, democratic theory mistakenly identifies the root of this as the people. It is therefore not just populism scholarship that asserts that the people are a problem for democracy. Democratic theory is itself yet to come to terms with its own object and as a result has failed to grasp the strategic significance of the relationship between the people of democracy and time. This conceptual confusion feeds an elitist fear of the people that restricts political analysis. If we continue to utilise the democracy/populism cleavage in place of thinking the politics of left and right, we may, perhaps irrevocably, contribute to the decline of the liberal-democratic historical juncture.

What does this mean for political analysis today? First, populism studies is too often unwittingly contributing to the rise of authoritarianism. Its establishment of a democracy/populism cleavage, even in some of the more self avowedly radical scholarship, and association of democracy with liberalism rather than the liberal-democratic regime type present liberalism as the sole democratic political alternative to so-called populist politics, whilst ignoring the curtailment of democratic institutions and disavowing the dependency of liberal values on democracy for the liberal-democratic regime type. This cuts off liberalism from its gestaltic relation with democracy, leaving it to minimise the logic of equivalence and strengthen the play of the logic of difference that Laclau and Mouffe identify as a key feature of authoritarianism. It further delegitimises recourse to the liberal-democratic tradition in order to construct alternatives to authoritarianism. Scholars who wish to support rather than undermine the liberal-democratic regime type would do well to cease using the term populist as a pejorative term that indicates anti-democratic politics, as this undermines the role of the people in democracy. If we think a certain politics is problematic it is not enough to simply claim that this is because it is populist. Instead, it is necessary to identify what it is precisely that we find problematic, and then, by locating that politics on the left/right spectrum, identify whether it is liberal-democratic or not in order to theorise how it might best be opposed. This is necessary because forms of politics that are rather too readily referred to as fascist or authoritarian may be more liberal-democratic than we realise. They may just comprise an articulation of liberal democracy that we oppose. This does not mean that we cannot oppose them, but that, if they articulate a politics which is still within the liberal-democratic regime, a different oppositional strategy may be required than if they were fascist or authoritarian. Finally, this means that if we wish to effectively oppose the rise of right-wing authoritarian politics today, instead of simply acquiescing with the neoliberal politics of the elites, raging impotently against the material toothlessness of liberal politics, or engaging in ceaseless justification of democracy, we would be best served by re-entwining the liberal and democratic traditions in the liberal-democratic regime type by articulating new left-wing social democratic alternatives.

## Notes

1. Thank you to Andy Knott for his patience and insightful feedback on this chapter, and to the British Academy Brighton (CAPPE)–Buenos Aires Populism network for inspiring the argument developed here. All remaining errors are my own.
2. In its serial investigation of populism *The Guardian* has claimed that it accepts Cas Mudde's definition of populism but condenses this to: 'Populists tend to frame politics as a battle between the virtuous "ordinary" masses and a nefarious or corrupt elite – and insist that the general will of the people must always triumph.' Although this adds a little nuance to Henley's definition, it is still not clear, without reference to Mudde's own research, how these claims distinguish populists from democrats (Barr et al., 2018).

## References

Abromeit, J. (2018) 'Frankfurt School critical theory and the persistence of authoritarian populism in the United States', in Morelock, J. (ed.) *Critical theory and authoritarian populism*. London: University of Westminster Press, pp. 3–28.

Abts, K. and Rummens, S. (2007) 'Populism versus democracy', *Political Studies*, 55, pp. 405–424.

Arditi, B. (2003) 'Populism, or politics at the edges of democracy', *Contemporary Politics*, 9 (1), 17–31.

Barr, C., Clarke, S. and Lewis, P. (2018) 'Measuring populism: how *The Guardian* charted its rise', *The Guardian*, retrieved from https://www.theguardian.com/world/2018/nov/20/measuring-populism-how-guardian-charted-rise-methodology (last accessed 18 April 2024).

Betz, H. G. (1994) *Radical right-wing populism in Western Europe.* London: Palgrave Macmillan.

Canovan, M. (1999) '"Trust the people!" Populism and the two faces of democracy', *Political Studies,* 47 (1), pp. 2–16.

Canovan, M. (2005) *The People.* Cambridge: Polity Press.

Cavell, S. (1991) *Conditions handsome and unhandsome.* Chicago: University of Chicago Press.

Derrida, Jacques (2008). *The beast and the sovereign, vol. 1.* Chicago: University of Chicago Press.

Economic Intelligence Unit (2021) *Democracy Index (2021)*, retrieved from https://pages.eiu.com/rs/753-RIQ-438/images/eiu-democracy-index-2021.pdf (last accessed 18 April 2024).

Freedom House (2022) *Freedom in the World 2022.* Washington, DC: Freedom House.

Hawkins, K. A., Aguilar, R., Castanho Silva, B., Jenne, E. K., Kocijan, B. and Rovira Kaltwasser, C. (2019) 'Measuring populist discourse: the global populism database'. Paper presented at the 2019 EPSA Annual Conference in Belfast, UK, 20–22 June.

Henley, J. (2018) 'Populist voters less likely to trust news media, European survey finds', *The Guardian*, 14 May 2018, retrieved from https://www.theguardian.com/politics/2018/may/14/populist-voters-less-likely-to-trust-news-media-european-survey-finds (last accessed 18 April 2024).

IDEA (2021) https://www.idea.int/news-media/news/democracy-faces-perfect-storm-world-becomes-more-authoritarian.

Ionescu, G. and Gellner, E. (1969) *Populism: its meaning and national characteristics.* London: Weidenfeld and Nicholson.

Laclau, E. (2005a) *On populist reason.* New York and London: Verso.

Laclau, E. (2005b) 'Populism: what's in a name?', in Panizza, F. (ed.) *Populism and the mirror of democracy.* New York and London: Verso, pp. 32–49.

Laclau E. and Mouffe, C. (2001) (2nd edn) *Hegemony and socialist strategy.* London: Verso.

Lefort, C. (1981) *Democracy and political theory.* Cambridge: Polity Press.

Lefort, C. (1986) *The political forms of modern society: bureaucracy, democracy, totalitarianism*. Cambridge, MA: The MIT Press.

Linz, J. L. (1964) 'An authoritarian regime: Spain', in Allardt, E. and Littunen, Y. (eds) *Cleavages, ideologies and party systems*. Helsinki: Transactions of the Westermarck Society, pp. 291–341.

Moffitt, B. (2016) *The global rise of populism*. Stanford, CA: Stanford University Press.

Mouffe, C. (2000) *The paradox of politics*. London: Verso.

Mouffe, C. (2018) *Towards a left populism*. London: Verso.

Mounk, Y. (2019) *The people versus democracy: why our freedom is in danger and how to save it*. Cambridge, MA: Harvard University Press.

Mudde, C. (2004) 'The populist zeitgeist', *Government and Opposition*, 39 (4), 541–563.

Mudde, C. (2015) 'Conclusion: some further thoughts on populism', in de la Torre, C. (ed.) *The promise and perils of populism: global perspective*. Lexington: University of Kentucky Press, pp. 431–452.

Mudde, C. and Rovira Kaltwasser, C. (2017) *Populism, a very short introduction*. Oxford: Oxford University Press.

Müller, J. (2017) *'What is populism?'*, London and New York: Penguin.

Pew Research Centre (2021) 'Global public opinion in an era of democratic anxiety', retrieved from https://www.pewresearch.org/global/2021/12/07/global-public-opinion-in-an-era-of-democratic-anxiety/.

Pitkin, H. (1967) *The concept of representation*. Berkeley: University of California Press.

Rancière, J. (1999) *Disagreement*. Minneapolis: University of Minnesota Press.

Rancière, J. (2004) *The philosopher and his poor*. Durham, NC and London: Duke University Press.

Rancière, J. (2009) 'The aesthetic dimension: aesthetics, politics, knowledge', *Critical Inquiry*, 36 (1), 1–19.

Rancière, J. (2010) 'Ten theses on politics', in *Dissensus: on politics and aesthetics*, S. Corcoran (trans). London: Continuum, pp. 27–44.

Rancière, J. (2011) (2nd edn) *Proletarian nights*. London: Verso.

Rancière, J. (2013) '"The people are not a brutal, ignorant mass" Jacques Rancière on Populism', retrieved from https://www.versobooks.com/blogs/1226-the-people-are-not-a-brutal-and-ignorant-mass-jacques-Rancière-on-populism.

Rancière, J. (2017) 'Attacks on populism seek to enshrine the idea that there is no alternative', retrieved from https://www.versobooks.com/blogs/3193-attacks-on-populism-seek-to-enshrine-the-idea-that-there-is-no-alternative.

Rosanvallon, P. (2008) *La légimité démocratique: Impartalité, réfl exivité, proximité*. Paris: Seuil.

Sondrol, P. C. (2009). "Totalitarian and authoritarian dictators", *Journal of Latin American Studies*, 23 (3), 599–620.

Stavrakakis, Y. (2014) 'The return of "the people"', *Constellations*, 21 (4), pp. 505–517.

Taggart, P. (2000) *Populism*. Buckingham: Open University Press.

Urbinati, N. (2014) *Democracy disfigured*. Cambridge, MA: Harvard University Press.

Woodford, C. (2017) *Dis-orienting democracy*. London: Routledge.

Woodford, C. (2022) 'Too left-wing or not populist enough? Using Laclau and Mouffe to rethink Corbynism and future left strategy in the UK', *British Politics*, retrieved from https://doi.org/10.1057/s41293-022-00212-z.

Woodford, C. (2024) 'Democracy, sovereignty and the people', *Journal of Social and Political Philosophy*, 3 (1), pp. 97–101.

Woodford, C. and Devenney, M. (2022) 'Logics of equality in the work of Ernesto Laclau and Jacques Rancière', in *Populism and the People in Contemporary Political Thought*. London and New York: Bloomsbury.

Zakaria, F. (2003) *The future of freedom: illiberal democracy at home and abroad*. London: W. W. Norton & Company.

# 4

# Politics and Time: The Nostalgic, the Opportunist and the Utopian. An Existential Analytic of Podemos' Ecstatic Times[1]

*Adrià Porta Caballé*

The time is out of joint
William Shakespeare, *Hamlet* (2003, p. 52)

When the past speaks it always speaks as an oracle:
only if you are an architect of the future and know the present will you understand it
Friedrich Nietzsche, *Second Untimely Meditation. On the Uses and Disadvantages of History for Life* (2004, p. 94)

## 1. Introduction: Podemos and Time

After the economic crisis of 2008 and the cycle of social mobilisations that opened up in 2011 with the 15M *Indignados* Movement, in 2014 Spain saw the birth of a new left-populist party called *Podemos*. In its original manifesto, 'Mover ficha' [*First Move*], a diverse group of activists and intellectuals called for 'turning outrage into political change' (Público, 2014), since there was the fear that the peak of popular protests against austerity measures implemented by the conservative government led by Mariano Rajoy would progressively slow down (Portos, 2019, p. 49, figure 1) unless the struggle was taken to the institutional level, in a position to dispute the elections to the European Parliament of 2014. Podemos' surprising success – achieving more than 1 million votes and five seats in parliament– showed, amongst other lessons, that the 15M had already realised to a great extent a certain cultural *transformation*, and it was now just a matter of political *translation*. Indeed, at some point even 80 per cent of the Spanish population supported the demands shouted in the squares (Europa Press, 2011), with slogans like: 'Que no nos representan!'

[*They don't represent us!*], 'Democracia Real Ya!' [*Real Democracy Now!*] or 'No somos mercancía en manos de políticos y banqueros' [*We are not commodities in the hands of politicians and bankers*]. The future Political Secretary of Podemos already analysed in those days the 'transversality', 'counter-hegemony' and 'winning dimension' of that new and democratic discourse (Errejón, 2011b, 2015). Moreover, Podemos never claimed to be the 'representation' of the 15M Movement – which was always called, in fact, 'unrepresentable'– nor a social experiment in the laboratory; rather I propose that the best way to understand it might be as a (political) *translation*. 'Traduttore, traditore' [*Translator, traitor*], it is said in Italian, therefore accepting that there is always a certain remnant which is lost in any translation, but it still aims at the same time to move from one plane to another –in this case, from the streets to the institutions. *Mutatis mutandis*, that is the same aspect that Kioupkiolis attempts to grasp with regards to populism when he states that Podemos represents a 'unique reflexive application' of Laclau's theory (2016, p. 103).

The *subjective* conditions were in place as much as the *objective* ones for such a great leap forward. In 'Understanding Podemos', Pablo Iglesias, then already General Secretary, reviewed the three main ingredients that formed part of what would be called the 'Podemos hypothesis' (2015, p. 14). First there was the application of the 'populist hypothesis' to the European context, as theorised by Íñigo Errejón primarily drawing on the work of Ernesto Laclau. Although the future Political Secretary of Podemos foresaw the 'latinamericanisation of Southern Europe', he made three important amendments to the 'populist hypothesis' if it had to be applied to the Spanish case: (1) the resistance of the state despite its legitimacy, representation and economic weakening (which turned the pure Gramscian case of an 'organic crisis' into a more nuanced 'regime crisis'); (2) the *nominal* survival of the middle classes despite the frustration in their *expectations* (which made Podemos always add 'citizenship' to 'the people'); and (3) the pluri-national character of the Spanish state (which, alongside its parliamentary system, made any attempts at a 'direct assault' more difficult than in a Latin American presidential election) (Errejón, 2011a, p. 106). The second ingredient that formed part of Podemos' recipe was the testing and experimentation of the populist discourse around two new and far-left TV programmes called *Fort Apache* and *La Tuerka* [*The Screw*]. This was mainly Pablo Iglesias' own effort, which saw him achieve a great audience and popularity among what he called the 'TV Nation', thus paving the way for the charismatic *hyper-leadership* required in the first Podemos. In his article, Iglesias stops here, but I believe it would be fair to also add a third ingredient: the supply of Izquierda Anticapitalista's [*the Anticapitalist Left's*] organisational muscle, which was crucial at least in Podemos' early stages. Indeed, not only was its leader, Miguel Urbán, part of the original circle, but to have the support of at least one already-existing far-left party's base became decisive after meeting Izquierda Unida's [*the United Left's*] 'coldness, not to say open hostility (... and) stubborn conservatism' at the beginning (Iglesias, 2015, p. 15).

Like Plato's tripartite theory of the soul, then, we could say that the original Podemos was conformed by three subjective factors –Errejón's populist theorisation (*head*), Iglesias' charismatic hyper-leadership (*face and voice*), and Izquierda Anticapitalista's organisational force (*muscle*) – which at the very beginning worked as one sole body in a kind of symbiotic unity. Of course, this is a simplification, since the main topic of politics is *power*, no group can ever accept to hold a vision enclosed by a certain division of labour and which would not ambition to impose its particular worldview onto the rest. Perhaps this is the reason why, after the surprising success of the European Parliament elections in 2014, it became more visible that there were in fact three currents within Podemos, which were colloquially called *Pablistas*, *Errejonistas* and *Anticapitalistas*. Since politics revolves around *conflict*, these original differences began to accelerate once important strategic decisions had to be made, leading to the setting-aside of the *Anticapitalistas* from the Citizen's Counsel after the first General Assembly in 2014 (which took place at the Vistalegre Stadium in Madrid) and the subsequent setting-aside of the *Errejonistas* after Vistalegre 2 in 2017, until it is accurate to say that today the leadership of Podemos can only be aligned with the *Pablistas*. Now, how are we to understand this *diremption* of Podemos into three currents when it was precisely their *unity* which has to be found as the original source of its success?

Before we put forward the *temporal* dimension, it might be useful to say that all the significant secondary literature on Podemos' internal conflicts can be subdivided into three different explanatory realms: *ideology, politics* and *class*. Chazel and Fernández Vázquez offer a paramount example of the first kind. Whereas they start by recognising that 'the dispute has been described as a conflict between a traditional left-wing (Iglesias) and a classic populist strategy (Errejón)' – and, we could also add, Trotskyist Marxism (Izquierda Anticapitalista) – Chazel and Fernández Vázquez conclude by stating that in fact 'they both intended to implement a populist logic (as defined by Ernesto Laclau) but had different understandings of it' (2019, p. 2). I would only add here that perhaps the difference between Iglesias and Errejón's readings of *On Populist Reason* had to do with the former interpreting it merely as a *tactical* move (subordinated to the objective of winning the first general election) whereas the latter understood it as a full-blown strategy (the construction of 'a people' as a long-term process). Furthermore, Chazel and Fernández Vázquez also add that 'most of the academic literature on Podemos emphasizes the importance of the ideological dimension (e.g. Franzé, 2017a; Gómez-Reino & Llamazares, 2019; Kioupkiolis, 2016) when studying the party. In line with those works, we argue that the importance of the ideas as an explanatory factor to internal conflicts is largely amplified as Podemos was created by political science professors' (2019, p. 4). Chazel and Fernández Vázquez develop this ideological dimension of the factional struggle by recognising a fundamental difference between Iglesias's *negrist* version of the 'populist hypothesis' placing the emphasis on 'how to maintain the *autonomy* and heterogeneity of the different struggles', and Errejón's amendment to Laclau's theory about the relationship between populism and institutionalism – falling in line with the works of Gerardo Aboy, Javier Franzé and Francisco Panizza – which led him to focus on 'how to *unite* those same struggles' (Chazel and Fernández Vázquez, 2019, pp. 7, 13).

Unsatisfied with a purely *ideological* analysis, Kioupkiolis (2016), on the one hand, and Mazzolini and Borriello (2021), on the other, turn their gaze towards broader *political* reasons, and particularly to the competition around power. The former identifies a certain 'ambiguity' in Podemos' 'hybrid mix' between *egalitarian* and *authoritarian* tendencies, or, as he puts it: 'the horizontal, open, diverse, networked and assembly-based mobilizations of the multitude on the streets and the web, on the one hand, and the vertical, hierarchical, unified, formal and representative structures of party formations, on the other' (Kioupkiolis, 2016, p. 100). On the other hand, Mazzolini and Borriello do not place so much emphasis on the constitutive tension between populism and radical democracy as on the dilemma between *rupture* and *normalisation* – let us remember, for instance, that Gramsci's newspaper had the double meaning of 'order' and 'novelty': *L'Ordine Nuovo*. Their overall assessment is optimistic since they considered Podemos' original expectations to have been excessive in the first place, so that 'they have perceived as a relative failure what would otherwise have been considered as a resounding success. In short, they have endured a process of "normalisation"' (Mazzolini & Borriello, 2021, p. 3).

Thirdly, and lastly, Rendueles and Sola would surely consider all these interpretations of Podemos' internal conflicts to be too 'cultural', since they perform a more quantitative and class-based analysis, coming from a clear Marxist inspiration. Their point of departure is that 'behind "the people" there are very different class realities' (Rendueles and Sola, 2017, p. 7). Furthermore:

> Faced with the dominance of middle-class politics and the weakness of the labour movement, Podemos has assumed many elements of hegemonic discourse and has avoided conflicting issues in terms of class. This option was electorally profitable but runs the risk of perpetuating the dominance

of middle-class politics, especially since most of the leadership of Podemos has that social background. Without the political articulation of the popular classes and the reactivation of the labour movement, the making of a 'plebeian' historical bloc is fatally flawed. (Rendueles and Sola, 2018, p. 44)

The term 'middle-class politics' was first coined for the purposes of analysing contemporary Spain by the sociologist Emmanuel Rodríguez López, who reduced 'the followers of the new "populism"' to the 'the social origin of the professional middle-class, and even the old socialist caste' (2016, pp. 107–108). Now, having reviewed the most significant interpretations of Podemos' internal conflicts, we think that each of these analyses – the ideological, the political and the class-based – has a certain *moment of truth*, but they all share a common denominator, which is *the almost complete neglect of temporality in politics in general and in populism in particular*. We will now thus proceed to explore this pathway. Our most general and initial hypothesis is that *Podemos' diremption into three different groups may coincide with a tearing-apart of (political) time itself*. Now, this hypothesis is not completely new or surprising – perhaps only in its application to politics – or at least it is part of a broader (modern) predicament. Indeed, in Shakespeare's *Hamlet*, the Prince of Denmark cries at the end of the first act, after having sworn to his father's ghost that he will avenge the killing by his uncle Claudius: 'time is out of joint. O cursed spite / that ever I was born to set it right!' (Shakespeare, 2003, p. 52). Lacan interprets here that what distinguishes Hamlet from Oedipus – and thus modernity from antiquity – is that whereas the latter can act because he *does not know*, the former cannot act because he *already knows too much* (2013, p. 288). For Derrida, on the other hand, there must be something 'ontological' or, even better, *hauntological*, about the disjointed time that Hamlet experiences and suffers (2006, pp. 10, 20), since, as Laclau summarises in a brilliant review: 'anachronism is essential to spectrality: the spectre, interrupting all specularity, desynchonizes time' (2007a, p. 68). Lastly, despite the animosity that Derrida and Laclau share for Hegel, I will also be using here the terms *diremption* and *tearing-apart* – both applied to the populist political party and to temporality itself – in the very precise sense that Hegel, too, in a work of youth, identified them with the necessity to think and reflect. He writes: 'dichotomy is the source of the need of philosophy' (1977a, p. 89).

Now, if we assume that the tearing-apart of Podemos has something to do with a certain diremption of (political) temporality, and any kind of dichotomy of this sort expresses the need of philosophy, it logically follows that we need a *theoretical framework* about the effect of time in politics in general and in populism in particular. That we are not violently forcing this topic on our particular case study finds its paramount justification at first glance in the figure of Íñigo Errejón. There is perhaps no other politician in recent Spanish history who has strategically thought so much in *temporal* expressions: when the elites, for instance, decided to place three different elections before the general ones, he called it a 'short and accelerated cycle'; he also named 'short track' the realm of political intervention, and 'long track' that of cultural transformation; following Bruce Ackermann, he characterised as 'hot moments' those when one can say *we the people*, and 'cold moments' when institutionalisation reigns (Errejón, 2016). One of the objectives of this chapter will be precisely to make *manifest* what is already *latent* in these temporal metaphors. However, we are in the dark beyond these diffuse appearances, since where should we even start to look for such a theoretical framework?

The argument of this chapter can be roughly summarised as follows. Famously, in his *Second Untimely Meditation. On the Uses and Disadvantages of History for Life*, Nietzsche distinguishes between three 'species of history': the antiquarian, the monumental and the critical (2004, p. 67). However, and as brilliant as this thought may sound, Nietzsche offers no justification for such a distinction. Moving forward, when Heidegger undertakes a revision of the history of ontology with temporality as the horizon for the question of Being, he will also discover the existential foundation of Nietzsche's triad. Indeed, in *Being and Time* it is said that 'the threefold character of historiology is adumbrated in the historicality of *Dasein*' (Heidegger, 2008, p. 448), which means that the tripartite distinction between the antiquarian, the monumental and the critical finds its ground in *Dasein*'s three ecstatic times: past, present and future (respectively). Should this radical thought be confined to the realms of 'historiology' or 'ontology', or would its application to *political theory* also offer us three different characters, depending on which ecstatic time is primary? We will call them the *nostalgic* (past), the *opportunist* (present) and the *utopian* (future). Through a detailed analysis of the Spanish left-populist party Podemos as a case study, we will propose that its internal conflict between the followers of Pablo Iglesias, Íñigo Errejón and the Anticapitalist Left may not only be explained by recourse to the traditional categories of ideology, politics and class, but also by attending to its temporal dimension, where the *pablistas* represented the primacy of the past (nostalgia), the *errejonistas*, the present (opportunity), and the *anticapitalistas*, the future (utopia). Since these three characters are equally one-sided if taken separately, we will end with an attempt at a reconciliation of the three ecstatic times in a political reformulation of being-as-a-whole-within-time-ness.

## 2. Nietzsche's *Second Untimely Meditation*: **The Antiquarian, the Monumental and the Critical**

As indicated, Nietzsche introduces the main argument of the *Second Untimely Meditation*[2] when he distinguishes between three 'species of history': the monumental, the antiquarian and the critical. Indeed, 'history pertains to the living man in three respects: it pertains to him as a being who acts and strives, as a being who preserves and reveres, as a being who suffers and seeks deliverance' (Nietzsche, 2004, p. 67). In his 'Introductory Study' to one of the Spanish collected works of Nietzsche, Germán Cano interprets that he is after a certain kind of *atmosphere* or *metabolism* in the appropriation of history so that it does not degenerate (2014, p. lxxiv), and therefore Nietzsche's analysis will attempt to show from now on at which point the *uses* and *advantages* that these three different kinds of history might have for life turn out to be *abuses* or *disadvantages*. To put it in the German philosopher's own botanical terms:

> Each of the three species of history which exist belongs to a certain soil and a certain climate and only to that: in any other it grows into a devastating weed. If the man who wants to do something great has need of the past at all, he appropriates it by means of monumental history; he, on the other hand, who likes to persist in the familiar and the revered of old, tends the past as an antiquarian historian; and only he who is oppressed by a present need, and who wants to throw off this burden at any cost, has need of critical history, that is to say a history that judges and condemns. Much mischiefs caused through the thoughtless transplantation of these plants: the critic without need, the antiquary without piety, the man who recognizes greatness but cannot himself do great things, are such plants, estranged from their mother soil and degenerated into weeds. (Nietzsche, 2004, p. 72)

Nietzsche first assures us that history belongs to the person who acts. The monumental sees history as a certain 'mountain range' or 'relay race' of great moments. Indeed, the monumental tries to impose the commandment that 'everything great must be immortal' upon a resigned society that, in apathetic routine, cries as a whole: 'No!' The only goal here is happiness – not one's own, but that of others – and there is no other salary than fame, honour or eternal glory. Whereas the masses just want to live at any price, the monumental historian knows that one lives best if one has no respect for existence. 'That the great moments in the struggle of the human individual constitute a chain, that this chain unites mankind across the millennia like a range of human mountain peaks, that the summit of such a long-ago moment shall be for me still living, bright and great' (2004, p. 68) – this is the fundamental idea of monumental history. For Nietzsche, the advantage that this kind of history must have for the active personality is clear: 'he learns from it that the greatness that once existed was in any event once possible and may thus be possible again; he goes his way with a more cheerful step, for the doubt which assailed him in weaker moments, whether he was not perhaps desiring the impossible, has now been banished' (2004, p. 69). For the revolutionary, for instance, who reads about the French or the October Revolutions, this is no idle endeavour, since she needs models for her great struggle against resignation, and she cannot find them in the present. However, if this is the *use* that monumental history might have for life, what could be its *abuse*? Since history has now been reduced to a mountain range or a relay race, its disadvantage can be no other than that 'monumental history deceives by analogies' (2004, p. 71). To compare Germany in the nineteenth century with the Renaissance, for example, is more than just an inexact comparison: it erases all substantial differences to create a violent conformity, it only relates to approximations and generalities, and it makes what is dissimilar look similar. To add insult to injury, if these seductive analogies are used by an established power, they might become so distorted that one is incapable of distinguishing between a monumental past and a mythical fiction. That is why the veracity of history and the past itself are endangered by an excess of monumental history.

Secondly, history belongs to the person that 'preserves and reveres – to him who looks back to whence he has come, to where he came into being, with love and loyalty; with this piety he as it were gives thanks for his existence. By tending with care that which has existed from of old, he wants to preserve for those who shall come into existence after him the conditions under which he himself came into existence – and thus he serves life' (2004, pp. 72–73). Different from monumental history, which only relates to the past instrumentally for action in the present, the antiquarian serves the past for its own sake, and as such she does more justice to it. The goal here is to 'be at home in the whole' by reappropriating the history of the world spirit as one's own – all of which has clear Hegelian overtones (1977b, p. 277). It is not difficult to see what use or advantage this feeling of reconciliation might have for life, and it can be comprised in the relief that 'here we lived, he says to himself, for here we are living; and here we shall live, for we are tough and not to be ruined overnight' (Nietzsche, 2004, p. 73). Indeed, the antiquarian is after a kind of self-justification for her own existence, the reassurance that one is not wholly 'accidental and arbitrary', which is found through the 'flower and fruit' of a whole tradition. What could possibly be the *disadvantage* or *abuse* of this sigh of relief? Nietzsche is able to locate it in the fact that antiquarian history 'knows only how to preserve life, not how to engender it' (2004, p. 75). Therefore, it tends to underestimate what still has to come into existence. Now, in this extremely restricted field of vision, there is no present criteria to distinguish between past events, so everything is considered equally worthy of reverence. But if everything is equally important, only magnitudes and degrees are left, which is the reason why there might be a lack of discrimination, of sense of proportion, in antiquarian history that renders it incapable of distinguishing between what is relevant in the past from what is not. Moreover, this insatiable thirst for antiquity can be problematic not only because it might lead to a blind and restless obsession for collecting, but even more importantly because it hinders the new and it paralyses action.

Finally, this twofold distinction would be incomplete if it did not have a third genre, *the critical*, which has 'the strength to break up and dissolve a part of the past: he does this by bringing it before the tribunal, scrupulously examining it and finally condemning it; every past, however, is worthy to be condemned –for that is the nature of human things' (2004, p. 75). Of course, Nietzsche himself, the greatest critic of morality that has ever been, does not believe this judging force to be *moralising*, but emerging from life itself. Finding recourse again in Goethe, the hero of this meditation, Nietzsche quotes his maxim 'for all that exists is worthy of perishing', although we could even find the first precedent of this thought in the first philosophical sentence uttered in the West, what is known as 'Anaximander's sentence', and which Nietzsche translated at an early age as follows: 'where existent things have their coming-to-be, thereto must they also perish, "according to necessity, for they must pay retribution and penalty for their injustices, in accordance with the assessment of time"' (Nietzsche, 2006, p. 33). The idea, coming from Anaximander up to Goethe, that life is inherently unjust and that hence it must perish is where Nietzsche locates the heart of the *critical* relationship towards history. However, he warns us that 'if we condemn these aberrations and regard ourselves as free of them, this does not alter the fact that we originate from them' since 'it is always a dangerous attempt because it is too hard to know the limit to denial of the past and because second natures are usually weaker than first' (2006, p 76) – that would be the *disadvantage* of the critical. Nevertheless, its *advantage* for life is still clear, 'that of knowing that this first nature was once a second nature and that every victorious second nature will become a first' (2006, p. 77).

To briefly recapitulate, then, the monumental sees history as a mountain range or relay race of great moments: its use for life is that it shows that greatness was once possible and thus it can be possible again, but in so doing it also deceives by analogies – that can be its abuse. Secondly, the antiquarian aims at feeling at home in the world by preserving and revering the past, which has the advantage of showing that we can live here because here we have lived, but it also has the disadvantage that it only knows how to preserve life, not how to engender it. Thirdly, and finally, critical history knows that everything that has come to be must perish and it has the arrogance to propose a second nature, but it runs the risk of denying the past because condemning an aberration does not change the fact that we originated from it. These, therefore, are the uses and ab-uses, the advantages and dis-advantages, of history for life – according to Nietzsche.

As brilliant as this analysis may sound, something is still missing from it, perhaps what is most important even coming from a philosopher. What is lacking is not so much the *distinction* between the monumental, the antiquarian and the critical itself, but the *foundation* for such a distinction. Indeed, why should there only be three kinds of history? Why not five instead? Why not just one? Moreover, as commonsensical as the subdivision between uses and abuses, advantages and disadvantages may also sound, we could legitimately ask why this should be the best way to look at history. What is the *ground* for such a subdivision? This is characteristic of a great deal of Nietzsche's philosophical oeuvre which, like *lightning*, sometimes offers the most brilliant ideas without giving sufficient reasons for them. This trait not only relates to his suspicions about 'Reason' but also with his style resembling that of his old master Heraclitus, who said in a fragment 'lightning steers everything', and Heidegger interprets that it must be because it 'surveys and shines over the whole of beings in advance and permeates this whole preluminously in such a way that, in the blink of an eye, the whole joins itself, kindles itself' (Heidegger, 2018, p. 123). With Nietzsche's blink of an eye, then, *time begins to be conjointed*.

## 3. Heidegger's *Being and Time*: Past, Present and Future

So, can we explain this lightning? Can we find a justification for Nietzsche's brilliant but unfounded threefold distinction in the *Second Untimely Meditation*? As the last reference already anticipates, we will have to wait for Heidegger's *Being and Time* (1927) in order to suture this gap. Indeed, when Heidegger undertakes a revision of the history of ontology with temporality as the horizon for the question of Being, he will also discover the existential foundation of Nietzsche's triadic structure. At the end of the book, in the chapter on 'Temporality and Historicality', Heidegger also recognises that Nietzsche distinguishes between three kinds of history 'without explicitly pointing out the necessity of this triad or the ground of its unity' (2008, p. 448). At the same time, Heidegger also admits that 'Nietzsche's division is not accidental.

The beginning of his "study" allows us to suppose that he understood more than he has made known to us' (2008, p. 448). So, what is this missing ground? Heidegger writes: 'the threefold character of historiology is adumbrated in the historicality of *Dasein*' (2008, p. 448). What does this mean? What meaning is hidden behind all this 'ontological' phraseology? Simply put, it means that the tripartite distinction finds its ground in *Dasein*'s three ecstatic times: past, present and future (respectively). Indeed, the fact that time conforms the horizon for the question of Being or, even more succinctly, that *Being 'is' time* – and not just *the present* – implies that any question regarding temporality, such as Nietzsche's on historiology, has to be taken back to *Dasein*'s three ecstatic times. An important warning has to be made here which will also be relevant later: to state that the monumental standpoint *corresponds* with a certain *privileging* of the present, the antiquarian, of the past, and the critical, of the future, *does not mean* that each of these types of history is *solely and exclusively* focused on *just one* ecstatic time, *completely neglecting* the other two; rather, it means that the other two are 'disclosed' or 'opened up' from a time that in each case stands as *primary* or *privileged*. To put forward some examples: it is not the case that the antiquarian despises the present or the future, these are precisely what she wants to *preserve*, but what gives the criterium on what deserves to be preserved is the past. Similarly, the monumental is not inattentive towards the past and the future, they are precisely what constitute history as a mountain range of great moments, but her focus is still to act in the present. Thirdly, and finally, the critic does not forget the past and the present, since that is exactly what she wants to criticise, but the standpoint from which she can derive that criticism can only come from the future.

Moreover, Heidegger continues, 'the possibility that historiology in general can either be "used" "for one's life" or "abused" in it, is grounded on the fact that one's life is historical in the roots of its Being, and that therefore, as factically existing, one has in each case made one's decision for authentic or inauthentic historicality' (2008, p. 448). Here we encounter, besides the previous *temporal* distinction between past, present and future, the second most important *existential* distinction in *Being and Time*, which is the one drawn between *authenticity* and *inauthenticity*. The original neologism in German is pretty self-explanatory since *Eigentlighkeit* not only means 'genuine', but it also implies a sense of 'propriety'. 'Authentic', then, in *Being and Time*, designates that *Dasein* which, in its being-towards-death (the possibility of impossibility), has decided to choose-itself in contradistinction with the 'inauthenticity' characteristic of saying what 'They say', or thinking what 'One is supposed to think', where 'everyone is the other and no one is himself' (2008, p. 165).[3] It is at this precise moment that we are in disposition to recognise that Heidegger not only grounds Nietzsche's triadic distinction between the antiquarian, the monumental and the critical in the threefold character of *Dasein*'s ecstatic temporality, but he is also able to find an explanation for the distinction between the *uses* and *abuses*, or the *advantages* and *disadvantages*, of history for life (which before might have seemed arbitrary) but now we realise that it is founded on the existential difference between *authenticity* and *in-authenticity*. Since we do not have the space here to go into the details on how the former *temporal* axis crosses with the latter *existential* one, we will use the table of one of the greatest experts on *Being and Time*, Reiner Schürmann, which summarises the fundamental intersections (2008, p. 110):

**Table 4.1**

| Structure of care | Primary ecstasis | Inauthentic mode | Authentic mode |
| --- | --- | --- | --- |
| Attunement | Past | Forgetting | Retrieve |
| Falling | Present | Making-present | Instant |
| Understanding | Future | Awaiting | Anticipation |

Another important warning has to be made here. Schürmann's table has the virtue of simplifying and clarifying the basic structures of *Being and Time* for our own purposes, but it also runs the risk of petrifying them into *dead* categories. That temporality is 'ecstasic' means, fundamentally, for Heidegger, that it is *outside-of-itself*, which implies that it *moves* from one time to the other, and nobody could better describe this movement in this case than Heidegger himself:[4]

> As historical, *Dasein* is possible only by reason of its temporality, and temporality temporalizes itself in the ecstatico-horizonal unity of its raptures. *Dasein* exists authentically as futural in resolutely disclosing a possibility which it has chosen. Coming back resolutely to itself, it is, by repetition, open for the 'monumental' possibilities of human existence. The historiology which arises from such historicality is 'monumental'. As in the process of having been, *Dasein* has been delivered over to its thrownness. When the possible is made one's own by repetition, there is adumbrated at the same time the possibility of reverently preserving the existence that has-been-there, in which the possibility seized upon has become manifest. Thus, authentic historiology, as monumental, is 'antiquarian' too. *Dasein* temporalizes itself in the way the future and having been are united in the Present. The Present discloses the 'today' authentically, and of course as the moment of vision. But in so far as this 'today' has been interpreted in terms of understanding a possibility of existence which has been seized

upon – an understanding which is repetitive in a futural manner – authentic historiology becomes a way in which the 'today' gets deprived of its character as present; in other words, it becomes a way of painfully detaching oneself from the falling publicness of the 'today'. As authentic, the historiology which is both monumental and antiquarian is necessarily a critique of the 'Present'. Authentic historicality is the foundation for the possibility of uniting these three ways of historiology. But the ground on which authentic historiology is founded is temporality as the existential meaning of the Being of care. (Heidegger, 2008, pp. 448–449)

What is crucial to retain from this fragment is that Heidegger does not see 'authentic historiology' as the *priority* of either the antiquarian, the monumental or the critical *per se* – he regards each of these standpoints, considered by itself, as equally *one-sided* – but rather as the 'ecstatico-horizontal unity of its raptures'. This argument will come back by the end of this chapter, when we will also attempt to find a 'being-as-a-whole-with-in-time-ness' in politics.

## 4. Politics and Time: The Nostalgic, the Opportunist and the Utopian

Now we have a robust theoretical edifice and all the necessary instruments to pose the decisive question of this chapter: Should these reflections on temporality made by Nietzsche and Heidegger be restricted to the spheres of 'historiology' and 'ontology' respectively, or could they also be applied to political theory? As the *ontologisation* of the *Second Untimely Meditation* undertaken in *Being and Time* already suggests, there should be something *fundamental* and *constitutive* about the distinction between the antiquarian (past), the monumental (present) and the critical (future) that could be applied at least in principle to any particular *region* of Being, and therefore also to politics. However, we cannot just import Nietzsche's distinction to political theory as it is, since we cannot forget that it was originally thought in relation to history. And, although 'the monumental' and 'the critical' retain a certain degree of universality as categories, what would it mean to be 'antiquarian' in politics? It seems that there would not be a way to operationalise that particular concept in political theory that would not do violence both to politics and to Nietzsche's own reflection. So, I propose a *corresponding equivalent* to the distinction between the antiquarian, the monumental and the critical that would do justice to the political moment: one that we will call the *nostalgic*, the *opportunist* and the *utopian*. This threefold distinction should also correspond to the primacy of the past, the present and the future, respectively.

Another important note of caution should be signalled here. I have deliberately attempted to find in each case a word that would have a *double meaning*, with both 'good' and 'bad' connotations in order to follow Heidegger's thought that each standpoint, taken by itself, is equally *one-sided*. The 'opportunist' is clearly the term that has worse overtones but which, like Nietzsche and Heidegger's distinctions, it is not used conceptually here in a *moralising* way. It is true that in everyday language an 'opportunist' is usually someone who tries to take advantage or power in every given situation without thinking about the potential side effects, but it is equally undeniable that it refers to someone who is attentive to 'windows of opportunity' – a crucial concept as we will see later for the neo-Gramscian interpretation of the 'Podemos hypothesis'. Similarly, the etymology of the word 'nost-algia' takes us back to ancient Greek, where *nóstos-* means 'return' and *-àlgos* means 'pain', and the conjoined term was recuperated during Romanticism as a form of *melancholy*. 'Nostalgia' is clearly an ineradicable phenomenon (like Proust's madeleine); however, someone who is *solely and exclusively* 'nostalgic' is someone trapped in the past that cannot move on. Thirdly, and finally, the term 'utopia' also brings us back to the ancient Greek where it would literally mean a 'no-place' (*oú-tópos*), although it was actually coined by Thomas More (2003; see also: Fernández Buey, 2007, p. 73ff.). It is clear that a certain kind of 'utopianism' in the sense of *idealism* is necessary for any social transformation worthy of that name, but it is equally undeniable that, taken to the extreme, it leads to the same criticism that Marx and Engels once made of 'utopian socialism': 'personal inventive action' and 'fantastic conditions' (2010, p. 515). With such double meanings I have tried, then, at first glance, to replicate Nietzsche and Heidegger's own double gestures when they distinguish between uses and abuses, advantages and disadvantages, and authenticity from inauthenticity.

With this theoretical framework in mind, which should cross the *horizontal-temporal* distinction between the nostalgic, the opportunist and the utopian with the *vertical-existential* distinction between authenticity and inauthenticity, we will move now to the development of each and every one of these (six) political standpoints. But how should we proceed so that such an existential question regarding temporality in politics does not remain purely at the abstract level? Now we turn to Podemos as a case study. As the introduction hinted, Podemos represents a particularly illuminating example of the effect that time might have in politics in general and in populism in particular, since the three main currents in which the party was finally torn apart – *Pablistas*, *Errejonistas* and *Anticapitalistas* – can be said to correspond, *mutatis mutandis*, with the three political modes of the nostalgic, the opportunist and the utopian.

With the birth of Podemos in January 2014 both Iglesias and Errejón shared the same *opportunist* outlook in the very precise sense that we have defined here; that is, they gave pre-eminence to the demands of the *present* over those of the past and the future. We have to begin to use here everything that we have learnt before from Nietzsche and Heidegger, since it is obvious that what we are calling now 'opportunism' in relation to politics is clearly reminiscent of what Nietzsche understood under the banner of the 'monumental' with regards to history. Now, the monumental view of history proper to the person who wants to act in the present stands as diametrically opposed to what Nietzsche names as the *supra-historical*, characteristic of an Heraclitus or a Hegel with such a strong plastic power as to simply lean back and assimilate all the dialectical movements of the past, while being wholly incapable of moving a finger in the present. This is because they lack the 'blindness and injustice in the soul of that who acts' (Nietzsche, 2004, p. 65). Nietzsche perhaps best summarises the whole spirit of this moment in the *Second Untimely Meditation* when he claims: 'not respect for history; instead, you should have the courage to *make* history!' (1995, p. 180). Already we can acknowledge the first analogy between our Nietzschean reflection and Podemos' own story. Indeed, in the years that led up to the formation of the party after the 15M Indignados Movement (2011–2014) the left seemed to be well-established in a 'supra-historical' outlook that contrasted with the highest peak in social mobilisations in the last few decades (Portos, 2019, p. 49, figure 1). Either the 'objective conditions' were not ready yet from a Marxist point of view, or 'we should go slowly because we are going far away' from an autonomist logic of *accumulation* of forces; in each case, the question of *power* (both as potency and seizure) was constantly deferred. This is reminiscent of what Žižek says about the obsessional neurotic, who is 'frantically active in order to prevent the real thing from happening' (2006, p. 26). By contrast, once Podemos started walking by itself, Errejón kept repeating that any political revolution takes place 'without handbooks' (Errejón and Mouffe, 2016, p. 78) – repeating Gramsci's move in 'The Revolution against *Capital*' (1988, pp. 32–36) – and Iglesias famously proclaimed Marx's expression of 'storming heaven' in the first General Assembly at Vistalegre (2010, p. 132). These two gestures can be seen in the Nietzschean struggle to *make* history, perhaps blindly and unjustly, against any supra-historical point of view: 'then we will gladly acknowledge that the supra-historical outlook possesses more wisdom than we do, provided we can only be sure that we possess more life' (Nietzsche, 2004, p. 66).

So, at the very beginning both Iglesias and Errejón shared the same opportunist-monumental viewpoint, whereas Izquierda Anticapitalista seemed to only accept this general outlook as a tactical concession for the time being, since its more futural anticapitalist demands could not be completely accommodated in the present. Paraphrasing Napoleon's famous dictum, quoted by Lenin, one could say that they thought 'we run for the elections, and then we see' [*on s'engage et puis ... on voit*] (1965, p. 480). For Iglesias and Errejón, however, at least at this moment in time, opportunism was a much more *authentic* decision: they both saw, and intended to develop and expand, what they called the *window of opportunity* in the party system, and so running in the elections was not just an *instrumental* means that necessarily had to be exchanged at the end of the day by social capital. As Knott already pointed out in the introduction: 'populism does not emerge within a vacuum but, rather, within a very specific context: the context of crisis' (Knott 2024, p. 8). As Mazzolini and Borriello point out, 'another crucial difference lies in the fact that the radical left treated elections as simply mirroring the political capital accumulated in the social sphere; conversely, Podemos thought of elections as moments of "political acceleration", thus displaying a talent for engineering explosive and successful electoral campaigns' (2021, pp. 5–6). The *temporal* conflict signalled here between elections as *accumulation* and as *acceleration* is in its turn the expression of a more fundamental difference between authentic and inauthentic opportunism. Indeed, now we can clearly see that to live the present authentically in politics means to seize the 'window of opportunity', as opposed to merely seeing it as an *instrumental cost-benefit calculus*. This is an attempt to translate to the sphere of politics Heidegger's distinction between inauthentic and authentic presents as *making-present* and *instant* (see Table 4.1 above). As a matter of fact, when the present is lived inauthentically it is experienced as a series of 'nows' – therefore paving the way towards *instrumental rationality* – whereas, to quote *Being and Time*, 'that Present which is held in authentic temporality and which thus is authentic itself, we call it the "moment of vision". (…) It means the resolute rapture with which *Dasein* is carried away to whatever possibilities and circumstances are encountered in the Situation as possible objects of concern' (Heidegger, 2008, p. 367). So, the inauthentic 'making-present' is *closed* in the 'now', whereas the authentic 'instant' is open to the possibilities of the situation. As Knott also pointed out in his own analysis of Heidegger: 'populism entails the announcement of the end of a political "now-time", and the entry of reflections on significance by growing sectors of the public' (Knott 2024, p. 8). Another word for the latter is 'moment of vision' [*Augenblick*], a term that Heidegger extracts from Kierkegaard (2009), but more importantly for our argument is its resemblance to the 'window of opportunity'. Let us see one of the clearest examples of this 'blink of an eye' [*Augenblick*] in politics:

This is only possible in *exceptional* situations, such as the one we are now in. It demands a specific strategy to identify the frameworks that could define this *new setting*, as well as the discourse to *project* it in the media sphere. When we insist on talking about *evictions, corruption and inequality*, for example, and resist getting dragged into debates on the form of the *state (monarchy or republic), historical memory or prison policy*, it doesn't mean that we don't have a stance on those issues or that we've 'moderated' our position. Rather, we assume that, without the machinery of institutional power, *it makes no sense at this point to focus on zones of struggle that would alienate us from the majority*, who are not 'on the left'. *And without being a majority, it is not possible to get access to the administrative machinery that would allow us to fight these discursive battles in other conditions*. (Iglesias, 2015, p. 16, my italics).

Now, this short fragment from 'Understanding Podemos' is an absolute manifesto of the *opportunist* kind in the precise sense that we are using it here, since it has all the ingredients characteristic of the *authentic present*. To begin with, the present is not seen as a series of 'nows' (*chronos*), therefore paving the way to an instrumental cost-benefit calculus (inauthentically), but as an 'exceptional moment' (*kairós*). Thus, in the 'blink of an eye', the present shows itself as open to the possibilities of the situation – or what Iglesias calls here the 'projection' of a 'new setting'. Perhaps what is most interesting for our purposes here is how this authentic opportunism leads to *prioritising the demands of the present* (evictions, corruption and inequality) above those that in Spain are usually associated to the past (state form and historical memory), although they should not necessarily have to, and the future (prison policy). Iglesias' justification is opportunist in our sense through and through: it makes no sense to focus on demands (*past or future*) that would alienate us from what the majority is *in the present*, since it does not make any sense either to raise demands (*in the present*) for which we do not have the power to resolve (*in the present*). Now, such an opportunist justification is precisely what was untenable for a party like Izquierda Anticapitalista which, at some point, would like to, understandably and legitimately, raise some demands that are more systemic and far-reaching – that is, 'utopian' (*utopian* here is not used in the colloquial sense of 'unrealistically fantasising', but in the precise temporal sense of prioritising the demands of the future over the past and the present). Our new theoretical framework, then, is able to explain, by virtue of the temporal dimension *alone*, why there was a certain inevitability in the conflict between the present-populists Iglesias and Errejón with the futurist-Marxists of Izquierda Anticapitalista.

This is the reason why in Vistalegre 1 in 2014, the dispute between the former, under 'Claro que Podemos' [*Of Course We Can*], and the latter, called

'Sumando Podemos' [*Adding Podemos*], was not raised so much in ideological or political principles but, most interestingly for our argument, in *temporal* ones. The question, which the registered members of the party had to resolve in open primaries, was in fact raised in the following *temporal* terms: What is the best model for a new and young party that has to face three elections in less than a year with a strategy that was called *Blitzkrieg* [War of Manoeuvre or Frontal Attack], in contradistinction to a longer-term 'war of position' – which is defined by Gramsci, for instance, as 'demanding enormous sacrifices by enormous infinite masses of people (... so that it is) concentrated, difficult and requires exceptional qualities of patience and inventiveness' (Gramsci, 1988, p. 230)? No wonder that the present of an 'electoral war machine' won with 80 per cent, although the anticapitalists had their *moment of truth* in pointing out the necessary measures for renewal: their proposal 'established the creation of a citizen's counsel elected via direct vote to individual candidates, which should have guaranteed its plurality and representativity, the election by lottery of a 20% of its members and the creation of a coordination team elected by the counsel and at least three spokespeople' (Rodríguez López, 2016, p. 94). As we can also see in this case, *utopianism*, in the exact sense of a prevalence of the future above the rest of time, also has both an authentic (it establishes a *horizon*) and an inauthentic mode (a mere *resolutive fiction*). Again, 'horizon' and 'resolutive fiction' designate here our attempt to transpose to the sphere of politics the Heideggerian distinction between authentic and inauthentic future: *anticipatory resoluteness* and *awaiting* – see Table 4.1. In effect, politicians are *utopian* in an *inauthentic* mode when they talk about *the future* by uttering empty promises such as 'we have to move forward, not backward'; however, one can also reappropriate the future in an *authentic* way by setting up a *horizon*, thereby reintroducing meaning and purpose into what is to come. This difference also coincides with the distinction in French between *futur* (future) and *a-venir* (to-come) that Derrida introduces to democracy (2006, p. 81). 'Resolutive fiction' as inauthentic future was proposed by Pablo Bustinduy and Jorge Lago – two members of Podemos' original Citizen's Counsel, one responsible for international relations and the other for culture – who define it as 'the attempt to narratively resolve something that would otherwise be experienced as a present and untenable social contradiction (...) a way of representing social conflict as something that has already been resolved or is in the process of being resolved' (2023, p. 6, my translation). The anticapalists did not get deceived by such resolutive fictions, and they authentically and conflictually proposed a horizon for the democratisation of Podemos. At this precise instant they had their moment of truth, but they lost, overwhelmed by the urgencies of the present.

Now, in order to move from Vistalegre 1 in 2014 to Vistalegre 2 in 2017, and therefore also from the *utopian* to the *nostalgic*, we have to ask what is the problem with the *present opportunist*? This question is crucial since it will explain why Iglesias adopted a nostalgic point of view, leaving Errejón alone in the 'window of opportunity'. Our proposal is that, in the present experienced authentically, as much as it opens up possibilities in the situation, it also produces a feeling of existential *Angst* if it remains completely one-sided. Indeed, by following any *new* demands just by the fact that they are accepted by the majority *in the present*, there is the risk of falling into what Heidegger calls *curiosity*: 'the possibility of understanding everything without previously making the thing one's own', at which point, '*Dasein* gets entangled in itself' (Heidegger, 2008, pp. 213, 223). I have tried to develop elsewhere why the concept of 'emptiness' is the most central and radical category in Laclau's theory of populism (Porta Caballé, 2021); for now, it suffices to say that it might also be the most *anxious* if there is not enough 'plastic power' in a political group in order to constantly maintain *open* the 'chain of equivalences'. The introduction highlighted the different readings of Laclau by Iglesias and Errejón and entailed the former interpreting it as *tactical* (subordinated to the objective of winning the first general election) whereas the latter understood it as *strategic* (the construction of 'a people' as a long-term process). Now, in the general election of December 2015 Podemos achieved 5 million votes, which would have been an outstanding success if it were not that the expectation was *to win*. This defeat in expectations necessarily recalibrated the *benefits* of the opportunist outlook, which had come at the great *cost* of breaking with tradition. As Chazel and Fernández Vázquez point out:

> Martin (2000), leaning on the work of Mancur Olson, showed that the split within a party can emerge for two reasons: (1) if the cost–benefit ratio is not beneficial anymore (in Podemos' case, Errejón considered the party had reached its glass ceiling by making an alliance with IU in the Unidos Podemos coalition); (2) because the 'individual aspirations grow over time' (Errejón thought the strategy with IU condemned Podemos to be an opposition force) (…) Electoral disappointments will develop 'intra-party disagreement' (Greene & Haber, 2016). (…) Errejón blamed Iglesias for defending an alliance with IU (leaving aside the broad-appeal strategy); while Iglesias started to see the limits of the 'transversal' strategy firstly defended by Errejón. (Chazel and Vázquez, 2019, p. 3)

This is the reason why, I want to argue, there is a retreat to a *nostalgic* point of view, epitomised in the *Pablista* return to the 'traditional left' in the aftermath of 2015, as a certain guarantee of stability, certainty and tradition, in contradistinction with the *Errejonistas*, who were left alone in the 'window of opportunity'. Such a retreat can be said to have culminated in the last meeting of the electoral repetition campaign before 26 June 2016, when Iglesias said that 'even more important than Podemos is the historical encounter with the traditional left' (La Sexta, 2016). Such a primacy of the past in politics is absolutely understandable and legitimate, and it can even be praised for its authentic *retrieving* of tradition beyond any inauthentic *forgetting* – see Table 4.1 – but it is equally undeniable that it moved away from the 'populist hypothesis' with its focus on present demands. In our attempt to translate Nietzsche and Heidegger's temporal categories to politics, note that the original 'Podemos hypothesis' did not merely and inauthentically *forget* the past; it understood it as more than a *sedimented tradition* (with its unchangeable symbols, fetishist words and flags), but also as an authentic *reactivation* of the conflict that originated that same tradition. It is important to remember, for instance, that the Bolsheviks did not name themselves as communists until Lenin *decided* to change the name from the original 'Social-democracy' in 1919, after the insurmountable betrayal of the SPD during the First World War. Sometimes one has to break with tradition precisely in order to remain *faithful* to the *truth-content* of that same tradition, and perhaps that is what Laclau is after when he borrows from the idea that 'Husserl called the routinization and forgetting of origins "sedimentation", and the recovery of the constitutive activity of thought "reactivation"' (1990, p. 34). In this last sense, Javier Franzé brilliantly summarises how Podemos originally attempted to reactivate the past:

> The Podemos discourse, therefore, principally associates the Transition with the old, those from above and the oligarchy. The past is no longer seen as the fratricidal spirit of the Second Republic and Franco's dictatorship as in the transition discourse; it is resignified in the light of the democracy/the people–oligarchy/the caste dichotomy. With democracy in this leading role, the historical context of the Transition discourse is diluted by another: that framed by the interests of those from below or those from above. The Second Republic is reclaimed as a time when popular-democratic politics has come to the fore, while the Transition is linked more to the Civil War in terms of the defeat of the people and the hijacking of democracy. This resignifying of the Second Republic, which links democracy with the empowerment of those from below rather than with anti-monarchism, denotes another defining characteristic of the Podemos discourse during this phase: the way in which it distances itself – in the light of 15M – from the traditional Spanish Left, with its strong attachment to the Left–Right

dichotomy and, at the same time, from the monarchy versus republic, secularism versus confessionalism, and proletariat versus bourgeoisie debates. (Franzé, 2018, pp. 55–56).

However, once Iglesias realised that what was most important was 'the historical encounter with the traditional left', Podemos was finally torn apart into the three ecstatic times – *Pablistas* (past), *Errejonistas* (present) and *Anticapitalistas* (future) – whose symbiotic synergy used to be the source of its original unity and force, and we may consider the 'populist hypothesis' to have ended in Spain (2014–2016). Note that Iglesias had not only been the General Secretary of Podemos, but also the leader (face and voice) of all the historic bloc that had attempted to 'turn outrage into political change' since 2011, and so his personal retreat into nostalgia had profound effects on Spanish political culture more broadly. Podemos had always said that the 15M Indignados Movement had been the best 'vaccine' against any kind of fascist reaction to the economic crisis, and Podemos' national-popular strategy surely continued to help contain that possibility; but once the 'window of opportunity' was left unattended due to a relapse into nostalgia, alongside the increasing Catalan conflict in 2017, the far-right party VOX began to rise into that void. 'Behind every fascism there is a failed revolution', as Žižek echoes Benjamin, and so the movement from privileging the present to putting the past first also implied a change of mood in the Spanish left itself, which had moved from outrage to hope, from hope to frustration, and now from frustration to *resentment*. This displacement enthroned the nostalgic paradigm as hegemonic in Spanish politics as a whole but also in the left in particular and turned *ressentiment* into the general category that can explain and illuminate the new cycle. *Ressentiment* quite literally means to 'feel again' a harm or damage caused *in the past*, by projecting onto the outside its blame or guilt in a moralising way as a result of one's own weakness or impotence *in the present* (Nietzsche, 1989, 36ff.). Now, the fall of 'the people' as an empty signifier capable of uniting the different *present* demands in a chain of equivalences against 'the caste' turned this hatred inward onto the left itself, fragmenting those same struggles and forcing them to compete with each other on who was to blame for the 'failed revolution' in the *past*. The obsession for finding 'when exactly did it all go wrong in the past' has produced, for instance, brilliant Proustian analyses such as Eduardo Maura's *The 90s*, which locates in this decade the origin of the simultaneous 'fear and euphoria', 'violence and consensus', which becomes constitutive of the 'Spanish democratic modernisation' (2018, pp. 12–13, 16). But the retreat into nostalgia has also found a series of more political 'returns', such as the usual 'return to Marx' undertaken by a certain revival of workerism, or the return to traditional values like 'the family' or Catholicism led by a new redbrown cultural sector. Although both of these movements are opposed politically, we think that our theoretical framework developed here can explain, by virtue of the *temporal* dimension *alone*, why a general tendency towards *nostalgia* in Spanish politics appeared, as a reaction to the fall of Podemos's exclusive focus onto *the present*.

Clearly, our analysis cannot claim to be fully *objective* since, like any other, it emerges from a *situated* point of view. But we have at least attempted to be *equable* by recognising that each of the three temporal positions is equally *one-sided* if taken separately; at the same time that each of them has its own *moment of truth*. And we are now able to summarise the results of our investigation in Table 4.2.

**Table 4.2**

| History (Nietzsche) | Antiquarian | Monumental | Critical |
|---|---|---|---|
| | It feels at home in the world by preserving and revering the past | It sees history as a mountain range or relay race of great moments | It knows that everything that has come to be must perish |
| *Abuse / Disadvantage* | It only knows how to preserve life, not how to engender it | It deceives by analogies | It forgets that condemning an aberration does not change the fact that we originated from it |
| *Use / Advantage* | It shows that we can live here because here we have lived | It shows that greatness was once possible and thus it can be possible again | It has the arrogance to propose a second nature |
| **Time (Heidegger)** | **Past** | **Present** | **Future** |
| *Inauthentic* | Forgetting | Instant | Awaiting |
| *Authentic* | Retrieving | Moment of vision | Anticipatory resoluteness |
| **Politics** | **Nostalgic** | **Opportunist** | **Utopian** |
| *Inauthentic* | Sedimented tradition | Instrumental rationality | Resolutive fiction |
| *Authentic* | Reactivation | Window of opportunity | Horizon |

## 5. Conclusion: Being-as-a-whole-within-time-ness in Politics

In the end, we are finally in a position to ask a crucial question: Are our results restricted to populism in particular, and even specially to our case study, Podemos in Spain (2014–2016), or could they also be extrapolated to political theory in general? Against the background of Arditi's well-known criticism that Laclau sometimes confounds 'populism' with 'the political' (2003), if one takes the position of Biglieri and Cadahia, there might be a productive 'mutual contamination' rather than just a mere 'semantic overlap' (2021, p. 16). It should come as no surprise that if populism stands effectively as the 'royal road' to the political (Laclau, 2007b, p. 67), then the categories developed here with regards to the case of Podemos could be easily operationalised for the purposes of political theory in general. Is not Marxism, for instance, also divided into three souls: the nostalgic (historical materialism), the opportunist (theory of revolution) and the utopian (communism)?

Finally, what is the most general conclusion that we can extract from our concrete temporal journey? That, *at least in the Spanish case, there was a strong correlation between populism and the present, so that, when the latter prevailed as the primary temporality, the former also followed as its most adequate political form; and, conversely, when the priority of the present collapsed, populism also faded away.* Whether this is a general law that could apply to populism itself would require a broader comparison with other contemporaneous case studies – the 'pink tide' in Latin America, Syriza, La France Insoumise, Jeremy Corbyn and Bernie Sanders. However, if this were to be the case more broadly, a work should be done in order to study the profound link that might be binding the 'metaphysics of presence' of the Derridean type with the 'instrumental rationality' that the Frankfurt School so fiercely criticises – and which we have used here as the defining factor of the *inauthentic opportunist*. How these two apparently opposed schools could work together in favour of a critique of *presentism* (in politics, in our case) is not a completely unexplored terrain, and some work has been done recently in this direction (Macdonald & Ziarek, 2007).

This chapter has demonstrated four theses. Firstly, time is not just an object that is *presently* 'there', but it *temporalises itself* in the 'unity of its ecstases', which necessarily include the past and the future. Secondly, for this very reason, politics is not, and it can never be, merely 'what goes on *now*', the decisions taken by political actors *in the present*, but it is also the *inheritances* and *expectations* that these actors hold at the instant of taking them. Thirdly, the existential decision between inauthenticity and authenticity traverses the whole relationship that politics establishes with time in each case. An inauthentic politician, for instance, resignedly negotiates with the symbols of the past (*sedimented tradition*), makes a cost/benefit calculus in the present (*instrumental rationality*), and utters empty promises with regards to the future (*resolutive fiction*). By contrast, an authentic politics that is still *to come* would require to reappropriate the truth-content and the original conflict within the past (*reactivation*), see the exceptional possibilities that open in a situation in order to act in the present (*window of opportunity*), and project a new setting of meaning and purpose into the future (*horizon*). Fourthly, and lastly, we hope to have sufficiently shown that each of the three temporal figures that constitute the political – the nostalgic, the opportunist and the utopian – are equally one-sided if taken separately in-and-for-itself, and that an authentic politics would require being-as-a-whole-within-time-ness by integrating the past, the present and the future with an equal weight. Only then will populism be able to cry, like Hamlet, 'time is out of joint. O cursed spite / that ever I was born to set it right!' (Shakespeare, 2003, p. 52).

## Notes

1. An embryonic part of this essay was presented at the 6th Populist Specialist Group (PSA) Workshop at the University of Brighton 22–23 September 2022 under the title 'Politics and Time: The Nostalgic, the Opportunist and the Utopian. The Case of Podemos'. I would like to thank especially Andy Knott, Giorgos Venizelos, Emmy Eklundh, Lazaros Karavasilis, Óscar García Agustín and Nicolás Ortiz Ruiz for their insightful comments, suggestions and criticisms, without which this essay would not have looked the same. This essay could not have been possible either without the umbrella offered by the research project 'Post-foundational Contemporary Thought: Theoretical-Critical Analysis of Contemporary Ontologies of Negativity and the Question of the Violence of the Foundation' (PID2020-117069GB-I00), funded by the Spanish Ministry of Science and Innovation, and with Laura Llevadot as Leading Researcher at the University of Barcelona.
2. We could ask ourselves at this point: Why are these meditations 'un-timely'? *Unzeitgemässe* perhaps is one of the most difficult Nietzschean terms to translate into English. In this case, it does not mean 'eternal' or 'out-dated', in the sense of being '*out* of [its] time'. Actually, if one takes a look at the other *Untimely Meditations* one realises that Nietzsche is not uninterested in his *own* time, the present: *David Strauss: The Confessor and the Writer* [1873], *Schopenhauer* as Educator [1874] and Richard Wagner in Bayreuth [1876]. In fact, Nietzsche's deliberate intention in each and every one of these meditations is to ruthlessly criticise a certain fashion or trend that has achieved fame or success in modern culture – particularly German culture – and to

show that their importance vanishes when they are looked upon from a certain *distance*. We have thus clarified that 'un-timely' does not mean completely 'out of time', but rather to look at the present from a certain distance. Now, from *what* distance does Nietzsche intend to look at the present of modern German culture? It is not only a *geographical* distance, considering the fact that Nietzsche had just had to renounce to his Prussian citizenship in order to accept the offer of a full Professorship at the University of Basel in Switzerland at twenty-four. Rather, his *exile* is more profound than that of a simply stateless person because he already had been *estranged* first by the study of classical philology. Nietzsche then compares his own time with that of Greece, more than any other epoch, and he starts to get in a bad mood. And there is no other reason as to why he then moves to ruthlessly attacking his own education (historicism), his master (Schopenhauer) and his friend (Wagner). This (self-)criticism is what the *Untimely Meditations* are meant to accomplish. No wonder that when Nietzsche reflects upon them in his autobiography, Ecce Homo, he appropriates the maxim of his dear Stendhal: 'always enter into society with a duel' (1989, p. 280). No wonder either that when he began to brandish the sword in his Unpublished Writings against his first enemy, David Strauss, he presented his attacks as a series of 'letters from a foreigner' (Nietzsche, 1995, pp. 155, 159, 162, 173). So, to begin with, we have thus clarified that Nietzsche's *Meditations* are *untimely* not in the sense of being 'in-actual' but rather in the sense of having become estranged or exiled from their *own* time, by 'an-*other* time' (that of Greece, especially) (Llinares, 2018, pp. 9–13). In this chapter we will also attempt to look at politics in an *untimely* fashion, as a 'foreigner' of the present, since politics is not just what 'goes on now', the decisions taken by political actors, but also the *inheritances* and *expectations* that these actors hold at the instant of making them.

3. After Lucien Goldmann's pathbreaking work *Lukacs and Heidegger: Towards a New Philosophy* (2009), it is difficult not to recognise that Heidegger's conception of 'inauthenticity' in *Being and Time* [1927] is nothing more than a copy of Lukacs' use of 'alienation' or 'reification' in *History and Class Consciousnes*, published only four years before ([1923] 1971). If we have decided to maintain Heidegger's terms in this chapter in the end it is only for two reasons: (1) because it is Heidegger in *Being and Time* who most explicitly links (in-)authenticity with *temporality* (which is the main topic of this essay), whereas in Lukacs it still remains restricted to a great extent to the economy of work and production; and (2) because it is Heidegger who explicitly draws the link with Nietzsche's *Second Untimely Meditation* (which serves as the base for the present chapter). Nonetheless, the reader should

keep in mind that, from a left-Heideggerian point of view, 'authentic' time is just the same as 'non-alienated' time, to the extent that the definitive hegemony of the 'time of the clock' as a series of now-moments also corresponds with the peak of the capitalist Industrial Revolution. To the four kinds of alienation defined by Marx in the *Philosophical and Economic Manuscripts*, then, one is tempted to add a fifth one: the worker's alienation from time itself.
4. For a longer, more developed and detailed reading of this, Heidegger dedicates volume 46 of his *Gesamtausgabe* exclusively to the *Interpretation of Nietzsche's Second Untimely Meditation* (2016).

## References

Arditi, Benjamín (2003) 'Populism, or, politics at the edges of democracy', *Contemporary Politics*, 9 (1), pp. 17–31.
Biglieri, Paula and Cadahia, Luciana (2021) *Seven essays on populism. For a renewed theoretical perspective*, George Ciccariello-Maher (trans). Medford and Cambridge: Polity Press.
Bustinduy, Pablo and Lago, Jorge (2023) *Política y ficción. Ideologías de un tiempo sin futuro*. Unpublished manuscript.
Cano, Germán (2014) 'Estudio introductorio', in *El nacimiento de la tragedia. El caminante y su sombra. La ciencia jovial*. Madrid: Gredos.
Chazel, Laura and Fernández Vázquez, Guillermo (2019) 'Podemos, at the origins of the internal conflicts around the "populist hypothesis": a comparison of the theoretical production, public speeches and militant trajectories of Pablo Iglesias and Íñigo Errejón'. *European Politics and Society*. DOI: 10.1080/23745118.2019.1582256.
Derrida, Jacques (2006) *Spectres of Marx. The state of the debt, the work of mourning and the new international*, Peggy Kamuf (trans). London and New York: Routledge.
Errejón, Íñigo (2011a) 'También en Europa: posibilidades populistas en la política europea y española. Política, conflicto y populismo (II)', *Viento Sur*, 115/March, pp. 105–114.
Errejón, Íñigo (2011b) 'El 15-M como discurso contrahegemónico', *Encrucijadas. Revista Crítica de Ciencias Sociales*, 2/December, pp. 120–145.
Errejón, Íñigo (2015) '*We the People*. El 15-M: ¿Un populismo indignado?', *ACME: An International E-Journal for Critical Geographies*, 14 (1), pp. 124–156.
Errejón, Íñigo (2016) 'Del asalto al cerco: Podemos en la nueva fase', *Eldiario.es*, 17 July, https://www.eldiario.es/opinion/tribuna-abierta/asalto-cerco-podemos-nueva-fase_129_3897988.html.

Errejón, Íñigo and Mouffe, Chantal (2016) *Podemos: in the name of the people*. Preface by Owen Jones, Sirio Canós Donnay (trans). London: Lawrence & Wishart.

Europa Press (2011) 'El 15M tiene el apoyo de más del 80% de los ciudadanos, sobre todo entre la izquierda, pero un 60% cree que no triunfará', *Europa Press*, 6 July, https://www.europapress.es/madrid/noticia-15m-tiene-apoyo-mas-80-ciudadanos-todo-izquierda-60-cree-no-triunfara-20110606172146.html.

Fernández Buey, Francisco (2007) *Utopías e ilusiones naturales*. Barcelona: El Viejo Topo.

Franzé, Javier (2018) 'The Podemos discourse: a journey from antagonism to agonism', in García Agustín, Óscar and Briziarelli, Marco (eds) *Podemos and the new political cycle. Left-wing populism and anti-establishment politics*. Cham: Palgrave Macmillan, pp. 49–74.

Goldmann, Lucien (2009) *Lukács and Heidegger: towards a new philosophy*, William Q. Boelhower (trans). London and New York: Routledge.

Gramsci, Antonio (1988) *An Antonio Gramsci reader. Selected writings (1916–1935)*, David Forgacs (ed.). New York: Shocken Books.

Hegel, G. W. F. (1977a) *The difference between Fichte's and Schelling's System of Philosophy*, H. S. Harris and Walter Cerf (trans). Albany: State of New York University Press.

Hegel, G. W. F. (1977b) *Phenomenology of spirit*, A. V. Miller (trans), with a Foreword by J. N. Findlay. Oxford: Oxford University Press.

Heidegger, Martin (2008) *Being and time*, John Macquarrie and Edward Robinson (trans), with a New Foreword by Taylor Carman. New York: HarperCollins Publishers.

Heidegger, Martin (2016) *Interpretation of Nietzsche's second untimely meditation*, Ullrich Haase and Mark Sinclair (trans). Bloomington: Indiana University Press.

Heidegger, Martin (2018) *Heraclitus. The inception of occidental thinking. Logic: Heraclitus doctrine of the logos*, Julia Goesser Assaiante and S. Montgomery Ewegen (trans). New York: Bloomsbury.

Iglesias, Pablo (2015) 'Understanding Podemos'. *New Left Review*, 93, May/June, pp. 5–22.

Kierkegaard, Søren (2009) *The moment and late writings*, with Introduction and Notes by Howard V. Hong and Edna H. Hong (ed and trans). Princeton, NJ: Princeton University Press, pp. 87–354.

Kioupkiolis, Alexandros (2016) 'Podemos: the ambiguous promises of left-wing populism in contemporary Spain', *Journal of Political Ideologies*, 21 (2), pp. 99–120. DOI: 10.1080/13569317.2016.1150136.

Knott, Andy (2024) 'Introduction: populism, metaphor, temporality', supra, pp. 1–24.

Lacan, Jacques (2013) *Le Séminaire, Livre VI: Le désir et son interprétation*. Texte établi par Jacques Alain-Miller. Paris: Éditions de la Martinière et le Champ Freudien.

Laclau, Ernesto (1990) *New reflections on the revolution of our time*. London and New York: Verso.

Laclau, Ernesto (2007a) *Emancipation(s)*. London and New York: Verso.

Laclau, Ernesto (2007b) *On populist reason*. London and New York: Verso.

La Sexta (2016) 'Pablo Iglesias: "más importante que Podemos es el encuentro histórico con la izquierda de toda la vida"', *La Sexta*, 25 June, https://www.lasexta.com/noticias/nacional/elecciones-generales-2016/pablo-iglesias-mas-importante-que-podemos-encuentro-historico-izquierda-toda-vida_20160625576db3426584a88907b6222a.html.

Lenin, V. I. (1965) 'Our revolution'. *Collected Works. Volume 33* (2nd English edn). Moscow: Progress Publishers, pp. 476–480.

Llinares, Joan B. (2018) 'Prefacio'. In Nietzsche, Friedrich, *De la utilidad y los inconvenientes de la historia para la vida. Segunda consideración intempestiva*. Madrid: Tecnos, pp. 9–27.

Lukács, Georg (1971) *History and class consciousness. Studies in Marxist dialectics*, Rodney Livingstone (trans). Cambridge, MA: The MIT Press.

Macdonald, Ian and Ziarek, Krzysztof (eds) (2007) *Adorno and Heidegger. philosophical questions*. Stanford, CA: Stanford University Press.

Marx, Karl (2010) 'Letter to Ludwig Kugelmann', in Marx, Karl and Engels, Friedrich. *Collected Works. Volume 44: Letters 1870–1873*. Electronic book: Lawrence & Wishart, pp. 131–132.

Marx, Karl and Engels, Friedrich (2010) 'Manifesto of the Communist Party'. *Collected Works. Volume 6: 1845–1848*. Electronic book: Lawrence & Wishart, pp. 477–519.

Maura, Eduardo (2018) *Los 90. Euforia y miedo en la modernidad democrática Española*. Madrid: Akal.

Mazzolini, Samuele and Borriello, Arthur (2021) 'The normalization of left populism? The paradigmatic case of Podemos', *European Politics and Society*. DOI: 10.1080/23745118.2020.1868849.

More, Thomas (2003) *Utopia*, with an Introduction and Notes by Paul Turner (trans). London: Penguin Books.

Nietzsche, Friedrich (1989) *On the genealogy of morals. Ecce homo*, with Commentary by Walter Kaufmann (ed). New York: Vintage Books.

Nietzsche, Friedrich (1995) *Unpublished writings from the period of unfashionable meditations*, with an Afterword by Richard T. Gray (trans). Stanford, CA: Stanford University Press.

Nietzsche, Friedrich (2004) *Untimely meditations*, Daniel Breazeale (ed) and R. J. Hollingdale (trans). Cambridge: Cambridge University Press.

Nietzsche, Friedrich (2006) *The pre-Platonic philosophers*, Greg Whitlock (trans). Urbana and Chicago: Illinois University Press.

Porta Caballé, Adrià (2021) 'El vacío del populismo latinoamericano frente a la ontología política europea', *Res Publica. Revista de Historia de las Ideas Políticas*, 24 (1), pp. 63–74. https://doi.org/10.5209/rpub.70315.

Portos, Martín (2019) 'Keeping dissent alive under the Great Recession: no-radicalisation and protest in Spain after the eventful 15M/*indignados* campaign', *Acta Politica*, 54, pp. 45–74. DOI: 10.1057/s41269-017-0074-9.

Público (2014) 'Intelectuales y activistas llaman a "recuperar la soberanía popular" con una candidatura para las europeas', *Público*, 14 January, https://www.publico.es/politica/intelectuales-y-activistas-llaman-recuperar.html.

Rendueles, César and Sola, Jorge (2017) 'Podemos, the upheaval of Spanish politics and the challenge of populism', *Journal of Contemporary European Studies*. DOI: 10.1080/14782804.2017.1304899.

Rendueles, César and Sola, Jorge (2018) 'The rise of Podemos: promises, constraints and dilemmas', in García Agustín, Óscar and Briziarelli, Marco (eds) *Podemos and the new political cycle. Left-wing populism and anti-establishment politics*. Cham: Palgrave Macmillan, pp. 25–48.

Rodríguez López, Emmanuel (2016) *La política en el ocaso de la clase media. El ciclo 15M-Podemos*. Madrid: Traficantes de Sueños.

Schürmann, Reiner (2008) 'Heidegger's *Being and time*', in Critchley, Simon and Schürmann, Reiner, *On Heidegger's* Being and Time, Steven Levine (ed). London and New York: Routledge.

Shakespeare, William (2003) *Hamlet*. Fully annotated, with an Introduction by Burton Raffel and an Essay by Harold Bloom. New Haven, CT and London: Yale University Press.

Žižek, Slavoj (2006) *How to Read Lacan*. London: Granta Books.

# Part II
# Populism and Technology

# 5

# Populisation: Populism – Temporary Dysfunction or Modernity's Revenge?[1]

*Simon Tormey*

It's not often that the ontology of a concept comes to be questioned, but amongst the myriad debates concerning what populism is, as well as what it is not, clearly lies a deeper question taking us beyond the analytical demand for precision. Populism is elusive as a concept, not just because we find it difficult to pin down in terms of key attributes or characteristics, but also because we don't seem to be able to find agreement on what kind of 'thing' populism really is (Moffitt, 2016; Pappas, 2019). What's going on?

'Populism studies' is dominated by comparative political scientists who see populism as a distinct regime, political system, party or movement (Moffitt & Tormey, 2013). This is to say that they see populism in terms of certain features or characteristics, which when taken together constitute the object in question. They include typically an ideology that talks about The People as a single homogenous entity in opposition to elites, a charismatic leader, and a repertoire of behaviours such as contempt for various minorities, and a vitriolic approach to addressing political opponents (Tormey, 2019). Some condense this to a more parsimonious definition such as 'democratic illiberalism' (Pappas, 2019).

By contrast with this approach, those identifying with the 'Essex School' see populism much less as a set of features, and more as a way of thinking about how politics functions under contemporary conditions (Simons, 2011). They see populism less as a set of family resemblances, and more in terms of a political strategy based on certain invariable qualities of democratic life. They include a system of political representation where the *demos* or people is central to political discourse and to its rhetorical qualities. Those who want to effect change must challenge those in power on grounds that they better understand the needs and interests of the people, in turn understanding that the people cannot represent itself, but must be represented. So, on this reading populism is a latent feature of democratic life. It is both a description of how politics functions ('We the people'), but also an admonition to those who want to challenge existing power structures in the name of something new. It is both a presence and a promise, something to come as well as something in the here and now.

This doesn't exhaust how populism is described, and thus how we might frame its ontology. Since 2016 we have heard a great deal about populism in specifically temporal terms, that is as some sort of event. Populism 'explodes'. Populism is an 'age, a 'moment', an 'epoch' (Badiou, 2012; Judis, 2016). And so on. Such a tendency is particularly prevalent in media reporting of contemporary politics. The election of Corbyn as Labour leader, the Brexit vote, and the election of Trump in November 2016 provide an assemblage of events that underpins this sense of the event-ness of populism. Populism is not in this sense just a set of distinguishing features, a strategy, or a way of thinking about politics, it is a way of thinking about what our politics has become. There is considerable debate about how long this will last, about whether this is a cycle, and whether we can expect a return to more sober professional styles of politics once the clamour dies down. But the sense of an event that alters the political landscape is difficult to escape.

So what is it to be? Is populism a regime, a strategy or an event of some shape and force?

My suggestion is that there's still something important missing in these various ways of thinking about populism, which is the sense of populism as a symptom for underlying changes in the nature of politics under contemporary conditions. Populism is also and perhaps primarily a symptom of a crisis that has enveloped liberal democracy, advanced capitalism and the emergent security-surveillance apparatus that has emerged out of it. Populism on this reading is less an aberration, a deviation or disruption to the norm, which is often the impression we get from the populism studies literature. It is more the working out of tendencies that are endemic to liberal capitalist modernity.

This is not to say that populism is inevitable or that it appears in the same guise in every social setting. It is more that we need to think of populism less as something special or of limited duration as is implied in the explosion metaphors. I don't think populism will give way either to the 'old normal' or some dramatically different way of doing politics. Populism is the result of the interplay of trends and tendencies, which means that our politics is becoming louder, more vulgar, less technocratic, more 'immediate', more spectacular. These are the hallmarks of populism, and the hallmarks of the political culture being created. Populism may once have been 'special' or extraordinary in some sense, but its ontology is I think closely bound up with that of globalisation and indeed modernity more generally. Globalisation's remorseless profit-driven imperative has disrupted the cosy certainties that underpinned an earlier age with its relatively settled hierarchies of class and identity. It has promoted flows of people, whilst at the same time opening the global economy to greater risk, in turn leading to savage recessionary swings and insecurity. It has been accompanied by a media revolution that has underpinned an increasing sense of crisis and dislocation. This is fertile ground for a politics of resentment and the scapegoating of those seemingly responsible for the mess we find ourselves in. The populist politics that emerges out of it is thus no longer exceptional, but to an increasing degree ordinary, banal. It is a politics for a world that senses itself as in crisis, a crisis moreover that seems to be endemic to globalisation.

It's for the reasons above that I propose we see populism not only, or not merely, as a kind of regime or a 'moment', but as a process – hence the admittedly ungainly reference to 'populisation' in the title of the chapter. The suggestion here is that our politics is becoming less technocratic, less moderate and less embracing of complexity, opportunity/cost and trade-offs. It is becoming 'hotter', more emotive, more simplistic and affective in tone. Since these are, on most accounts, hallmarks of populist as opposed to 'normal' politics, I think populism is not merely here to stay, it increasingly defines politics as we experience it, and as it is prosecuted by key actors.

## 1. Finding Some Common Ground

Given the radically different ways in which populism is thought about, it should hardly come as a surprise to find that there is a good deal of contestation concerning even basic definitions of what populism is. Nevertheless, there are certain themes that come through strongly in most accounts. Chief amongst these is the concept of the People, the populace, from which populism gets its label. Populism is a politics of 'the People', *as opposed to* the establishment, the elites, Washington, Westminster (Canovan, 2005). In other words, the point of invoking the people is as a contrast to those who exercise power. So, populism is not just any kind of democratic discourse. It's a discourse that starts from a sense of rupture between those who represent and those who are represented (Laclau, 1990). The simple premise that sets populism in motion is the idea that somehow and to some degree those who govern have ripped off the rest of us, the people.

Following on from this observation is a sense of populism as a politics driven by a sense of crisis, by a sense that politics is 'letting us down' and thus that something has to change. Moreover, that change needs to come from without, as opposed to from within the existing parameters of representative politics. From this point of view populism is a politics driven by 'outsiders'. Whether those outsiders are really outside, in the sense of coming from beyond the elites, is a question that need not detain us here for long. Merely to note that some of today's most compelling outsider figures are objectively and even subjectively members of the elites they can be so critical of. One of the puzzles of populism is how it is that figures such as Donald Trump, Nigel Farage and Marine Le Pen, all in narrow class terms members of the establishment, are able to convince large swathes of the electorate that they can represent the interests of ordinary citizens.

What the above indicates is that populism doesn't challenge the basic assumptions that inform representation. Rather, populism is a form of *hyper*-representation for those who no longer feel represented but who are looking for a meaningful or authentic representative to take up their needs and interests. So populism may include some radical demands, but its radicalism rarely threatens a break or rupture to the system that it appears to be so critical of. Indeed, in many respects not only does populism reaffirm representation, in recent times it has been responsible for its reinvigoration, presenting what is in effect a new set of claims to be able to represent the people more effectively than 'the representatives'. The appearance of populism can thus have the paradoxical effect of reinvigorating political systems that might otherwise have seemed rather moribund (Arditi, 2007). Populism ups the political stakes, in turn grabbing the attention of a perhaps somnolent electorate, forcing it to re-engage with the electoral process and indeed with politics more broadly. So whilst populism can appear more or less threatening to democracy, it can act as a stimulus or catalyst to mobilisation and awakening political interest.

Populism is a politics that invokes the people for a particular purpose, that is to highlight the deficiencies of the elites. This is prompted by and feeds off crisis. Where there is no sense of crisis there is rarely any populism (Moffitt, 2015). Populism is a form of politics that remains within the logic of representation, moving towards hyper-representation. It's a politics of outsiders, though those outsiders may themselves be insiders, or members of some other set of elites, whether that be from business or, as is increasingly the case, from the world of celebrity. The question then is why are we seeing more of this style of politics? What does the appearance of populism tell us about the nature of politics across the advanced democracies?

## 2. Explaining Populism

Surveying the vast literature on the causes of populism it becomes evident that two approaches dominate when it comes to trying to explain why we are seeing the increasing prevalence of this style of politics. They are respectively economic grievance and cultural grievance (Tormey, 2019).

Economic grievance takes its cue from the global financial crisis of 2008, which led to deep recessions across the capitalist world and the adoption of austerity measures. The political price of austerity was often felt by the centre-left and by social democratic regimes, rather than the centre-right and Conservatives. Nevertheless the overall effect was to create an atmosphere of bitter resentment against the elites, in turn preparing the way for new parties and political figures who promised a way out of the economic crisis. Left-wing parties did well in countries such as Spain and Greece, attributing austerity to Conservative-liberal regimes, corrupt politicians obsessed with megaprojects at the cost of public services. Right-wing parties targeted the recent inflow of migrants and refugees, knowing that this would find a receptive audience amongst those who are unemployed or perhaps excluded from benefits and services, and therefore receptive to a story about how they had denied their just entitlements.

The idea that populism arises out of economic crisis is compelling if we are thinking that populism is something of recent vintage and in particular something associated with the events of 2016. 'Global Trumpism', as Mark Blyth puts it, received enormous impetus from recession and the inability of the elites to come up with a formula to restart the economy and get people back to work. However, whilst this helps us understand why populism appeared in 2016 it doesn't help explain the appearance of populism as such, which on most readings pre-dates the 2008 financial crash. How do we account for the emergence of the Le Pens in the 1990s, the likes of Geert Wilders and Pim Fortuyn in the 2000s, and the persistence of populism in regions such as Latin America and Australia over many decades, and so on? How do we account for the continuing appeal of populist leaders and movements a decade and half after the financial crisis, as marked for example by the election of Giorgia Meloni in Italy and the dramatic emergence of outsider figures such as Eric Zemmour, the 'French Trump' who whilst ultimately unsuccessful in the 2021 French presidential election, underscored the appeal of an anti-elites, anti-mainstream messaging for many voters. Clearly there must be something more to the story than just economic crisis precipitated by the collapse of banks.

What about cultural grievance? This is an argument associated with the likes of David Goodhart and Pippa Norris who argue that over the course of the past few decades there has been a significant but growing divergence between what the former calls 'anywheres' and 'somewheres' (Norris & Inglehart, 2019; Goodhart, 2017). This latter group have felt themselves under threat through the processes celebrated by anywheres. They do not see globalisation as something positive. They do not welcome inflows of new migrants into their communities. They do not want to be part of a multicultural melting pot, but rather see culture in zero sum terms. The more we celebrate diversity, the greater the threat to that sense of identity and belonging which they feel to be integral to their own sense of well-being. Populism, as we have heard, is a politics of resentment, of crisis, and here it is crisis precipitated by the sense of loss and thus nostalgia for how things were: 'Make America Great Again.'

Cultural grievance makes a lot of sense if by populism we mean primarily movements of a right-wing or nativist kind. It certainly seems to be the case that across the advanced democracies we have seen a significant backlash against trans-nationalism, immigration and globalisation. This is expressing itself in political terms with the rise of the anti-immigrant far right. It also helps to explain why it is that we see these movements arising in contexts that were relatively unscathed by recession and austerity, such as Germany, Austria and the Nordic countries. On the other hand, cultural grievance doesn't help us explain the rise of *left-wing* populisms of a kind associated with Syriza, Podemos or Jean-Luc Mélenchon.

So, we are left with at best a partial account that helps us explain some part of the populism story, but not all of it. It helps explain why we are seeing the rise of the political *right*, less so the political left. Nor does it seem to help explain why politics is taking the particular form it does: its anti-elitism, its focus on narratives of betrayal, its quest for charismatic leadership, and so forth.

Neither the economic grievance argument nor the cultural grievance argument seems able to explain why we are seeing more populisms of both left- and right-wing variety arising across the democratic world. They capture part of the picture, but not all of it. How then to account for the rise of populism in more general terms as a style or form of politics?

These narratives need to be supplemented with an account of 'democratic grievance' and the collapsing measures used to gauge our engagement with representative institutions and processes (Tormey, 2015). The key features here include the decline of engagement with mainstream politics, and mainstream political parties, which have suffered a precipitous decline in membership since the 1960s in the advanced democracies. They include a decline in the status and standing of politicians, and a waning of trust in democratic institutions and processes. Finally, they include a declining interest in and knowledge about how politics works, as measured in for example the number of hours devoted to politics in the mainstream media and column inches in serious newspapers.

Over the past half-century or so citizens have become more impatient with politicians, and less convinced that mainstream or centrist politics has much to offer them individually or collectively (Hay, 2007; Keane, 2009;

Flinders, 2012). Those who retain an interest in politics and the conviction that politics may help us to resolve collective problems have moved away from mass membership parties, towards self-consciously 'outsider' parties and figures who promise a radical break with the present. Less formal modes of organising, including protests, demonstrations and varieties of online engagement such as campaigns via social media platforms have also increased in frequency and impact particularly amongst the young looking for something more engaging than involvement with the usual committees and campaigning. Participation in politics is in this sense often expressed in terms that implicitly challenge the legitimacy or primacy of conventional forms of political mobilisation. They take place on 'the street' or through various forms and modes of informal networking. For those less inclined to activism they take the form of interest in outsiders and heterodox figures from beyond the political mainstream, offering a 'fresh start', a 'new beginning', a 'break with the past'. As we have noted, all of this is part of the repertoire of populist movements, parties and leaders. The question remains: What is driving all this? What is the cause of democratic grievance?

## 3. Towards a Sociological Approach

As noted, populism studies is dominated by comparative political science, which is interested in the study of differences between regimes, movements, parties. The key point is to understand what is *distinctive* about populism, as opposed to where populism comes from, or what causes it. Populism studies is thus long on descriptions of how these regimes differ, but shorter on what *causes* the differences, and why it is that we seem to be seeing an increase in populism. This isn't a criticism, so much as an explanation for why it is that we seem to lack a compelling narrative about why populism is arising more frequently, becoming more prevalent as a mode or style of politics. I think we need an approach that acknowledges certain key secular changes happening across democratic societies to explain why democracy has found itself in crisis and why we are seeing the rise of outsider movements and politics. In short, we need to adopt a sociological approach to get to the heart of a *political* crisis.

This is not it should be added a particularly fashionable approach amongst populism studies scholars; but it is I think a necessary approach given the shortcomings of the dominant approaches already discussed. The comparative and country study approach tends to treat populism as an idiosyncratic and disruptive phenomenon, imagining a norm – the functional democracy with high levels of trust and engagement with the mainstream – that looks increasingly anachronistic. The Essex approach by contrast has a tendency to see populism as built into the DNA of democratic discourse, which in turn loses the specificity of populism, as opposed to other varieties of politics. Implied in a sociological approach on the other hand is that populism is an incipient tendency of contemporary society, and thus something that can be discussed as part of the more general crisis provoked by globalisation and modernity.

### 3.1 The Decline of Traditional Structures of Authority and Hierarchy

One of the bedrock observations in the sociology of modernity, one that features in the work of theorists as diverse as Marx, Weber and Nietzsche, is the decline of traditional structures. As Marx memorably puts it, under capitalist modernisation 'all that is solid melts into air; all that is holy is profaned' (Marx, 1988). No one has been able to improve on this formula as a shorthand for the corrosive impact of new technologies, new ways of organising ourselves, and the new belief systems and ideologies that support technological and social advance. Marx was hopeful that all of this would produce a certain clarity as we were 'compelled to confront the true conditions of our existence'. But the effect has been corrosive on every truth claim, not the least of which has been on the communist truth claim itself.

Lyotard memorably described the resulting scepticism as 'incredulity towards meta narratives' and by extension the post-modern condition (Lyotard, 1984). This is a condition of deep scepticism and doubt, the liberating consequences of which are well documented, but which also carries certain risks. Amongst the latter is the declining status of experts and expertise. We increasingly query and question the sources of authority, leaving ourselves as arbiters not only of our own interest but of everyone else's.

With the proliferation of sources of information and the increasing ease with which they can be accessed, so we have, in Lyotard's phrase, become 'pagans', non-believers in official narratives, whether offered by the Church, the state or by some other source of authority. Conspiracy theorising proliferates and is no longer confined to the margin. We exist in an atmosphere of disbelief, scepticism and doubt fuelled by an absence of a single point of truth. If that becomes tiresome, then we construct an arbiter for ourselves, or find one in the various fundamentalisms that proliferate around us in the vacuum created by the waning of orthodoxy, however defined (Heller & Feher, 1988). Such an atmosphere is fertile ground for narratives of hurt, injustice, conspiracy and by extension for the need for a 'new beginning' or a new start from the metaphorical 'outside'. It leads to a redemptive mindset and the demand for simple solutions to complex problems. It's a stance of impatience with the present and a hunger for change from the old messages and the familiar tunes.

## 3.2 Individualisation and the Decline of Collective Identities

The corrosive effect of modernisation processes extends beyond belief structures, towards our very sense of who we are and where we belong in society. Reference to Marx is again useful in this respect. Marx documented how technological change led to a change in the composition of classes and by extension class identity. The myriad identities of the feudal world give way increasingly to identification in terms of membership of either the bourgeois class or the working class, that is until the working class accepts its historic destiny as destroyer of class society. However, as Marx also realised, the bourgeois class has a great advantage in this struggle. It has the means to convince many of us that the primary unit of social life is not social class, but the individual. Freedom is the freedom of the individual to realise her potential. Rights belong to people, not to classes. Opportunity is 'what we make of it', not a birth right nor entitlement (Heller, 1999).

The 'new spirit of capitalism' emphasises self-realisation, and an escape from the clutches of group identities so that we might express 'who we are' (Boltanski & Chiapello, 2005). Hence the contemporary obsession with self-improvement, forging our own destinies, fulfilling 'the American dream'. This is not to say that group identity is unlikely or undesirable. It's more that we now choose the groups that we identify with. Identity is now performative rather than functional. It relates to what or who we think we are, as opposed to how we are seen or relate to others (Castells, 1997).

We are encouraged to embrace fluidity and the possibility for a reimagining of ourselves as that whom we would like to be, as opposed to that whom others expect us to be. By extension, politics is losing its anchoring as the mechanism by which groups defend or advance their own interests and needs. Political parties were once the bearer of distinctive group identities, whether as defenders of the working class, or of distinct ethnicities, or ideological projects. Loyalty to political parties was handed down from generation to generation, and maintained on the back of low mobility, local and tribal identities, and the perpetuation of family loyalties.

Much of this has been eroded in the passage towards a post-Fordist economy which favours a 'liquid' subjectivity based on high mobility, the promotion of self-reinvention and self-improvement, and a corresponding willingness to jettison the anchors that once made for more predictable political behaviours (Bauman, 2000). Post-Fordism and an increasingly globalised economy have also resulted in greater precarity and class polarisation, albeit along new lines. Inequality intensifies, throwing ever larger numbers into a world of deep existential as well as financial uncertainty. The middle class is becoming squeezed and so are the prospects of the young, who once hoped to follow their parents and grandparents into the relative security of a middle-class profession.

The price paid for the creation of this emerging 'precariat' is, as Guy Standing has argued, greater anxiety, and less certainty in terms of our understanding of our place in the world (Standing, 2011). Anxious subjects lead to anxious politics, a politics that trades on a sense of despondency, fear and insecurity to drive an agenda of blame and culpabilisation (Eklundh et al., 2017; Furedi, 2006). Anxiety, a generalised and non-specific dread, searches for someone or something to blame. It lends itself to the primacy of affective or emotive styles of politics – something that at once pins the blame for our condition on something with the offer of a soothing remedy in return. Politics 'as usual' becomes politics as 'exception' and the quest for rupture.

### 3.3 Bureaucracy and Complexification

A further dimension of the modernisation story is the emergence of the modern state in the passage from feudal to modern modes of governance, and by extension increasing bureaucratisation, managerialism and complexity. Michel Foucault has perhaps gone the furthest in exploring this aspect of modernity, documenting the myriad mechanisms by which we move from overt, muscular systems of control and domination through increasingly subtle modes of 'governmentality' that come to penetrate and shape every aspect of our now biopolitical lives (Foucault, 1980).

The sense of our world being increasingly moulded, shaped, governed by hidden or discrete forces paves the way for what Richard Hofstadter terms the 'paranoid style' in politics (Hofstadter, 2008). This is the adoption of a posture that assumes the worse, that sees politics as a dark, Machiavellian enterprise disguised by warm words and noble sentiments. He was himself building on a raft of critiques of the increasing bureaucratisation of life as well as its centralisation in the hands of what Eisenhower famously termed 'the military industrial complex', memorably capturing the dominant forces shaping the nature of the emerging state. C. Wright Mills similarly described a 'power elite', one remove from the public eye, and able to shape outcomes in accordance with its own interests (Mills, 1956). Herbert Marcuse analysed an emergent 'one-dimensional' society in which the mere contemplation of social alternatives becomes impossible in the totalitarian universe of 'instrumental rationality' (Marcuse, 1964).

Moving to the present, many of these themes re-emerge in the trope of the 'deep state', implying layers of unaccountable, hidden officials running our lives behind our backs. Its most recent incarnation is the idea of an invisible alliance of global institutions and corporations conspiring to advance a 'Great Reset' that will leverage the COVID-19 panic to re-engineer an even more authoritarian future for us collectively.

These themes concerning unaccountable elites operating in unseen ways to determine the content of our lives were once marginal or heterodox, and thus easily dismissed. Today they are increasingly mainstream, as the paranoid style comes to define how we think about the nature and form politics takes in our societies. The threat lies in undercutting the premise of mainstream democratic politics, which is that we can exercise power by using our vote. This in turn fuels a narrative about the need for an approach that challenges elites as a whole from without or outside. This is grist to the populist mill, which is built on a sense of grievance not only about the outcomes of politics, but also about how politics functions and for whom.

### 3.4 Globalisation and its Discontents

Globalisation describes an increasingly unified global system underpinned by international law. Over the past half-century the flow of goods, capital and people has greatly intensified, disrupting inherited political and social structures, and giving rise to global cities, global culture and global problems such as climate change and migration (Beck, 2000). Our societies have become increasingly multicultural, cosmopolitan and less predictable as recent migrants bring with them different values, norms and expectations. More or less homogenous societies have become increasingly marked by *metissage*, complexity, hybridity (Bhabha, 1994).

Globalisation has brought a raft of problems with it as far as many citizens are concerned. The increasing interconnectedness of our world also increases the sense of powerlessness at the level at which politics is being conducted, which as far as many citizens are concerned is at the level of the nation-state. The 'crisis' literature of the 1990s and 2000s is full of themes around the powerlessness of the state, the hollowing out of politics, and 'post democracy', 'ruling the void', and so on (Crouch, 2004; Mair, 2013). Globalisation has, it is argued, undermined democratic politics. It has abstracted power to distant global elites, corporations and bureaucracies. It has also opened borders, permitting an influx of migrants, refugees, tourists threatening the sense of certainty of place and identity that underpins the 'somewhere' worldview.

Globalisation is thus perceived as transforming citizens lives in ways that appear to be beyond or outside our control. Our ability to shape or influence what happens 'in our name' appears ever more limited. In short, many citizens feel themselves to be losers in this great reordering of social life. Not only that, but contesting or influencing the nature of its outcomes seems ever more demanding. Globalisation not only creates generations of the 'left behind', it also denies them any meaningful mechanism for catching up. Globalisation creates its own path dependency and sense of inevitability famously articulated by Margaret Thatcher in her phrase 'There is no alternative', or TINA for short.

The fact that politicians of both left and right used the same argument throughout the 1990s and 2000s to produce the same 'Third Way' outcomes was not lost on the electorate, much of which decided that a contest between identikit politicians peddling similar-sounding policies meant that the electoral contest had become a spectacle without substance (Hay, 2007). Politics had become a grey process dominated by grey people in grey suits. Only a jolt from the political outside therefore could regain that sense of contingency and indeterminacy which at one level is the very essence of political contestation. That jolt has taken many forms over the past decade, from the Brexit vote and the rise of the nativist right such as Trump and Johnson to the emergence of anti-austerity left populisms represented by Podemos, Syriza and the Corbynite resurgence. Even the centre has had to adopt a more militant populist style as perhaps best represented in the emergence of Emmanuel Macron and his activist sounding *République en Marche*. Populism represents the 'return of the political' as Chantal Mouffe puts it, a return of something repressed in the attempt to render politics technocratic and instrumental (Mouffe, 1993).

### 3.5 Towards a New Media Galaxy

Less commented upon in theories of modernisation is the radical change in the media ecology over the past half-century or so. During this period we have moved from a moment where the media could be compellingly characterised as an 'ideological state apparatus' (ISA) enforcing a particular worldview through exclusive use of a limited number of channels, to a complex interplay of technologies promoting the sense that the media is something we create for ourselves (Althusser, 2001). As Indymedia once intoned 'don't read the media, be the media'. Where once we chose from a handful of TV channels, now we can choose from scores of different media outlets. Where once the state exercised a near monopoly on reporting and thus on what counted as 'fact', now increasingly we ignore these once trusted sources in search of materials that confirm our own increasingly idiosyncratic beliefs and worldviews. Where once the news involved the careful creation of content under the elite gaze, now we are able to follow events in real time in an apparently unmediated way via interactive technologies that permit anyone in possession of a smartphone to broadcast live over mass communication channels such as Twitter and Facebook.

The impact of such changes on our perception of reality cannot be underestimated. We have moved from the relative simplicity of ISAs exercising a monopoly over how we perceive the world, to an unruly plurality of images, sources, narratives. On the plus side, it's clear that new media technologies have been a democratising force in terms of defining what the media is and how it operates. All of us have the ability to generate content and to share that content in potentially consequential ways. This has been seen across the world in terms of increased capacity of citizens to reveal the workings of the state, increasing our collective 'monitory' capacities through 'sous-veillance' (Keane, 2011). It has also greatly enhanced collective or rather 'connective' mobilisation as witnessed at Tahrir Square, in Spain during #15M, via the Occupy movement, and more recently as seen in Hong Kong in protest at the clamping down of civil liberties, and in many Chinese towns and cities in protest at Zero Covid and authoritarian surveillance, and in Russia against conscription and the prosecution of war in Ukraine (Bennett & Segerberg, 2013).

The downsides of these momentous changes are however just as apparent. The possibility for superimposing digital images, circulating conspiracy theories, generating fake news and creating 'echo chambers' is progressively undermining trust in mainstream media sources (Morozov, 2012). New social media enables us to influence behaviour in both positive and negative ways. It also amplifies our sense of threat or crisis, thereby further exacerbating that sense of anxiety that permeates our culture, especially amongst the young (Haidt and Lukianoff, 2017). With the benefit of a smartphone we can now flick through a catalogue of disasters, crises, human misery. Without a contextual narrative of a kind associated with elite-driven media, actors vie to translate these images into an accommodating narrative. The unholy nexus of diminishing concentration levels and commercial imperatives means a media constantly hungry for 'eyeballs' leading to clicks on strategically positioned advertising. What matters is less our understanding of what is going on around us, and more our consumption of the image and by extension the 'product', whether commercial or political, lurking within.

As is often remarked upon, populism has proved highly adept at using new media technologies to generate a sense of hiatus, anxiety and panic which in turn fuels the desire for simplistic solutions to chronic crises (Moffitt, 2016). This reflects the fact that crisis is vital to populism. Without the perception of crisis, populists lack the dynamic that fuels the desire to look outside or beyond existing political choices. The new media galaxy serves this purpose well. It is both a mechanism for inducing panic and anxiety, but also a means for tapping in a direct and unmediated way our desire for a comforting message, and a redemptive figure to show us the way out of the mess.

## 4. Democratic Crisis and Populism

It's often noted that liberal-democratic or representative politics appears to be in crisis, albeit of a chronic rather than acute kind. This is to say that it reflects deep-lying shifts in the nature of modernity and how we come to experience it as citizens. Our crisis is one marked by the long-term decline of those elements we use to assess the measure of a vital and healthy democracy. They include a faltering interest in elections, the collapse of the mass 'catch-all' political party, a waning interest in the minutiae of political life however measured, and finally and most damningly a decline of trust in politicians. These are the symptoms of chronic crisis. They won't in and of themselves bring down democracy. Rather they create a fertile ground for populism. How? There are several dimensions to explore here:

*The rise of outsider politics* – As we have noted, ours is a sceptical age. What kind of politics is appropriate for sceptics or 'pagans'? It's a politics in a negative register that seeks to pin the blame for current ills on a compelling object that cannot speak for itself. Who better in this respect to blame for our abject condition than 'elites' or 'Westminster', *La Casta* or 'Washington'. The rich are profiting at the expense of the poor. The insiders are having their own way to the detriment of us, the people, the outsiders. Henrik Bang makes a similar point when he talks about the 'uncoupling' of representatives from those being representatives (Bang, 2004). Once a mechanism of inclusion, representation under contemporary conditions is increasingly seen as a mechanism for *excluding* us from our own system of governance – hence the kind of slogans commonplace in contemporary movements: 'Not in My Name', 'Real Democracy Now', 'For the Many not the Few', and so on.

The premise of this style of politics is that you don't have to *believe* in something; you just have to share the intuition that something has gone wrong and that it's the elites who are to blame. Populism promisingly allies that sense of indignation to a sense of our own power to change matters, a sense of collective agency of a non-specific but inclusive kind. In a democracy there is no more compelling or inclusive label than 'the People'. The people is both the subject and the object of democracy. From this point of view, it is logical for the people to be mobilised when the sense of threat is held to be general.

*The rise of the authentic leader* – We have lost our trust or faith in politicians, experts, people in any kind of position of authority. We have instead developed an appetite for those who seek to puncture the elite bubble.

This can come from the right, as authoritarian rebuke to the liberal cosmopolitan consensus that has reigned since the 1960s. Or it can come from the left, in the form of those offering a chastising critique of austerity politics inflicted on innocent populations since the financial crisis of 2008. But the key point about our new leaders such as Giorgia Meloni and Eric Zemmour, and more familiar figures such as Trump, Johnson and Le Pen, is that they are 'authentic'. They are not beholden to anyone or anything. They say what they mean, and they mean what they say. They are not the creatures of party machines, hidden factions, smoke-filled rooms. They offer accessible, media-friendly 'no-nonsense' critique coupled with compelling narrative for how we are going to make matters better.

An important feature of populism is thus its ability to produce as it were an unmediated form of mediation. The populist leader is presented as capable of representing the needs and interests of the people as a whole, directly, 'viscerally' as Marine Le Pen puts it. The leader is 'us' and we are 'them'. It is for this reason that populism is implicitly, and sometimes explicitly, held to presage the end of pluralism and thus of liberal democracy itself (Müller, 2016). This is however taking populist rhetoric for political reality. Whilst it is undeniable that some populist leaders develop or display authoritarian tendencies, authoritarianism is not intrinsic to populism. What is intrinsic is the gesture of representing oneself as the 'true' representative of the people against those, the political elite, who have been mandated to represent. Populism thus uses the repertoire of representation to mount a critique of how representation works and for whom under democratic conditions. It is not in this sense anti-democratic, so much as anti-mainstream, anti-insider, anti-establishment.

*Mediatisation and the populist style* – Politics is supposed to be about the pursuit of the common good and getting things done. But as we have heard, getting things done is really no longer the province of politics. Politics is now much more about *performance*, which is one of the reasons why it can appear an extension of the logic of celebrity culture. We are becoming accustomed to celebrities becoming politicians, and politicians becoming celebrities. What do they have in common? An embrace of the logic of a mediatised age: it is the performativity of the performance that matters, much less its efficacy in producing results or something concrete, which is the usual measure for assessing how well politicians are doing.

What the public wants is a compelling narrative. We want a spectacle, a drama with a clearly delineated sense of who is to be trusted with the people's needs and interests, and who isn't. This is why the populist narrative is so compelling. Populists understand the attraction of dramatic form, the need for clarity, and the potency of a clear delineation of who or what is to be blame and who will bring redemption. This continual reference to inside and outside sustains the dynamic of populism in the face of stasis, boredom, ennui, indifference, which if allowed to take hold represent the main threat to populism and populist leaders.

Populism collapses the space between campaigning and governing to the point where they become a continuum. It does so quite deliberately, because populists know that politics is about hard choices and the zero sum ('Do we spend money on X or Y?'). Populists would rather avoid the inevitable compromises and negotiations of democratic governance in favour of simplification: 'Get Brexit done', 'Build a Big Beautiful Wall', 'Remettre La France en Ordre' (Get France back on its feet). It's an emotive or affective politics that thrives because politics has itself become increasingly about style and performance. Populism is less a radical break from the tendencies that we are observing under the heading of modernisation than the culmination of those trends and tendencies. Far from representing something disruptive or extraordinary, populism appears to be an increasingly banal feature of life in many advanced democracies as well as in the developing world. It is sober, competent, technocratic governance of a kind associated with the likes of Angela Merkel, Mario Draghi or Joe Biden that appears increasingly idiosyncratic.

## 5. Conclusion

The above brief narrative cuts against the grain of much of the received wisdom about populism and what it represents. We have become used to the claim that populism is an exception or disruption to the normal state of affairs. This is a reading that displays a nostalgia for the 'lost thing': elite-led technocratic liberal democracy. In this process of continual erosion of 'normality' as far as our definitions of democratic institutions and processes are concerned, populism fills the void. Populism becomes the new normal.

At the same time, it would be wrong to say that populism is inevitable or that the experience of these changes will be the same for everyone. Some political cultures and political systems display features that mean populism may remain a weak force or may never arise at all. An unexceptional observation in this respect is to note that some electoral systems offer greater potential for populist breakthroughs than others. Presidential and 'first past the post' systems are in this respect more susceptible to the emergence of a compelling outside, comprising figures or movements than are systems based on proportional representation or systems where there is no direct election for the president or prime minister. Many of those political systems, as for example is the case in Germany, were expressly designed to prevent the emergence of radical or heterodox figures who might destabilise political institutions.

Equally, some political cultures for whatever reason are less given to the 'populist temptation' than others. Scandinavia tends to come to mind in this respect, though this has not prevented the emergence of far-right and indeed populist figures in response to the perception of societies that they are becoming 'overrun'. Less obviously, there are countries such as Ireland that have a history of political radicalism but where for a variety of reasons populism has yet to gain any real traction.

What nevertheless seems increasingly to be the case is that populism is becoming unexceptional. This is I have argued because of deeper-lying trends and tendencies that have a secular aspect to them as far as the modernising process is concerned. It is these trends and tendencies that have brought about the much discussed 'crisis of democratic politics', one of whose symptoms is the emergence of populism. From this point of view populism is less the source of the crisis, and more a symptom of deeper-lying issues that have yet to be resolved. Given that many of these issues are endemic to the modernising process, one has to doubt that there is a 'cure' for populism.

What does this tell us about the nature of populism? What is populism's ontology? At one level this is a question of genre. Political scientists study types and species of regime. Historians are interested in moments, eras, epochs. Political theorists are interested in strategies and social change. On the other hand, this leaves us with the problem of indeterminacy. Populism cannot be 'all things to all people'. It must mean something, be something. This meaning is, I have argued, located in the trends and tendencies of contemporary society. These trends are making us more sceptical, less accepting of authority, more short-termist and less committed to particular ideologies or parties. Our culture is more brusque, less thoughtful, more given to immediacy, visuality. It is by extension more affective and emotive in tone and content. The ontology of populism is thus located in the ontology of late modernity itself, a world marked by a preoccupation with crises of every type, amplified by new social media technologies producing anxious subjects looking for simple solutions to complex problems; problems produced by modernity, but which modernity seems ever more ill-equipped to manage let alone resolve. In short, it is the nature of the modernity we are creating, consciously and unconsciously, that is leading to the normalisation of populism, or the populisation of politics.

## Note

1. This chapter features many sections that appeared in an earlier article published in 2020 entitled 'No going back? Late modernity and the populisation of politics', *ProtoSociology*, 37, pp. 77–98.

## References

Althusser, L. (2001) 'Ideology and ideological state apparatuses', in *Lenin and Philosophy and Other Essays*. London: New Left Books.

Arditi, B. (2007) *Politics on the edges of liberalism: difference, populism, revolution, agitation*. Edinburgh: Edinburgh University Press.

Badiou, A. (2012) *The rebirth of history: times of riots and uprisings*. London: Verso Books.

Bang, H. (2004) 'Culture governance: governing self-reflexive modernity', *Public Administration*, 82 (1), pp. 157–190.

Bauman, Z. (2000) *Liquid modernity*. Cambridge: Polity.

Beck, U. (2000) *What is globalization?* Malden, MA: Polity Press.

Bennett, W. L. and Segerberg, A. (2013) *The logic of connective action: digital media and the personalization of contentious politics*. Cambridge: Cambridge University Press.

Bhabha, H. (1994) *The location of culture*. London: Routledge.

Boltanski, L. and Chiapello, E. (2005) *The new spirit of capitalism*. London: Verso.

Canovan, M. (2005) *The people*. Cambridge: Polity.

Castells, M. (1997) *The power of identity*. Oxford: Blackwell.

Crouch, C. (2004) *Post-democracy*. Cambridge: Polity.

Eklundh, E. et al. (eds) (2017) *The politics of anxiety*. London: Rowman & Littlefield.

Flinders, M. (2012) *Defending politics: why democracy matters in the twenty-first century*. Oxford: Oxford University Press.

Foucault, M. (1980) *Power/knowledge: selected interviews and other writings, 1972–1977*. New York: Random House.

Furedi, F. (2006) *Culture of fear revisited: risk-taking and the morality of low expectation*. London: Continuum.

Goodhart, D. (2017) *The road to somewhere: the populist revolt and the future of politics*. Oxford: Oxford University Press.

Haidt, J. and Lukianoff, G. (2017) *The coddling of the American mind: how good intentions and bad ideas are setting up a generation for failure*. Penguin: London.

Hay, C. (2007) *Why we hate politics*. Cambridge: Polity.

Heller, A. (1999) *A theory of modernity*. Oxford: Blackwells.

Heller, A. and Feher, F. (1988) *The postmodern political condition*. Cambridge: Polity Press.

Hofstadter, R. (2008) *The paranoid style in American politics, and other essays*. New York: Vintage Books.

Judis, J. B. (2016) *The populist explosion: how the great recession transformed American and European politics*. New York: Columbia Global Reports.

Keane, J. (2009) *The life and death of democracy*. London: Simon & Schuster.

Keane, J. (2011) 'Monitory democracy?', in Alonso, S., Keane, J. and Merkel, W. (eds) *The Future of Representative Democracy*. Cambridge: Cambridge University Press, pp. 212–235.

Laclau, E. (1990) *New reflections on the revolution of our time*. London: Routledge.

Lyotard, J. F. (1984) *The postmodern condition: a report on knowledge*. Manchester: Manchester University Press.

Mair, P. (2013) *Ruling the void: the hollowing of western democracy*. London: Verso Books.

Marcuse, H. (1964) *One dimensional man*. London: Sphere Books.

Marx, K. (1988) *The communist manifesto*. London: Norton.

Mills, C. W. (1956) *The power elite*. New York: Oxford University Press.

Moffitt, B. (2015) 'How to perform crisis: a model for understanding the key role of crisis in contemporary populism', *Government and Opposition*, 50 (2), pp. 189–217.

Moffitt, B. (2016) *The global rise of populism: performance, political style, and representation*. Stanford, CA: Stanford University Press.

Moffitt, B. and Tormey, S. (2013). 'Rethinking populism: politics, mediatisation and political style', *Political Studies*, 62 (2), 381–397.

Morozov, E. (2012) *The net delusion: the dark side of internet freedom*, London: Penguin.

Mouffe, C. (1993) *The return of the political*. London: Verso.

Müller, J. W. (2016) *What is populism?* Philadelphia: University of Pennsylvania Press.

Norris, P. and Inglehart, R. (2019) *Cultural backlash: Trump, Brexit, and authoritarian populism*. Cambridge: Cambridge University Press.

Pappas, T. S. (2019) *Populism and liberal democracy*. Oxford: Oxford University Press.

Simons, J. (2011) 'Mediated construction of the people: Laclau's political theory and media politics', in Dahlberg, L. (ed.) *Discourse theory and critical media politics*. London: Palgrave.

Standing, G. (2011) *The precariat: the new dangerous class*. London. Bloomsbury.

Tormey, S. (2015) *The end of representative politics*. Cambridge: Polity.

Tormey, S. (2019) *Populism: a beginner's guide*. Oxford: Oneworld.

# 6

# Populism and the Mirror of Technology

*Michaelangelo Anastasiou*

In this chapter, I examine the relationship between the spatiotemporality of populism and technology. My efforts are geared towards a social history of populism that effectively situates the latter within the social and political modalities of modernity by accounting for its diachronic institution in time. I begin by examining how notions of temporality are conventionally understood in studies of populism. I demonstrate that existing works tend towards synchronic understandings of populism, where populism's dynamics are accounted for episodically, in the absence of a theory of social change. I argue that synchronic understandings of populism underemphasise the political dimensions of populism, that is, the operational acts that are implicated in its (re)constitution in time. I proceed in a brief examination of the historical emergence of populism, identifying how populism, as a political logic, hinges on processes of inter-territorial connectivity that are associated with particular social and political modalities of modernity. By employing a post-Marxist approach, I then delineate a theoretical framework with the aim of effectively accounting for the ontological dimensions of space and time and their relation to politics. I argue that space consists in relatively stable synchronic arrangements, while time consists in structural indeterminacy, understood as diachrony, which is implicated in political practice. I historicise such deductions by investigating populism's relationship with modern technology and modernity, concluding that populism, as an operational logic, is:

- An extension of the social and political potentials afforded by (modern) technology. From an ontological standpoint, technology can be understood as discursive configurations that enable subjects to exceed their corporeal limitations. This potential broadens the scope of political acts, enabling

modalities of inter-territorial connectivity (space) and social disruption (time) – both of which consist in necessary features of populist politics.
- Facilitated by social and political modalities that are closely associated with modernity. The ordering of social, political and technological life in modern times broadens the scope of political conflict. As a result, meaning becomes increasingly ambiguous, something which, as I will demonstrate, renders the use of political metaphors, such as 'the people', particularly effective.

## 1. Time in Studies of Populism

There is a surprisingly limited number of works that have explicitly examined the temporal dimension of populist politics. This does not mean that notions of temporality are generally absent from populism studies, but that they manifest implicitly 'beneath the text' and can only be explicated by inference. In the present section, I explicate these underlying assumptions, while examining the associated theoretical implications. I argue that populism is conventionally understood in terms of synchrony, with minimal attention paid to its diachronic constitution. What is consequently unaccounted for is the specifically political dimension of populism, that is, the very acts that are implicated in its ongoing constitution in time. Relatedly, synchronic understandings of populism tend to produce ahistorical accounts that are unable to effectively decipher populism's historical significance as a political practice.

The vast majority of existing studies typically afford us static understandings of populism, by retrospectively focusing on the instance(s) where populist configurations manifest. This can be likened to the efforts of a photographer who captures a moment 'in time'. Most commonly, authors delineate populism's presumably substantive characteristics in the format of fixed (and very often universal) definitions or typologies, following empirical observation (Ionescu & Gellner, 1969; Inglehart & Norris, 2016; Pappas, 2018). To this end, definitions of populism span the gamut, in the absence of any scientific consensus, while often involving sweeping generalisations. In assessing the associated theoretical implications, two general problems are encountered. Firstly, fixed definitions are invariably undermined by the diversity of empirical manifestations of populism, which do not conform to the rigid confines of univeralisms (De Cleen & Stavrakakis, 2017; Anastasiou, 2019). And, relatedly, the patterns of change that accompany populist manifestations are not effectively accounted for, whether the analytic focus is on current or historical patterns of change.

This paradigm is only minimally destabilised where efforts are made in situating populism within a relational sequence, by accounting for its underlying causes. While a suggestion of diachrony is injected in the analysis, it is nonetheless restricted to two 'temporal' instances: the cause and the effect. This approach is typically utilised in approaches that see populism as a by-product of demand or supply side factors (see Golder, 2016) or as a by-product of particular social, political or cultural factors (Kornhauser, 1959; Lipset, 1960; Ionescu & Gellner, 1969). Consider the logic of post-materialist theses, as an example, which see populism as a by-product of 'post-industrialism' (Ignazi, 1992; Betz, 1994; Inglehart & Norris, 2016), where incredibly complex and nuanced processes are compartmentalised, reified and sequenced according to the logic of linear causality. Consequently, populism's political *dynamics*, in the plurality of their manifestation, are underemphasised, because populism is assumed to 'automatically' outpour out of particular causes. What is absent are the precise political logics and practices, in their variable manifestations, that enable populism's emergence, constitution and re-institution in time.

The same can be said about theories that trace populism's emergence to the interplay between synchronic structures. Here, populism is conceived as 'springing out' of incongruent social configurations that give way to political mobilisation (Taggart, 2002). Margaret Canovan's (1999) influential thesis, as an example, understands populism as a phenomenon rooted in the tension between democratic institutionalism and democracy's redemptive promise of salvation. Similarly, Bødker and Anderson (2019) consider populism to outpour from the tension between accelerated societal speeds and the slowness of governance, where populist actors seek redemption through unmediated politics with a heightened sense of immediacy. Again, what is underemphasised are populism's diachronic political dynamics, which are implicated in its ongoing constitution in time.

The tendency to 'favour' synchronic understandings of populism is also reflected in a series of studies that have examined the temporal narratives of populist politics (da Silva & Vieira, 2018, pp. 20–21; Lazar, 2022, p. 160; Taş, 2022). The analytic focus here is not on time as such, but on how populist actors advance particular ideas about past, present and future. Taş (2022), for example, examines how populist leaders advance narratives of collective victimisation, by claiming that the 'good old days' have succumbed to a crisis-laden present. The future is consequently posited as beholding two opposing possibilities: either the demise of the people, or its rejuvenation. What is accounted for is not diachrony or populism's mechanisms of change, but how disparate historical and current events are meaningfully sequenced and synchronically institutionalised. The object of analysis is the social construction of time, that is, how *perceptions* of temporality come to be instituted.

There are thus considerable gaps in the literature concerning, specifically, the *operational dynamics* of populism. Populism appears as an 'automatic' effect of particular recursive arrangements, with minimal emphasis placed on the precise *constitutive practices* that enable populist articulations. In other words, what is unaccounted for is the specifically political dimension of populist politics – its *disruptive potential*, where attempts are made in re-ordering existing structures (of power). As Laclau and Mouffe (2001) suggest, 'the political' consists in those very instances where social arrangements, and by extension power relations, come to be disrupted and new ones instituted. The associated theoretical implications should be explicated: if political practice enables the instituting of *novel* relations, it *inheres in temporality*, since it is the necessary 'ingredient' that disrupts 'automatistic' synchronic practices.

This issue has been addressed, whether explicitly or not, by post-Marxist theorists whose analysis focuses on *how* populist manifestations come to be articulated through political practice. By relinquishing substantivist understandings of populism, post-Marxists understand populism as an operational logic. Populism entails the symbolic simplification of the social landscape, where diverse political demands and identities come to be incorporated as part of a political body, such as 'the people', where that political body is *antagonistically* counterposed to a constructed 'Other', such as 'the establishment' (Stavrakakis, 2004; Laclau, 2005b). The construction of the popular body thus entails the articulation of *symbolic equivalences* between otherwise disparate demands and identities. The analytic focus is thus directed towards the very practices that enable the symbolic articulation of the populist body, where the mechanisms of populist articulations are identified empirically as particular manifestations *in* time.

The inherently *indeterminate* character of the social is understood as the 'ground zero' of populist politics. The very fact that social structures are essentially incomplete, or 'failed structures', means that social configurations are governed by instances of indeterminacy that enable the possibility of choice and therefore agency (Laclau, 2005a). From this standpoint, indeterminacy is understood as being synonymous with temporality. Indeterminacy is what 'frees' actors from synchronic, that is, recursive practices, enabling creative forms of action and the instituting of novel social arrangements. This is why moments of crisis, where social arrangements come to unravel, are understood as breeding grounds for populist politics (Mouffe, 2018; Stavrakakis et al., 2018). Where indeterminacy proliferates, so do political choices and therefore populist potentials.

There are nonetheless certain theoretical absences from this body of literature. Post-Marxist approaches are remarkably effective in delineating the dynamics of populism in those instances where they manifest, but they are only partly effective in situating populism historically. Populism's historical emergence and trajectory, as well as its *longue durée*, while discussed, or assumed, is not accorded epistemological depth. It is my estimation that this can be attributed, in part, to Laclau and Mouffe's initial theoretical formulations, which set the grounds for subsequent post-Marxist analysis. In *Hegemony and Socialist Strategy* (2001), Laclau and Mouffe are explicit in that 'plurality' (i.e. indeterminacy) is not 'the phenomenon to be explained', but the starting point of social and political analysis (p. 140). This is because indeterminacy is conceived as inhering in *all* sociopolitical formations, while broadening in scope in modern times. What was under-thematised, however, is *why* the degree of indeterminacy fluctuates historically (Anastasiou, 2022, pp. 150–153) – more on this later. This is why post-Marxism is principally oriented towards performative analyses, examining how social and political arrangements come to be articulated *within moments* of synchronic structures, in the absence of any sort of elaborated historicisation of such deductions (see Vahabzadeh, 2003, pp. 54–56). It therefore comes as no surprise that, in his later works, Laclau collapsed the distinction between synchrony and diachrony (1990, p. 42) and, subsequently, the distinction between politics and populism (2005b), thus de-historicising the latter.

This issue was explicitly addressed within post-Marxism (Stavrakakis, 2004, pp. 262–264; da Silva & Vieira, 2018, p. 16; Vulović & Palonen, 2022), albeit not exhaustively, where efforts were made in re-historicising populism by 'injecting' ontic content into Laclau's formal theory of populism. While Laclau identifies the constitution of antagonistic political bodies as the key feature of populism, various other post-Marxist authors identify, specifically, the signifier 'the people' as a key element of populist politics (De Cleen & Stavrakakis, 2017; Katsambekis, 2017, p. 204). The antagonistic deployment of the signifier 'the people', around which diverse demands become articulated, is what differentiates populism from other forms of antagonistic politics, such as class, gender and race.

From this standpoint, populism's operational logic is analytically distinguished from its ontic content. The dual logic of equivalence and antagonism is posited as a universal political possibility (ontological), whereas the signifier 'the people' is posited as a historically contingent political category (ontic). In deducing the associated implications, we may suggest that a historical analysis of populism would be geared towards identifying instances where the signifier 'the people' came to incorporate disparate demands and identities as part of an antagonistic political body.

What is left outstanding, however, is the question of diachrony, as pertaining specifically to the *ontological* dimensions of populism in history. The challenge here consists in effectively establishing, from a historical standpoint, a theoretical connection between the dual logic of equivalence and antagonism and structural indeterminacy. Is populism's recurring emergence in modern times attributed solely to the politicisation of 'the people' and its associated family resemblances? Or might this recurrence be associated with underlying ontological parameters that 'exacerbate' political potentials? Existing post-Marxist works see populism as a potential incubated during periods of systemic failure and crisis of representation (see Stavrakakis et al., 2018), where the institutional order has failed to absorb the populace's demands (Laclau, 2005b, pp. 73–78). However, systemic failure and crises of representation are typically posited in terms of their ontic content, that is, in terms of the acts and structures that are implicated in structural indeterminacy and/or crisis (Stavrakakis et al., 2018). This is a perfectly viable and legitimate analytic approach. What is under-thematized, however, is how *ontological precepts, in particular, facilitate systemic failures, crises of representation and, more broadly, structural indeterminacy* – a question that of course warrants both theoretical and historical consideration.

The present work seeks to bridge this theoretical gap by examining the relationship between populism and technology, here understood as an ontological potential directly implicated in political practice and therefore social change. The argument I will advance is that political practice and, more specifically, populism mirror the operational potentials afforded by modern technology.

## 2. Populism in History

The historically contingent character of populism is widely registered in the literature (Greenfeld, 1992, 2006; Canovan, 2005). The emergence of populism is empirically related to the so-called 'democratic revolution' and its associated political features: the assertion of popular sovereignty, republican institutionalism, the popular pursuit of civil, political and social rights, and so on and so forth (Marshall, 1950; Greenfeld, 1992; Habermas, 1996; Canovan, 2005). Here, it is paramount to highlight two related historical features of populist politics. The first concerns its *relation to modernity*: even though the political notion of 'the people' can be traced to the *populous Romanus*, its generalisation as a salient political category coincides with the social and political revolutions of modernity (Greenfeld, 1992; Canovan, 2005). The second concerns its *symbolic breadth*: the increasing political significance of the category 'the people' involved its uneven and incomplete universalisation, as it came to symbolically incorporate more and more identities (Greenfeld, 1992; Canovan, 2005).

In the European context, in particular, the increasing political significance of 'the people' is intimately associated with the consolidation of nation-states and intra-state democratic pursuits (Greenfeld, 1992). Populism's *antagonistic dimension*, at least in its ontic manifestations, where 'the people' is counterposed to 'the establishment', is empirically associated with two related historical developments that are inextricably connected with the historical emergence of the nation-state. The first is the reconfiguration of power relations in modernity, which involved the (partial) transference of power from the aristocracy to the people (Hobsbawm, 2012, pp. 80–100). The second is the proliferation of intra-state democratic pursuits following the state's increasing control of social life (Giddens, 1985, pp. 201–205; Laclau & Mouffe, 2001, pp. 149–171; Mann, 2010, pp. 730–732; Hobsbawm, 2012, pp. 80–100). Historically, then, 'the people' emerges conceptually and empirically *in opposition to the centres of power*, in the context of heterogeneous political pursuits.

The associated territorial dimensions are of paramount significance. As post-Marxists highlight, populist configurations consist in the symbolic incorporation of plural identities, whose unfulfilled demands find an expression in the notion of 'the people'. Populism entails the articulation of *symbolic equivalences* between otherwise disparate identities and demands (Laclau, 2005b, pp. 73–74). This means that populism necessarily involves modalities of *territorial traverse* – as populist articulations expand, so do their territorial reach. In this sense, it is useful to enquire whether the emergence and expansion of populist articulations is related to the territorial consolidation of nation-states and the historical factors that enabled inter-territorial connectivity. The literature on nations and nationalism provides us with ample relevant data, typically highlighting the causal efficacy of technological forms. The consolidation of territorial networks is enabled by the potentials afforded by communication technologies (Deutsch, 1966; Anderson, 2006), transportation technologies (Weber, 1976), technologies of production (Giddens, 1985), technologies of governance (Giddens, 1985; Foucault, 2001), and so on and so forth. The crux of my argument is beginning to announce itself: populist politics hinge on the social and political possibilities afforded by modern technology. The expansion of populism's 'chains of equivalence', which come to incorporate disparate identities vis-à-vis processes of inter-territorial connectivity, necessitate technological forms that enable the articulation of symbolic equivalences over territories that exceed the immediate locale.

By implication, a historical understanding of populism warrants examination of the latter's relationship with technology. The task at hand is epistemological and concerns the ontological parameters of technology as they relate to politics and social change. If we are to sketch out the most prevalent epistemological logic in populism and nationalism studies, we would arrive at the conclusion that populism is accounted for *episodically*. History, in essence, appears as a movement between sequences of 'self-enclosed' synchronic arrangements – much like an animator imparts the illusion of movement by sequencing illustrations. The culprit here is cause-effect reasoning, where the 'causes' of populism are identified (e.g. American Revolution, economic factors, cultural factors) and the outcome (i.e. populism) is assumed, in the absence of a theoretical framework that can account for the qualitative intricacies of that 'in between'. What I am referring to here is not merely the 'events' that mediated between cause and effect, but the very *ontological precepts that enable the possibility of disruption and therefore change – what is here understood as temporality.*

My efforts are thus prefigured. By theoretically accounting for the ontological parameters of temporality, I endeavour to illuminate the intimate relationship between technology and populism, thus situating the historical emergence of the latter within specific ontological and ontic parameters.

## 3. Time, Space and Politics

Let us proceed by delineating our epistemological premises. The prime object of analysis concerns the ontological status of 'time' and its relation to politics. I demonstrated that existing theories are only partly effective in accounting for populism's temporal dynamics because they typically understand time in terms of recourse. Synchronic understandings of time underemphasise the political dimension of populist politics because they do not effectively account for the element of change through practice. To relate this to broader theoretical debates, we may suggest that what is unaccounted for is creative agency – how actors, in their political pursuits operate subversively, i.e. against structural constraints (see Anastasiou, 2022, pp. 92–94). The question of temporality is therefore not a theoretical issue with restricted significance but is at the heart of social and political theory.

It is my estimation that the nuances of temporality can only be illuminated when related to the question of the subject. The 'experience' of time emerges to the extent that thought and action cease to be subordinated to absolute recursive parameters (Laclau, 2005a; Anastasiou, 2022, pp. 140–141). Under perfect structural conditions, actors would merely amount to automatons operating as cogs within a fixed system, in the absence of deliberation and choice. Relatedly, no experience of time could emerge in a situation of total randomness. In such a hypothetical situation, the experience of 'change' could not be counterposed to anything outside of itself and would thus be unintelligible. Ergo, temporality germinates where the structure has failed to constitute fully, thus yielding indeterminate possibilities that enable the possibility of volitional action (Laclau, 1990, p. 41, 2005a, pp. 56–57). The temporality of subjectivity is to be located in what Laclau (2005a) calls the 'moment of the subject', where the subject *chooses* between alternative possibilities, precisely because its course of action is not fully predetermined (p. 57). Within this theoretical framework, 'space' is deployed to designate the dimension of social life that is governed by repetition, and thus stability (Laclau, 1990, p. 41). By implication, structures of power can be understood as operating within the spatial dimension of social life. But what accounts, specifically, for the indeterminate dimension of social life – to what do we attribute the failure of the social's full constitution?

In post-Marxism, social life is seen as a network of discursive operations, where discourse is understood as the relational field through which ideas and matter co-constitute one another (Laclau & Mouffe, 1987; Laclau, 2005b, pp. 68–69). The implications are twofold. Firstly, social life is undercut by meaningful modalities that order social and individual experience (Laclau & Mouffe, 2001, pp. 105–114). Secondly, the ideal and material elements that constitute social life acquire their meaning relationally (Wittgenstein, 1967; Laclau & Mouffe, 2001, pp. 105–114). This understanding of social life stands in sharp contrast with essentialist understandings of society, which explicitly or implicitly assume that ideas or processes behold inherent meanings that can on some level be abstracted from their relational context (recall the social scientist who conjures up universal definitions!) (Laclau & Mouffe, 2001, pp. 97–105). Meaning is thus constituted contingently, within networks of *differential and associated* ideas (Saussure, 1966; Laclau & Mouffe, 2001, pp. 127–134; Lacan, 2006; Laclau, 2014, chapter 3). The meaning of 'democracy', as an example, is established in reference to: historical meanings (revolutions, popular sovereignty), ideological meanings (ethnocentric *and* humanistic), public policy meanings (free *and* regulated market) and various other meanings of a contextual character. Its meaning is thus *polysemic* and at the same time ambiguous, since it incorporates a spectrum of ideas, which may be closely associated, but also 'contradictory', paradoxical, etc.

The notion of *overdetermination* is here deployed to register the constitutive polysemy and thus ambiguity of meaning, designating the symbolic spectrum of differential and associated ideas (Freud, 1955, pp. 301–302; Laclau & Mouffe, 2001, pp. 97–105). Indeterminacy is an extension of the overdetermined character of the social. This is because the overdetermined networks of meaning that are in discourse are invariably, albeit in part, 'incompatible' with one another. This 'incompatibility' between networks of meaning is precisely what enables, perhaps by fiat, the possibility of choice, conscious thought and volitional action (Laclau, 1990, pp. 41–45, 2005a; Laclau & Mouffe, 2001, pp. 97–114). The notion of 'democracy', as an example, can at the same time reference humanistic and ethno-centric narratives, an ambiguity that is expressed in the varied attitudes, actions and contextual *decisions* of individuals.

The inherent tensions in discourse as well as the changing contexts of social experience are what undermine the recursive dimension of social life, enabling the possibility of choice. We may very well suggest then that the temporality of social life, which outpours from indeterminate possibilities, is enabled by the overdetermined character of the social – what is identified in post-Marxism as the social's inherent *dislocation*. Diachrony is thus an expression of the irresoluble tension between space and time, *where space designates meaningful configurations that are relatively stable, and where time designates the dimensions of meaning that are 'dislocated', contested and thus subject to change*. The space-time dialectic is, in essence, the 'engine of history'. The logic of populism, as we will see, is situated on this very nexus, but it is facilitated specifically by the ontological modalities of technology. Technology's twofold potential either increases the scope of spatialisation, enabling the constitution of inter-territorial symbolic equivalences, or increases the rate of temporality, broadening political possibilities.

## 4. Populism and the Mirror of Technology

Conceptually positioning technology within a historical framework, so as to deduce the associated sociopolitical implications, requires us to first delineate a theory of technology. To this end, my efforts will in the first instance be geared towards a theory that reveals technology's ontological parameters. This will enable me to subsequently deduce technology's ontic manifestations in modernity and examine its sociopolitical significance specifically with regard to populist politics. My argument is that the logic of populism hinges on the ontological parameters of technology and their particular manifestation in modernity.

Our theoretical starting point is Karl Marx (1999), who identifies, as a key feature of capitalism, modern machinery's *usurpation of corporeal labour power*: modern machinery, in a chimeric fashion, enables the corporeal subject to increase its productive capacities. Now, Marx's theory situates the significance of modern technology specifically within economic activity. However, it is not difficult to deduce the full implications of Marx's argument, should we free it from the fetters of historical materialism. 'Modern technology', as machinery or *any other form*, enables forms of *empirical expedience*, when in discourse with corporeal subjectivities. In other words, technology, *in general*, enables subjects to exceed their corporeal limitations, whether in production or any other activity.

A caveat is here warranted. From a post-foundational standpoint, technology cannot be regarded as a particular 'object', but as the very ground of possibility (Anastasiou, 2022, pp. 143–148). In other words, technology consists in the *relational complexes* that enable increases in empirical expedience. A machine, for example, yields productive output within a very precise relational field that involves workers, managers, bureaucratic organisation, rationalised organisations of time, and so on. It is at the same time underpinned by a scientific and operational network that functions as its condition of possibility: from the mathematician to the physicist, to the chemist, to the workers who built it, and so on. So, too, the factory workers operate within a very precise relational field that functions as their condition of possibility: from the farmers who produce their food to the schoolteachers who educated them, to the workers who built their homes, to the workers who construct systems of mass transportation, and so on. This total discursive network of relations, all of which are *necessary* for the machine's higher output, is what I designate as technology – it is the intersubjective discursive field that, in its totality, enables increases in empirical expedience. By extension, particular technological forms such as 'machinery' or 'communication media' can be understood as nodes operating within the relational techno-discursive field.

Seen from this perspective, there is nothing *substantively* unique about modern versus pre-modern technology. The hammer, as an example, is a form of pre-modern technology that enables the worker to exceed their corporeal limitations, when situated within a particular social configuration that functions as the hammer's and the worker's condition of possibility. Technology thus beholds an ontological status – it is a universal possibility. There are, however, differences in terms of technology's ontic content, which *varies in scope and in the degree of empirical expedience it affords*. In examining the associated political implications, we may very well suggest that the technological potential, which operates intersubjectively, frees the subject from its corporeal limitations, thus enabling political acts that are broader in scope and of higher impact.

By implication, technology may enable broader forms of spatialisation, where ideal and material elements come to be incorporated in broader discursive networks. The wagon, the train, mass communication and social media technologies, albeit in different degrees, enable forms of interconnectivity between otherwise disparate or 'isolated' elements. The technological possibility also enables increases in the scope and degree of temporality – the empirical expedience afforded potentially allows for the introduction of dislocations that yield 'instances' of indeterminacy. Social media technologies, as an example, enable the circulation of associated, 'contradictory', ambiguous and incompatible ideas on a global scale, whose uneven interaction enables modalities of social 'disruption' and dislocation and, by extension, political contestation. It thus becomes clear that the technological potential, in and of itself, is *neither aprioristically geared toward forms of social control (spatialisation) nor forms of social disruption/dislocation (temporalisation)*. These are mere possibilities whose actualisation hinge on a wide array of 'factors' and activities that find their variable expression in a multifarious discursive network. In this sense, the era of profuse technological innovation we commonly call 'modernity' can be understood as an extension of the operational modalities afforded by the technological possibility: the concurrent expansion of spatialised discursive networks and the potentially heightened temporalisation of social life (Anastasiou, 2022, pp. 140–153).

The consolidation of nation-states and the subsequent 'globalisation' of societal processes can be understood in terms of cross-territorial spatialisation, wherein disparate networks came to be 'consolidated' in the form of 'mass' and 'global' networks. This entailed processes whereby otherwise isolated cultures came to be incorporated into broader interactive networks, enabling in turn the construction of larger cultural-territorial units and identities. But as spatialisation increases in scope so does, potentially, temporality. As social life becomes increasingly heterogeneous, where disparate cultures engage in discourse, and as the technological possibility broadens the scope of political practices, the terrain of indeterminacy proliferates in scope. 'Competing' ideas broaden the field of overdetermination, where ideas become increasingly polysemic and therefore ambiguous. The notion of 'religion', as an example, may be characterised by a relatively restricted scope of meanings within an isolated village. But once that village is incorporate into broader – national or even global – networks it will come to 'import' complexes of ideas that may overdetermine the meaning of 'religion', such as liberal, secular, fascist, agnostic and new age meanings. Consequently, 'religion' becomes increasingly ambiguous and polysemic. The notion of religion is here used paradigmatically, but it is easy to imagine the broader and associated implications. Intercultural connectivity necessarily results, at least in the 'first instance', in modalities of meaningful indeterminacy, as meaningful configurations begin overdetermining one another. This may concern not only political concepts, such as 'democracy', 'the family', 'the woman', 'class', 'sexuality', 'lifestyle', 'choice', etc., but mundane concepts that are associated with everyday activity.

In examining the associated political implications, we may suggest that as the terrain of overdetermination broadens, the taken-for-granted structures of the past, including modalities of political legitimacy, potentially become increasingly contested and ambiguous. This means that the terrain of (political) possibilities broadens. Ergo, new structures can come to be spatialised, instituting new forms of social control, or new forms of contestation can germinate, yielding further political potentials. It is my estimation that politics in modernity oscillate within this spectrum of possibilities. This is the reason why social configurations in modernity are characterised by increasing modalities of both control (space) and dislocation (time). This dialectic, as it unfolds in an increasingly interconnected and multifarious techno-social network, characterises the principal dimensions of social change in modernity.

In situating the significance of populism within this framework, we may very well suggest that populist politics hinge on the precise possibilities afforded by modern technology. As already detailed, populism entails processes of territorial traverse, wherein disparate identities and demands come to be symbolically 'consolidated' under the symbolic 'umbrella' of 'the people'. Technology allows corporeal subjects to exceed their bodily limitations, enabling them in articulating discursive linkages of a political character over wider territorial units. In the early phases of modernity, such processes were facilitated by technological forms such as print media, mass transportation, electronic communication, etc. – all of which should be understood as elements operating within broader discursive networks. In 'late' modernity, such processes are facilitated and exacerbated by technological forms of a more 'instant' character, which allow territorially broader discursive articulations. Examples include the Internet, social media technologies, smartphones, etc.

What should be emphasised here is that social configurations enabled by 'instant' forms of communication will not, in and of themselves, broaden political possibilities. In fact, the empirical expedience afforded by technology can very well subdue subversive efforts, through the institutionalisation of controlled social structures. Consider, as an example, how early forms of modern technology were often deployed by the state in efforts of constructing 'unitary' or 'cohesive' nation-states (Giddens, 1985). In other words, the 'compression of space and time' (Harvey, 1990), whereby discursive elements become interconnected, and where social processes 'work faster', does not in and of itself produce political potentials, such as populism. Political choices and thus populist potentials will germinate only when the scope of structural indeterminacy broadens, whereby modalities of social control and political legitimacy become weakened (Mouffe, 2018; Stavrakakis et al., 2018). In this sense, temporality can be understood as populism's necessary ingredient. Articulations of populist spaces thus require the concurrent dislocation of existing structures, and technology is the medium through which such endeavours can more effectively be actualised. 'Creative disruption', to play on words, inheres in the populist operation.

This should be theoretically related to the manner by which the technological field is ordered, in the sense that decentralising technological configurations potentially increase the field of political participation. Political contestation thus broadens in scope, whether territorially or temporally, in the sense that decentralising technological networks may allow increases in the rate of dislocation and thus the scope of novel political possibilities. To the extent that such potentials are utilised, the field of overdetermination broadens. We can cite here as relevant evidence, print media's political impact in early modernity (Anderson, 2006) and digital technology's political impact in contemporary life (Castells, 2009). These historical parameters do not have a determinate effect: they do not necessarily yield populist politics. They do, however, foster the necessary conditions that enable populist potentials, which invariably germinate in the space-time dialectic. Populist potentials will *only* materialise as precise products of political practice and nothing less.

Whether technology tends towards the 'direction' of social control (space) or indeterminacy (time) is contingent upon the totality of discursive operations, which steer the social in a particular direction. In detailing the relevant historical tendencies, certain conclusions can be deduced. From a strictly comparative standpoint, modern life is to a greater extent undercut by temporalisation. This has been extensively detailed in the literature and corroborated by a plethora of empirical evidence. 'The institutionalisation of social change', wherein social and political modalities become increasingly fluid, consists in a principal dimension of (post-)modern life (Marx, 1978; Bauman, 2000; Beck, Bonss & Lau, 2003; Rosa, 2013). However, the increasing temporality of social life is not an outcome of 'the speeding up' of social life, as it is typically understood, that is, as the institutionalisation of social arrangements that recur in shorter time intervals (Giddens, 1985; Elias, 1987; Rosa, 2013). The temporalisation of modern life can more accurately be described as increases in the *rate of dislocation*, where indeterminate possibilities broaden in scope, by virtue of the *increasingly overdetermined character of the social*. 'Social change' is a possibility that germinates in the field of overdetermination. By implication, the scope and degree of overdetermination is positively correlated with political and therefore populist potentials.

There is, however, an outstanding theoretical question that needs to be answered, regarding, specifically, the ontic content of populist politics and its historical significance. There is an increasing consensus in the literature that political reference to 'the people' constitute one of the principal features of populism (Mudde, 2004; Canovan, 2005; Stavrakakis, 2014; Moffitt, 2018). The political efficacy of 'the people' has been attributed to its linguistic structure (Stavrakakis, 2014, p. 506). While 'the people' is often framed particularistically, encapsulating particular identities, its linguistic 'excess' references the universal subject of 'the people'. This linguistic 'slip' symbolically posits 'the people' as an entity 'larger than itself' – a characteristic that lies at the heart of its political efficacy. As a member of the working class I can more effectively pursue my rights if I frame my identity in accordance with a universalism, such as 'the people', where I situated my identity not as a part within the whole, but *as the whole*.

But does the political efficacy of 'the people' inhere in the term itself, or is it an extension of multifarious discursive operations in history? The notion of popular sovereignty, as it finds expression in the notion of 'the people', is intimately associated with a series of processes, which were facilitated by technological possibilities that enabled radical reconfigurations of power relations in modern times: political revolutions, the state's increasing penetration in social life, the proliferation of democratic narratives, the consolidation of modern territorial states, the advent of nationalist politics, and so on and so forth (Kedourie, 1961; Gellner, 1983; Giddens, 1985; Smith, 1986; Greenfeld, 1992; Mann, 2010; Hobsbawm, 2012).

Now, in my estimation, something substantive about populism is missed, if we are to regard the above-noted 'variables' as mere causes that engendered populism as a determinate outcome. If, however, we are to understand them as a *plurality of relational acts in history*, through which the notion of 'the people' came to *unevenly proliferate*, certain productive theoretical conclusions can be deduced (see Anastasiou, 2022, pp. 112–122). The proliferation of the signifier 'the people', as a component of heterogeneous social and political processes meant that 'the people' became increasingly overdetermined. 'The people's' meaningful-symbolic chain broadened as it became increasingly institutionalised and politically deployed. The polysemy of 'the people' renders the notion highly ambiguous and thus politically malleable. In other words, 'the people' is a term that is to a large extent *undercut by temporal possibilities and can thus function as a catalyst for social change*. As a highly ambiguous notion, it can effectively facilitate, in a varied fashion, the whims of political imagination and desire (Anastasiou & Custodi, forthcoming).

The radical polysemy of 'the people' is what enables political processes of *nominal circumscription* (Anastasiou, 2022, p. 112), wherein disparate identities come to be incorporated under its 'symbolic umbrella'. As Laclau notes, the articulation of populist bodies entails the deployment of 'empty signifiers', which come to represent the symbolic equivalence between disparate demands and identities (2005b, pp. 67–128, 2007). The 'emptiness' of 'the people' is enabled by its productive polysemy, through which differential demands, identities, narratives, and so on, can be referenced. 'Emptiness' does not imply that 'the people' is devoid of meaning (Laclau, 2005b, p. 105, 2014, pp. 20, 119), but that it is highly overdetermined by a plethora of meaningful configurations

(Laclau, 2005b, pp. 131–133). It is this very characteristic that enables 'the people' to *exceed* the particularistic content of the identities it encapsulates, while coming to reference the mere equivalence between them, thus nominally circumscribing them as an 'empty' category. In other words, 'the people', by virtue of its radically overdetermined character comes to operate as a *metaphorical replacement* for each and every one of the identities and demands it incorporates under its symbolic umbrella (see Laclau, 2005b, pp. 106–109, 2014, pp. 53–78). 'The people' becomes 'split' between its particularistic meanings, as it is deployed contextually, and its 'emptiness', which references the *totality of the political body* (Laclau, 2005b, pp. 77–81). And therein lies its efficacy as a political category.

By implication, we may suggest that the increasing overdetermination of social life is positively associated with the efficacy of political metaphors. This is because metaphors, which exceed the particularism of rational reasoning, and which therefore tend to be of a 'simplistic' nature, are more effective in symbolically 'consolidating' the disparities of modern social life, whether those are narratives, identities, political demands, ideologies, acts, and so on and so forth. Let us consider, as an example, how disputes over state intervention are often framed as 'more' or 'less' government. From a rationalistic point of view, 'more' or 'less' government tells us nothing about the empirical realities that are underscored by these terms, which are incredibly complex and ambiguous, and neither quantitatively measurable in a sense where they could indicate the extent of government intervention. The notions of 'more' and 'less' government, as metaphors, have a mere 'aggregating' function, through which a plethora of heterogeneous elements come to be *unevenly symbolically 'consolidated' as equivalents*: government policies, political actors, ideological orientations, identities, political interests, democratic demands, and so on. We may very well suggest that political metaphors, as facilitated by the technological potential that *broadens their operational scope*, 'compensate' for the increasing complexity of modern life.

These deductions help us effectively decipher the emergent political patterns of our times. Much has been written lately, mostly in a derogatory fashion, about post-truth politics, fake news, simples truths, demagogy, and so on (Waisbord, 2018; Bergmann, 2020). These political modalities are very often cast as manifestations of 'populism', with the underlying implication that populism consists in an irrational and/or anti-democratic/anti-liberal phenomenon. Now, it is true that from the standpoint of empirical validation, particular political actors, whether populist or not, resort to inaccurate, if not altogether false claims. But this tells us nothing about the logic of their political practices. I believe that something substantive is disregarded if these political modalities are merely seen as an expression of an underlying irrationalism. Their efficacy lies in how emotionally-laden metaphors, which are broadly imbricated in the existing sociotechnical milieu (Anastasiou, 2020), are deployed with *the effect* of symbolically consolidating disparate – and perhaps a plethora of – social and political modalities. In this sense, the spectrum of metaphorical possibilities should be understood as spanning the ideological gamut. Emotionally laden metaphors can accommodate conservative ('homeland', 'immigrant threat'), conspiratorial ('foreign elite'), liberal ('integration', 'consensus') and progressive ('equality', 'justice') pursuits. Metaphors can also enable symbolic displacements *between* ideological types, such as when 'the nation' is deployed with progressive intentions (Custodi, 2021), or when 'democracy' and 'justice' are deployed ethnocentrically.

These deductions allow us to situate the development of contemporary political trends in a new light, while broadening our strategic horizons. The political significance of recent theoretical contributions (Stavrakakis, 2014; Mouffe, 2018), which seek to highlight the progressive potential in populist politics, should be understood in reference to the conclusions deduced in the present section. The effectiveness of political pursuits, whether populist or not, will, at least on some level, be contingent upon the deployment of political metaphors, which enable the symbolic incorporation of social disparities and, thus, the constitution of multidimensional alliances and political frontiers (see Laclau & Mouffe, 2001, pp. 159–193; Anastasiou, 2022, pp. 194–212). Political endeavours, particularly of the progressive variety, have for far too long hinged on the politics of rationalism, at the expense of their own success. Political pursuits cannot be successful without appropriately diagnosing the sociotechnological parameters in which they operate. Therein lies the trap, but also the promise.

## 5. Conclusion

I attempted to situate populism within the logic of particular ontological and ontic parameters. I revealed its spatiotemporal dynamics by relating it to the potentials afforded by modern technology. The operational dynamics of populist politics hinge on the spatiotemporal possibilities enabled by technology, which allow the subject to exceed its corporeal limitations and therefore the scope of its political practices. By extension, the subject is enabled in processes of inter-territorial connectivity, which broaden the operational scope of political antagonisms through the articulation of symbolic equivalences (space). It is also enabled in processes of disruption and dislocation, which broaden the scope of indeterminacy (time). As existing structures and modalities of political legitimacy become disarticulated, the scope of political and therefore populist possibilities broadens. Populism, as a political logic, is thus situated within the uneasy tension between space and time, as facilitated by the technological potential.

In detailing populism's ontic parameters, I identified cultural arrangements that facilitate institutionalisations of social change as key historical developments that enable populist possibilities, vis-à-vis the disarticulation of existing structures. These historical dynamics were related to the decentralising character of modern technological forms, which potentially broaden the sphere of political contestation and therefore the proliferation of social dislocations. I further argued that the political efficacy of 'the people' – populism's central signifier – is an extension of diachronic political processes that resulted in 'the people's' symbolic dispersion vis-à-vis technological modalities, as it came to be deployed and institutionalised variably and unevenly in time and space. 'The people' became increasingly polysemic, thus facilitating disparate political orientations and imaginaries. The radical polysemy of 'the people' underpins its political utility in populist pursuits, where disparate demand and identities come to be symbolically and antagonistically 'consolidated'. This is also the reason why populism manifests diversely, ranging from far-right to progressive and transnational variants, as detailed in recent literature (Anastasiou & Custodi, forthcoming; Custodi & Padoan, 2022).

The above-noted deductions prefigure future research on populism, highlighting the importance of populism's inextricable connection to modern technology and the associated implications specifically with regard to democratic and, more broadly, political pursuits.

## References

Anastasiou, M. (2019) 'Of nation and people: the discursive logic of nationalist populism', *Javnost – The Public*, 26 (3), pp. 330–345. DOI: 10.1080/13183222.2019.1606562.

Anastasiou, M. (2020) 'The spatiotemporality of nationalist populism and the production of political subjectivities', *Subjectivity*, 13 (3), pp. 217–234. DOI: 10.1057/s41286-020-00104-x.

Anastasiou, M. (2022) *Nationalism and hegemony: The consolidation of the nation in social and political life*. Abingdon: Routledge.

Anastasiou, M. and Custodi, J. (forthcoming) 'The populism-nationalism nexus', in Stavrakakis, Y. and Katsambekis, G. (eds) *Research handbook on populism*. Cheltenham: Edward Elgar.

Anderson, B. (2006) *Imagined communities: reflections on the origin and spread of nationalism*. London: Verso.

Bauman, Z. (2000) *Liquid modernity*. Cambridge: Polity Press.
Beck, U., Bonss, W. and Lau, C. (2003) 'The theory of reflexive modernization', *Theory, Culture & Society*, 20 (2), pp. 1–33. DOI: 10.1177/0263276403020 002001.
Bergmann, E. (2020) 'Populism and the politics of misinformation', *Safundi*, 21 (3), pp. 251–265. DOI: 10.1080/17533171.2020.1783086.
Betz, H.-G. (1994) *Radical right-wing populism in Western Europe*. Basingstoke: Macmillan Press.
Bødker, H. and Anderson, C. (2019) 'Populist time: mediating immediacy and delay in liberal democracy', *International Journal of Communication*, 13 (0), pp. 5948–5966.
Canovan, M. (1999) 'Trust the people! Populism and the two faces of democracy', *Political Studies*, 47 (1), pp. 2–16. DOI: 10.1111/1467-9248.00184.
Canovan, M. (2005) *The people*. Cambridge: Polity.
Castells, M. (2009) *Communication power*. Oxford: Oxford University Press.
Custodi, J. (2021) 'Nationalism and populism on the left: the case of Podemos', *Nations and Nationalism*, 27 (3), pp. 705–720. DOI: 10.1111/nana.12663.
Custodi, J. and Padoan, E. (2022) 'The nation of the people: an analysis of Podemos and Five Star Movement's discourse on the nation', *Nations and Nationalism*, pp. 1–18. DOI: 10.1111/nana.12865.
da Silva, F. C. and Vieira, M. B. (2018) 'Populism and the politics of redemption', *Thesis Eleven*, 149 (1), pp. 10–30. DOI: 10.1177/072551 3618813374.
De Cleen, B. and Stavrakakis, Y. (2017) 'Distinctions and articulations: a discourse theoretical framework for the study of populism and nationalism', *Javnost – The Public*, 24 (4), pp. 301–319. DOI: 10.1080/13183222.2017.1330083.
Deutsch, K. (1966) *Nationalism and social communication: an inquiry into the foundations of nationality*. Cambridge, MA: The MIT Press.
Elias, N. (1987) *Time: an essay*. Oxford: Blackwell.
Foucault, M. (2001) *Power, essential works of Foucault, 1954–1984; v. 3*, J. D. Faubion (ed). New York: The New Press.
Freud, S. (1955) *The interpretation of dreams: the complete and definitive text*, J. Strachey (ed and trans). New York: Basic Books.
Gellner, E. (1983) *Nations and nationalism*. Oxford: Basil Blackwell.
Giddens, A. (1985) *The nation-state and violence: volume two of a contemporary critique of historical materialism*. Cambridge: Polity Press.
Golder, M. (2016) 'Far right parties in Europe', *The Annual Review of Political Science*, 19, pp. 477–97. DOI: 10.1146/annurev-polisci-042814-012441.
Greenfeld, L. (1992) *Nationalism: five roads to modernity*. Cambridge, MA: Harvard University Press.

Greenfeld, L. (2006) *Nationalism and the mind: essays on modern culture*. Oxford: Oneworld.

Habermas, J. (1996) 'The European nation state. Its achievements and its limitations. On the past and future of sovereignty and citizenship', *Ratio Juris*, 9 (2), pp. 125–137. DOI: 10.1111/j.1467-9337.1996.tb00231.x.

Harvey, D. (1990) *The condition of postmodernity: an enquiry into the origins of cultural change*. Cambridge, MA: Blackwell. DOI: 10.2307/2072256.

Hobsbawm, E. (2012) *Nations and nationalism since 1780: programme, myth, reality* (2nd edn). Cambridge: Cambridge University Press. Available at http://www.cambridge.org/cy/academic/subjects/history/european-history-after-1450/nations-and-nationalism-1780-programme-myth-reality-2nd-edition-1?format=PB&isbn=9781107604629#iuqhKJ4oirE3oXpl.97.

Ignazi, P. (1992) 'The silent counter-revolution: hypotheses on the emergence of extreme right-wing parties in Europe', *European Journal of Political Research*, 22 (1), pp. 3–34. DOI: 10.1111/j.1475-6765.1992.tb00303.x.

Inglehart, R. and Norris, P. (2016) 'Trump, Brexit, and the rise of populism: economic have-nots and cultural backlash', *HKS Faculty Research* Working Paper Series. RWP16-026. Harvard, MA. Available at https://dx.doi.org/10.2139/ssrn.2818659.

Ionescu, G. and Gellner, E. (eds) (1969) *Populism: its meanings and national characteristics*. London: Weidenfeld and Nicholson.

Katsambekis, G. (2017) 'The populist surge in post-democratic times: theoretical and political challenges', *Political Quarterly*, 88 (2), pp. 202–210. DOI: 10.1111/1467-923X.12317.

Kedourie, E. (1961) *Nationalism*. London: Hutchinson.

Kornhauser, W. (1959) *The politics of mass society*. Glencoe, IL: The Free Press.

Lacan, J. (2006) 'The instance of the letter in the unconscious or reason since Freud', in *Écrits*, Fink, B., Fink, H. and Crigg, R. (trans). New York: W.W. Norton & Company, pp. 412–439.

Laclau, E. (1990) *New reflections on the revolutions of our time*. London: Verso.

Laclau, E. (2005a) 'Deconstruction, pragmatism, hegemony', in Mouffe, C. (ed.) *Deconstruction and pragmatism*. London: Routledge, pp. 49–70. Available at https://www.routledge.com/Deconstruction-and-Pragmatism/Critchley-Derrida-Laclau-Rorty-Mouffe/p/book/9780203431481.

Laclau, E. (2005b) *On populist reason*. London: Verso.

Laclau, E. (2007) *Emancipation(s)*. London: Verso.

Laclau, E. (2014) *The rhetorical foundations of society*. London: Verso.

Laclau, E. and Mouffe, C. (1987) 'Post-Marxism without apologies', *New Left Review*, (166), pp. 79–106.

Laclau, E. and Mouffe, C. (2001) *Hegemony and socialist strategy: towards a radical democratic politics* (2nd edn). London: Verso.

Lazar, N. C. (2022) 'Populism and time', in Manucci, L. (ed.) *The populism interviews*. Abingdon: Routledge, pp. 159–163. DOI: 10.4324/9781003250388-30.

Lipset, S. M. (1960) *Political man: the social bases of politics*. Garden City, NY: Doubleday & Company.

Mann, M. (2010) *The sources of social power: the rise of classes and nation-states, 1760–1914*. Cambridge: Cambridge University Press. Available at https://www.cambridge.org/core/books/sources-of-social-power/B7697E09 5085EDA5FD12BE9CBE778A68

Marshall, T. H. (1950) *Citizenship and social class*. Cambridge: Cambridge University Press.

Marx, K. (1978) 'Manifesto of the Communist Party', in *The Marx-Engels Reader* (2nd edn). New York: W.W. Norton & Company.

Marx, K. (1999) *Chapter fifteen: machinery and modern industry, Capital volume one*. Marxist Internet archive. Available at https://www.marxists.org/archive/marx/works/1867-c1/ch15.htm#S1

Moffitt, B. (2018) 'The populism/anti-populism divide in Western Europe', *Democratic Theory*, 5 (2), pp. 1–16. DOI: 10.3167/dt.2018.050202.

Mouffe, C. (2018) *For a left populism*. London: Verso.

Mudde, C. (2004) 'The populist zeitgeist', *Government and Opposition*, 39 (4), pp. 541–563. DOI: 10.1111/j.1477-7053.2004.00135.x.

Pappas, T. S. (2018) 'How to tell nativists from populists', *Journal of Democracy*, 29 (1), pp. 148–152.

Rosa, H. (2013) *Social acceleration: a new theory of modernity*, J. Trejo-Mathys (trans). New York: Columbia University Press.

Saussure, F. de (1966) *Course in general linguistics*, C. Bally, A. Sechehaye and A. Riedlinger (ed), W. Baskin (trans). New York: McGraw-Hill.

Smith, A. (1986) *The ethnic origins of nations*. Oxford: Blackwell.

Stavrakakis, Y. (2004) 'Antinomies of formalism: Laclau's theory of populism and the lessons from religious populism in Greece', *Journal of Political Ideologies*, 9 (3), pp. 253–267. DOI: 10.1080/1356931042000263519.

Stavrakakis, Y. (2014) 'The return of "the people": populism and anti-populism in the shadow of the European crisis', *Constellations*, 21 (4), pp. 505–517. DOI: 10.1111/1467-8675.12127.

Stavrakakis, Y. et al. (2018) 'Populism, anti-populism and crisis', *Contemporary Political Theory*, 17 (1), pp. 4–27. DOI: 10.1057/s41296-017-0142-y.

Taggart, P. (2002) 'Populism and the pathology of representative politics', in Mény, Y. and Surel, Y. (eds) *Democracies and the populist challenge*. Basingstoke: Palgrave Macmillan.

Taş, H. (2022) 'The chronopolitics of national populism', *Identities*, 29 (2), pp. 127–145. DOI: 10.1080/1070289X.2020.1735160.

Vahabzadeh, P. (2003) *Articulated experiences: toward a radical phenomenology of contemporary social movements*. Albany: State University of New York.

Vulović, M. and Palonen, E. (2022) 'Nationalism, populism or peopleism? Clarifying the distinction through a two-dimensional lens', *Nations and Nationalism*, (September), pp. 1–16. DOI: 10.1111/nana.12920.

Waisbord, S. (2018) 'The elective affinity between post-truth communication and populist politics', *Communication Research and Practice*, 4 (1), pp. 17–34. DOI: 10.1080/22041451.2018.1428928.

Weber, E. (1976) *Peasants into Frenchmen: the modernization of rural France, 1870–1914*. Stanford, CA: Stanford University Press.

Wittgenstein, L. (1967) *Philosophical investigations* (3rd edn), G. E. M. Anscombe (trans). Oxford: Basil Blackwell.

# 7

# Populism, Social Media and the Technospheric

*Jamie Ranger*

## 1. Introduction

The world has lost its friction and fallen into screens. Conversations with strangers, neighbours, and increasingly even friends and family members are becoming detached from the social expectation of shared assumptions. We are networked to more people, places and ideas than ever before, and yet the wires that stretch out and entangle themselves in the world also bind and entrap us in the solitude of bubbles, the social resembling pulsating foam rather than the reliable solidity of the public sphere. We are epistemically unmoored from a chaotic, paradoxical and hypocritical world of crises, scandal, complexity and insecurity: yet despite the appearance of a growing general agreement that society must change, we cannot agree on why, when and how. We have a general idea of how we got here: the impotent political response to the 2008 financial crisis that saw an unprecedented spike in class inequality in the West (Kuhn, Schularick & Steins, 2018); state austerity measures hit the poorest and most vulnerable the hardest (Oxfam, 2013); the primary response to looming ecological catastrophism on a planetary scale has been vague green individualism rather than acknowledgement of structural forces (Millman, 2019); the remobilisation of citizen activism, from Occupy and #MeToo to Black Lives Matter and Antifa, were hastily demonised or recuperated by a complicit press (Leopold & Bell, 2017); the return of political re-engagement with socialist ideas was met with immediate false-equivalence with the simultaneously emergent far-right nationalism (McTague, 2019); the younger generations, engaged with political discourse through grassroots movements and social media, were swiftly portrayed as entitled and ignorant (Milkman, 2017). Millennials have taken to the ironic term '*doomscrolling*' to refer to the endless stream of seemingly relentless, disconnected instances of bad news on social media feeds (Watercutter, 2020). For many, living in Western post-modernity may be characterised as the cultural condition of perceiving the world as a series of impositions rather than opportunities.

In response to these tendencies, much radical political theory read as sources of residual comfort for a counter-cultural intelligentsia than a practical resource for unmasking instances of social domination. I would also venture those radical democratic theorists, by contrast, many of whom would self-identify as Marxists, post-Marxists or communists of numerous stripes, were dashed against the rocks by a tide of anti-socialist sentiment across the West, as technocrats and 'Third Way' politics firmly replaced social welfarism and worker-aligned policies across centre-left political parties. It was during a period of liberal capitalist triumphalism that the apparent inevitability of our current systems had radical politics on the back foot, having to argue against the contention of 'the end of history' itself (Fukuyama, 1992).

I argue that we currently live in the technospheric condition, a series of social, cultural and technological factors that intersect with one another and produce certain subjectivities, the contemporary iteration of which is increasingly steered by social media. The technospheric condition distorts what is properly political (that is to say, democratically contestable) and makes it appear technical (an objective process grounded in efficiency to be deferred to experts). However, due to the global communications apparatus shifting towards the attention economy model of social media, unlike the post-political citizens of the 1990s, these subjectivities are open to the relitigating of all political questions. This state of affairs provides counter-hegemonic actors an opportunity to contest the neoliberal-capitalist status quo, but also contributed to the re-emergence of previously vanquished far-right forces, who regroup and attempt to normalise and integrate themselves into mainstream conservatism.

Political polarisation and intense contestation have returned, but erratically, characterised by a distrust of pre-existent political institutions, undermined by misinformation, debased by racism, sexism and xenophobia, and now political theory must map a hyper-connected world of motion, media and malaise.

Firstly, I will explain Ernesto Laclau's discursive approach to populism. Secondly, I will explicate the bundle of interconnected sociotechnical influences that I refer to collectively as the technospheric condition and explain the implications for Laclau's account of populism. Finally, I will argue that the logics of difference and equivalence central to the construction of the people required for politics are being increasingly steered by algorithmic interference on social media platforms, arguably undermining the purpose of politics itself.

## 2. Discursive Populism and Constructing the People

The philosopher Jacques Rancière claims that 'the foundation of politics is not in fact more a matter of convention rather than nature: it is the lack of foundation, the sheer contingency of any social order. Politics exists simply because no social order is based on nature, no divine law regulates human society' (1999, p. 16). From this acknowledgement of the radical contingency that grounds politics as a mode of human activity, Ernesto Laclau's discursive account of populist reason is primarily concerned with 'the nature and logics of the formation of collective identities' (2005a, p. ix). He argues that any process of social identity formation operates under a similar logic as populist politics, intending to demonstrate 'that populism has no referential unity because it is ascribed not to a delimitable phenomena but to a social logic whose effects cut across many phenomena' (p. xi). Populism lacks an inherent political agenda of its own and is better understood as a rhetorical strategy articulating unfulfilled demands and creating communities of solidarity, 'a way of constructing the political' (p. xi).

For Laclau, political identities are constructed through the process of articulation, in which diverse groups are brought together around a shared set of symbols, values and goals. Laclau argued that political identities are not fixed nor essential, but rather are continually negotiated and contested through a process of discourse and struggle. In his view, political identities are shaped by a variety of factors, including social and economic conditions, historical context and cultural influences, as well as the ways in which people interact with one another and by the ways in which they are represented in public discourse.

Populism emerges under circumstances in which politicians fail to deliver on a series of particular demands, at which point populism 'presupposes the constitution of a global political subject bringing together a plurality of social demands' (Laclau, 2005a, p. 116) and allows those who believe their voices were previously unheard to amass under a homogenous political mobilisation. He argues that populist discourses emerge from 'any place in the socio-institutional structure' (Laclau, 2005b, p. 44), but are always predicated upon the antagonistic relationship between the rhetorically and symbolically constructed categories of 'the people' and 'the elite'.

Laclau contends that populism ought to be understood as a 'political logic', given that any attempt to ascribe specificity to populist movements across the political spectrum is doomed to be crushed under the weight of an 'avalanche of exceptions' (Laclau, 2005a, p. 117). When a group of people find their political demands frustrated, 'some kind of solidarity will arise between them all: all will share the fact that their demands remain unsatisfied' (Laclau, 2005b, p. 37).

There are two pre-conditions for populism: '(1) the formation of an internal antagonistic frontier separating "the people" from power; and (2) an equivalential articulation of demands making the emergence of "the people" possible' (2005a, p. 74). There is always an unfulfilled 'we', a deserving group for whom political institutions are wilfully ignoring, unable to accommodate, or incapable of adequately addressing, and this 'we'-ness is forged by those competing sides – one side that stands with 'the people' and all their demands that are going unfulfilled (linked together to provide implicit legitimacy to all demands and solidarity between claimants) and that other side that stands with the pre-existing political settlement, usually framed as 'the elites' to emphasise an asymmetry of power relations.

Laclau argues that classic forms of populism presuppose a larger community going unheard and a smaller group of elites, 'so the equivalential logics will cut across new and more heterogenous social groups' (p. 77). Laclau suggests that there are two ways of constructing the social – 'either through the assertion of a particularity – in our case, a particularity of demands – whose only links to other particularities are of a differential nature ... or through a partial surrender of particularity, stressing what all particularities have, equivalentially, in common' (pp. 77–78). For example, wealthy rural voters who care about the state of their roads and how often the bins are collected, middle-class voters working as professionals in public services concerned about increasing privatisation and the urban rental market, and working-class voters concerned about increases in consumption taxes, may all be aligned under a joint anti-government banner that stresses the indifference of elites in addressing everyday concerns, or even more specifically conjoined as citizens demanding a more responsive, active and civically minded state. Laclau marks these two ways of constructing the social as a 'logic of difference' and 'logic of equivalence' (p. 78).

The distinctiveness of the rhetorical strategy of populism from articulations of the social in conventional politics can be found when populists address 'privileged, hegemonic signifiers which structure, as nodal points, the ensemble of a discursive formation', where an institutionalist discourse attempts to align the limits of any discursive formation with the limits of the political community (p. 81) – in the contemporary Western liberal context, there is no alternative; the money has run out; we can't have a nanny state. The populist response – and its subsequent invocation of a new 'we'-ness through its construction of the people – requires a transition from isolated, heterogenous demands to a holistic, global demand which articulates the formation of a political frontier (we stand for 'x') and the discursive construction of existing power as an antagonistic force (they want to deprive us of 'x') – populists must intervene with the naming of this new 'we'-ness to generate what Laclau terms 'radical investment' (p. 110).

Radical investment here refers to the act of ascribing a radical, transformative significance to certain political demands or symbols. In the context of populism, a shared, unified interest in challenging the existing power structures. This investment in a particular set of demands or symbols is acknowledged as radical in the sense that it seeks to fundamentally transform or upend the existing sociopolitical order – a break from conventional politics is articulated as necessary in order for any of the existing, unfulfilled demands to be met – it is always more than simply campaigning for a change in policy, because populism determines that any change must be systemic. If any change must be systemic, then it is the system, however newly articulated, that serves the populist's construction of a chain of equivalence – there must be something about the system, the elites, the political class that leaves the people necessarily unheard in a way that they cannot resolve themselves. This involves bringing together different grievances, issues and identities under a common umbrella forging unity and constructing a populist identity.

Populisms – left, right or syncretic – are constructions of the people, a logic of articulation and collective identification that resembles politics in its more institutionalised forms. If we accept the importance of human beings freely associating and determining their own interpretations of their social standing and the political trajectory they wish to endorse for their state, it stands to reason that our lines of reasoning are informed, as clearly as possible, by chains of equivalence forged together by human agency. In other words, if I believe in one cause, and I am led to believe that I ought to identify on an equivalential basis with another group of people advocating for another cause on the grounds that we share certain underlying political beliefs or similar political orientations, that causal link ought to have been established either by group associations or connections between causes articulated by political leaders and activists within my political purview.

In the next section, I will introduce the notion of the technospheric, which draws upon contemporary critical philosophy of technology to suggest a relationship between the technical and the political in the shaping of social space, and thus reframing technology more broadly as a contributory factor to social behaviours and structural challenges that politics must confront.

## 3. What is the Technospheric?

Technics is the anglophone reconstruction of the ancient Greek *techne*, defined by Aristotle as one of the virtues of thought (also referred to as the intellectual virtues) as a disposition that brings contingent things into existence by way of craft. Philosophers often use *technics* interchangeably with *technique*, or to distinguish technics in the broadest possible sense from technology as referring to something more historically specific, tied to industrialisation, modernity and/or capitalism. Lewis Mumford was first to retrieve technics from the ancients, using it to refer to the total technical equipment of a society (Mumford, 1934). Jacques Ellul, a prominent critic of technology writing later, referred instead to Technique, defined as 'the totality of methods rationally arrived at and having absolute efficiency (for a given stage of development) in every field of human activity' (Ellul, 1964, p. xxv). For Ellul, technique is a guided operation, replacing spontaneous forms with technical forms in order to maximise efficiency, adapt to new conditions and better operationalise certain aspects of a given form. He argues that in the eighteenth century, there was an *explosion of technique*. Ellul argues that globalisation caused technique to have universal transmissibility across the entire world: where once regional contexts provided distinctive approaches to problems or situationally specific tools, there is now an overarching hegemonic technique across the world. Ellul argues that the tendency towards universal, uniform techniques of human production globally imposed and normalised across cultures has emerged across all aspects of social life, albeit with varying degrees of success. *Technique* itself has replaced *Nature* as the hegemonic social *milieu* (for further analysis, see Durbin in Higgs, Light & Strong, 2000, p. 39).

Bernard Stiegler considers technics the repressed foundational aspect of the human condition, rather than a concrete practice of circulating standardised instructions on ways of making and doing – man is first and foremost a technical being that manipulates the environment to supplement its inability to confront the terms of nature directly. Technics is the process by which individual living beings exteriorise their modes of being into the world through crafting, the extension of the body into other objects: we see this process in toolmaking and the way in which tools function as supplements to our own human capacities. Technics allow for the implication of human life into the world to transcend life – not in the sense that all objects last forever, rather that a man can make a tool, die, and that tool stays in the world, to be used by another who may yet to have been born at the time the tool was made. For Stiegler, 'being is historial [not historical], and the history of being is nothing but its inscription in technicity' (Stiegler, 1998, p. 4). Historial is to be understood in the sense of being recorded, as opposed to historical, understood to mean that which is related to the past. For Stiegler, being is characterised by four traits: 'temporality, historiality, self-understanding and facticity' (p. 5). Being is temporal insofar as there is always a past to which we anticipate how our lives are different from our ancestors and in which way they will be similar. Being has an essential relationship with a heritage that exists prior to the establishment of our present, but this heritage is itself contestable: 'this historical, nonlived past can be inherited inauthentically: historiality is also a facticity' (p. 5). It is conceivable to imagine a world where the inherited past is a false one, a mythological tradition that exists solely as a bricolage of retrieved archaeological artefacts, imperfect historical inferences and narratives that develop from the needs of the present rather than the facts of the past. Technics, therefore, play a constitutive and reconstructive role in the production of cultural and social norms and their relation to political order – and make public memory possible.

Hannah Arendt defines a political community as a 'kind of organised remembrance' (Arendt, 1958, p. 198), in which its political sphere is considered 'more specifically "the work of man" than is the work of his hands or the labour of his body' (p. 208). Arendt's political public is sustained by its remembered words and deeds, which are considered integral to understanding the community's sense of shared identity. I wish to forge the link between technics and politics through memory, as the transmission of memory is integral to the constitution and continuity of society required for politics. Speech and action are considered necessary for establishing political relationships, as a record of ancestral speech and action establishes political continuity. For Arendt, it is humanity's individuality that means we cannot be understood exclusively in terms of our species-being as are plants and animals, and recalling Stiegler, this process of individuation is always-already technical. Stiegler's use of individuation is not – as one would expect – taken from psychology, but instead borrowed from the philosopher of technology Gilbert Simondon (see Simondon, 2020). In the absence of a shared history – which itself involves an account and archiving of what the community deems worthy of remembrance – the impermanence of the social undermines the establishment of a politics. Through the commemoration of past deeds, a coherent society can be 'founded', even if it is always provisional due to the radical contingency of the political.

Society is constituted by shared meanings in the present, and a collective expectation of its future direction premised upon those shared meanings, and so opting out of the way in which these shared meanings come to exist (and persist) through time merely incapacitates those individuals committed to radically transforming the social milieu. All knowledge, all collective recollections retained through time, are bequeathed by a common past written mostly by anonymous authors, 'projecting a common future that is always indeterminate, inaccessible and improbable, but which insists and remains open through works' (Stiegler, 2020, p. 24). Our technical inheritance influences our capacity to determine and anticipate our desires, including our political subjectivity.

The importance of technics as the transmission of memory, and with it the construction and continuity of political communities, calls for a renewed political focus on media. Couldry defines media as 'technologies that able regularly and reliably to transmit or preserve meanings across space and time' (Couldry, 2020, p. 4). Our society (and we as individuals) are constantly mediated and mediatised. Whilst mediation describes the ways in which transmitting ourselves into another space and time from our corporeal selves, for example, a photograph or a video clip, mediatisation describes the ways in which we are changing our behaviour because of the media surrounding us. Mark Deuze has argued that in contemporary life, we do not live *with*, so much as live *in* media. Media augment life, and as such, for Deuze, it is an illusion (or a delusion) that we can control our media (Deuze, 2009). Media cannot be switched off; it is pervasive and ubiquitous (even more so in the expansive sense of influencing technics). We cannot make sense of a world outside media because media is a key component in the construction of social reality itself. Media almost acts as its own discursive ecology, its culture industry seducing us with fantasies, stories and narratives that blur the clear demarcations between socially constructed reality and socially convenient fiction. As Couldry and Hepp remind us, 'the screen is not simply a "medium" … it is a building site on which a whole economic and epistemological world is erected' (Couldry & Hepp, 2016, p. 95). Furthermore, politics itself, through the circulation of political party advertising, televised speeches and debates, panel shows and partisan artistic endeavours, has become part of the broader media ecology, what Stiegler terms 'the absorption of politics into the market through the integration of the mnemotechnical system into the global techno-industrial system' (Stiegler, 2020, p. 193).

Technics and their media not only preserve history, but shape our sense of temporality itself, our sense of what is to *be* through time. Technics is inherently political insofar as it produces the conditions for both individual and collective self-understanding, mediating the 'we'-ness required for collective agency and the intergenerational continuity of 'we'-ness required for the emergence of political communities (societies with a shared sense of directionality). A healthy and accountable media landscape ought not be considered a democratic bonus, so much as a necessary precondition for any radical social transformation in the information age. However, the organisation of contemporary technologies is such that the unprecedented optimisation of information archival and retrieval destabilises the social cohesion reliant on collective memory.

Stiegler argues that all technical systems pose social problems that become political problems at the point of collective social disruption, which must be resolved with 'therapeutics' that are 'always a system of de-proletarianization'

(2020, p. 62). What does he mean by this? In the information age, technical novelty and planned obsolescence are often prioritised over innovation, as technology increasingly takes the commodity form of devices (and requires devices to provide screens of access to informational commodities). General proletarianisation describes a process by which all (across all classes) are impoverished in our overall knowledge of social systems, depriving the individual worker, consumer and citizen of the knowledge of how they fit into a broader structure that appears to operate dispassionately and imperviously even in the absence of their contribution. The more complex and comprehensive our modern digital communications technology become, the more distinct are the levels of specialisms required to be on 'the right side' of the knowledge barrier.

As proletarianisation detaches individuals from the broader technical aspects of the social system, it is inevitable that what media theorist Mark Poster referred to as 'information subjects', those specialists capable of understanding the niche technical frameworks that increasingly shape the contours of their particular industries and of society more generally, become valuable to both the public and private sectors. As Poster notes, 'information is presented as the key to contemporary living and society is divided between the information rich and the information poor. The "informed" individual is a new social ideal' (Poster, 2001, p. 8). Nevertheless, expertise is necessarily specialised due to the complexity of our systems, and as such, 'thought leaders' in their niche technical sectors and professional networks are not necessarily fluent in the broader social and technical system to which we are all generally proletarianised subjects. The technical system paradoxically leads to the destruction of knowledge that occurs when it is exteriorised, despite exteriorisation 'being the fundamental condition of the constitution of all knowledge' (Stiegler, 2020, p. 25).

General proletarianisation can be understood as the intensification and expansion of both proletarianisation at work and in leisure: employment is becoming more about performing bureaucratic or technical tasks divorced from value-producing interactions with raw materials, whilst leisure time is dominated by conspicuous consumption, the consumption of 'content' on numerous screens, and discourse surrounding the consumption of such aforementioned content, a systematic erosion of our sense of *savoir-vivre*, our sense of 'how to live'. The extent to which our understanding of social reality, especially concepts, objects and innovative processes outside of our immediate lived experience are shaped by media cannot be underestimated.

Returning to the notion of social stability and memory, it is the speed of information that tears at the social fabric as much as the sheer quantity of data, as the information economy is predicated on various analytical, statistical and probabilistic models that coalesce to form 'reticulated artificial intelligence' capable of information feedback loops capable of operating at speeds between two and four million times quicker than the human nervous system. Our dominant system operates beyond the limits of human thought, and although Stiegler's criticism of technological acceleration remains implicit, I argue that there exists an underlying observation that if technical apparatuses are communicating with each other at accelerating speeds, should anything go wrong, far more significant and far-reaching damage accrues before human intervention is possible. Furthermore, there are also certain systems where any abrupt halt causes serious aftershocks: an emergency stop often leads to whiplash.

Stiegler is not alone in framing social acceleration as a consequence of the technical configuration of social life that is cause for concern. For the sociologist Hartmut Rosa, 'acceleration is an irreducible and constitutive trait of modernisation' (Rosa, 2003, p. 27). For modern societies, capitalist economies dictate that productivity and growth must be continuous just in order to preserve what we already have, and it is this frenetic standstill as he refers to it, that leads to a state of individual and institutional inertia, insofar as these rapid changes undermine the belief that our lives and our actions are heading in some meaningful direction. Rosa wants us to consider that the lack of democratic transformation in our state of affairs is partially explained by a phenomenon guided by our relationship to technological systems, that our institutions feel unable to initiate change because change is continuously enforced from outside, and as such, the uncertainty built into the stability of the economic systems of modernity creates a sense of powerlessness, retrenchment and consternation.

Rosa describes three systems of social acceleration: technical acceleration, the acceleration of social change, and the acceleration of the pace of life. Technical acceleration refers to the rapid developments in transportation and communication technologies: we started on foot, and then we used wheels, then horses pulled carts with wheels, and now we deal in engines and flight. We used to send letters through the post, or telegrams through the wires, and now we can send electronic mail across the world in seconds.

The second system of acceleration is the acceleration of social change, related to this first system of technological change: prior to modernity, you would learn a skill that you could plausibly pass down the generations – everything from family recipes to my grandfather teaching me how to bleed a radiator. To be modern is to live through technological developments that fundamentally alter the ways in which people interact with their world, to shorten the lifespan of human relationships with particular technologies, and thus give life a sense of fast-paced movement, towards the direction of progress, or otherwise. Learning how to clean the VCR is a skill my father learned, but it became redundant before he even taught me, never mind my children. There are skills related to the technologies of our day that will be pointless in a generation, especially when we consider the gains being made in the field of artificial intelligence.

Modernity has produced a social rapidity, where social beliefs and actions are considered sensible, mainstream or acceptable, for shorter and shorter periods of time. Rosa refers to these rapid changes in 'attitudes and values as well as fashions and lifestyles, social relations and obligations as well as groups, classes, or milieus, social languages as well as forms of practice and habits' (Rosa, 2009, p. 83). Culture moves at a faster pace: fashion trends, music genres – even the articulation of political ideologies – are becoming harder and harder to catch up with and keep track of, a process that has become almost laborious, and exacerbated in the age of social media, where Internet memes and in-jokes can escalate within hours, disappear from relevance within a day and briefly resurface in an ironic, tired or even nostalgic reformulation by the end of a given week.

The acceleration of the pace of life can be understood as a form of subjectivity, an effect of feeling as if they are always running out of time, that there are never enough hours in the day; a subjectivity that views time as a commodity to be spent, and to be spent efficiently, a resource becoming scarce. Rosa defines it as 'an increase in the number of episodes of action or experience per unit of time, i.e., it is a consequence of trying to do more things in less time' (Rosa, 2010, p. 21).

The technospheric condition produces a sociotechnical milieu in which specialists – those with technical expertise in specific, isolated scenarios – thrive as structural necessities, the skilled labourers and enlightened managerial class that perform valuable work, the rest of us toiling without context and living without a coherent understanding of the rules of the game. This relationship between social life and the technological apparatus that supports its reproduction complements a neoliberal politics, as it allows hegemonic norms to be framed as specialist knowledge – known only by the consultant, the economist, the bureaucrat – and thus accommodates the contradiction between the disaffected mass of citizens and the minority of elites enacting deeply unpopular policies with little organised and cohesive resistance.

A critical political engagement with technics underscores the importance of co-presence for political deliberation, and the sharing of social spaces as integral to the communitarian spirit of democratic projects. In order to be present, for a space to command one's attention, people require spaces that accommodate and resonate with them, that afford them the capacity to give themselves the time to engage in the work of politics (and the accompanying theoretical knowledge to understand why they want to politically convene in the first instance). However, if the projection of a common future remains open, then accessibility to each other is an integral political issue of the information age. If in the age of information, our personal projects are increasingly computationally presented and algorithmically organised to serve corporate ends, then either the foundations of society will be constantly destabilised by technical disruption, or social stability is reliant on a technical configuration that operates outside of democratic accountability. Populism constructs a people, but it does so on the basis that the political actors are fellow citizens. Metaphors aside, populist politics involves human agents deploying a rhetorical strategy to coordinate various *real* demands (where real refers to their origins in human concerns) and as I shall argue in the next section, the logic of social media platforms disrupts the process.

## 4. Populism and the Technospheric

In *New Reflections on the Revolution of Our Time* (1990), Laclau argued that the contemporary rhythms of capitalism created new antagonisms in political life. Capitalism and rapid technological change are framed as the precondition for the neoliberal status quo that progressives must challenge. Nevertheless, radical politics should no longer be understood as a collective struggle against a dominant system, but as a series of disconnected but potentially linkable nodes of resistance – from this reading of the social, Laclau and Mouffe both argue for a left populism, a mode of politics capable of marshalling disparate demands under unified progressive sloganeering and identification. Laclau's concerns – and thus his accompanying methodological approach to populism – complements political engagement with the technospheric condition. The combination of neoliberal politics and a fragmented sociotechnical existence that reinforces such politics may be overcome by an organised, progressive, unified populist politics. However, as I shall argue, the emergence of social media as a disruptive and transformative force within the technospheric condition provides opportunities for counter-hegemonic political movements of all persuasions.

Political elites in a hegemonically neoliberal era are easily framed as much of a muchness – this idea is perhaps best articulated by the satirical animation *Futurama* (season 2, episode 3: A Head in the Polls, 1999). The characters Fry and Leela are watching a televised debate. The politician Jack Johnson announces, 'it is time for someone to say – I am against those things everyone hates!' The camera swerves to reveal his opponent is his clone named John Jackson, who responds 'now I respect my opponent, I think he's a good man, but quite frankly, I agree with everything he just said!' but with an intonation of disagreement. Fry is appalled, but Leela reassures him that despite sharing identical DNA, they disagree on key issues. Jack Johnson – 'I say your 3-cent titanium tax goes too far!' / John Jackson – 'and I say your 3-cent titanium tax doesn't go too far enough!' The humorous spectacle of attempted disagreement aside, of course both candidates propose raising taxes. Populisms latch on to these technocratic representations of liberal democratic politicians and purport to offer a radical alternative more aligned with the people's demands.

My contention is that neoliberalism and the technospheric condition have been uneasy but generally complementary bedfellows, at least until the widescale adoption of social media. The media and communications infrastructure and technological innovations at work and in leisure contributed to reproducing conditions of general proletarianisation and social acceleration. The increasingly globalised world became unwieldy and difficult to fully understand, systems of computerisation and bureaucratisation complicated working life, and the integration of the Internet into leisure time contributed to a goldrush for neoliberal values. In 2002, Don Heath, president of the Internet Society, said that 'if the United States government had tried to come up with a scheme to spread its brand of capitalism and its emphasis on political liberalism around the world, it couldn't have invented a better model than the internet' (Heath in Simon et al., 2002, pp. 5–6).

In this sense, the most unfortunate aspect of these forms of cyber-optimism is the way they laundered the triumph of financial capitalism, the disproportionate and growing inequality between capital and labour and the neoliberal retrenchment of the post-war social welfare states of the Global North, through a technological vision of global progress. Our everyday experience of technology is often the placement of a barrier between orders and the ordered, the absolute reduction of the political to the technical.

Wellman and Haythornwhaite (2002) argued that it is the quotidian and humdrum aspect of habitual Internet use that obscures its pervasive incorporation into people's lives. The generation raised by the television trapped the generation below them similarly in a world of screens, but these screens began to offer far more in the way of interpersonal connectivity, networks of immediacy and intimacy, and slowly these applications would become woven into conventional social activity: Facebook friends and Twitter feeds became routine and boring, but also formative, addictive and politically charged.

Social media did not develop into its current form until the advent of 'Web 2.0', a term denoting the period from around 2004 when there was an explosion of new globally popular websites such as YouTube, Myspace and Facebook that would have been practically implausible prior to widespread broadband connections. Social media attempts to map social reality such that a user may come to understand the social world, and their own place within it, and whether social media inculcates certain beliefs, behaviours or dispositions which serve the status quo either explicitly through discourse, or implicitly by operating within its parameters, is a test of its success at reproducing the status quo. As Wendy Chun argues, 'software, or perhaps more precisely operating systems, offer us an imaginary relationship to our hardware: they do not represent transistors but rather desktops and recycling bins. Software produces users. Without operating system (OS) there would be no access to hardware; without OS no actions, no practices, and thus no user. Each OS, through its advertisements, interpellates a "user": calls it and offers it a name or image with which to identify' (Chun in Lovink, 2019, p. 29).

Srnicek categorises social media as an advertising platform insofar as it operates to 'extract information on users, undertake a labour of analysis, and then use the products of that process to sell ad space' (2017, p. 49). Capitalist competition causes the Internet to fragment, as many different services, products and applications are being made available to online consumers every day; online platforms serve as the most scalable websites, because they attempt to impose a clear and cohesive streamlining of the disorder of cyberspace: 'the aim for Facebook is to make it so that users never have to leave their enclosed ecosystem: new stories, videos, audio, messaging, e-mail, and even buying consumer goods have all been progressively folded back into the platform itself' (p. 110). Social media was the market response to the problems of the technospheric condition, but, due to the adoption of the attention model as the means by which platforms would profit, the *quantity* of networking, content and user interaction is far more important than the *quality* of these connections.

Private media operates on the economic logic of acquiring attention, of 'selling' stories to consumer-readers, and populists thrive under conditions where they court controversy and make divisive declarations as part of a broader rhetorical strategy. The advertising economy of social media is the ultimate extension of the logic of attention, dissolving the barrier between the personal rhythms of everyday social life and media consumption. Social media can only exist in a context in which people are capable and willing to share, communicate, collaborate and identify with various communities, but that these actions, whilst encouraged online, are precisely what has been diminished by the individualist culture of Western societies. Platforms thrive as mediators of social life, harvesting our data and repurposing our own self-reported preferences back to us as targeted advertisements. In this context, the marketing strategy for the platform model of contemporary neoliberal capitalist social media relies on two supporting mythologies: social media platforms can generate and sustain social spheres equivalent to the physical spaces in which human beings interact with in the material world; and that neoliberal market logic – understood apolitically – is the natural way of organising such communities. That is to say, social media presents the social bonds that bind us together in the material world, e.g. the school where friends all met for the first time, with the market logic of choice and preference, e.g. friends are whomever you feel should be able to access your Facebook profile and those whose profile you'd like to access. Social obligations produced by intimate proximity are culturally reconfigured by the platform model as voluntary associations in the libertarian vein – communities that exist through persistent express consent that can be dissolved with the click of a cursor.

As the world becomes more increasingly mediated, the poorer our ability to communicate clearly and concisely, and arrange the information sent our way into a coherent pattern of activity; the wider our letterbox, the more junk mail will fall on our doormat, and the harder it is to separate urgent notices sent by friends from worthless drivel sent by con artists. On the individual level we are increasingly compelled to slowly adopt new technologies and change our habits to shape the broader needs of market society, but whilst these nudges occur, there remains the possibility of politicising technology through collective action such that digital platforms are reorganised, restructured and regulated to benefit the workers, end users and society more generally. Whilst users new to social media experience these platforms as disorientating and overwhelming, digital natives and proficient early adopters may marshal these systems and harness social media for their own creative ends.

Social media may be understood as the corporate capture of a digital project aiming towards increased democratisation, but in doing so, it becomes a useful reference point, a powerful metaphor and an everyday demonstration of the possibilities of global community, of instant and spontaneous connectivity, and of our desire to share our lives with others. The recuperation of an egalitarian impetus to collaborate, communicate and connect provides us with a virtual space brimming with counter-hegemonic potential, by laying both the literal and metaphorical network infrastructure between individualised, anxious and increasingly disenfranchised citizens. Social media shows that despite the so-called non-existence of society, whether argued from the neoliberal right (Thatcherite 'there is no alternative') or the socially weightless post-foundational left (society is merely a construction of the hegemonic discourse), we all wanted to 'be together' all along.

Nevertheless, the return of political contestation in all forms, encouraged by the need for as much attention-grabbing content as possible on social media platforms, results in the reopening of all previously closed matters, to the relitigation of all sociopolitical questions, by exposing the radical contingency of the social (albeit in an individualistic, virtual format). Consequently, hegemonic legacy media are now struggling to produce cohesive narratives, failing to legitimise the neoliberal occupation of the 'empty space' of democratic sovereignty. The result has been the rise of populisms of both the left and right, as well as strange, esoteric, paranoid political groups that prioritise their micro-communities' online perception over the broader offline shared reality. Social media political subjectivity ultimately produces fragile partisanship: incomplete, fragmented political subjectivities, occasionally untethered even from national ideological formations.

The consequences of the technospheric condition complicate the process of developing authentic affinities between political actors due to the imposition of algorithmic interference on social media platforms that steer and influence the chains of equivalence between political demands as much as any populist strategy. Populist politics already struggles with the difficulties of spinning many plates at once – accommodating differences under a unified identity, articulating chains of equivalence, challenging the status quo through the cultivation of solidary between disparate movements – and all this happens because of people constructing 'the people'. However, in a world of algorithmic steering, populism is both increasingly popular as a rhetorical strategy for political movements, and yet increasingly inauthentic, given that chains of equivalence are increasingly suggested, recommended or connected through algorithmic interference: Did you like this event? Perhaps you'd like this new group. Did you enjoy this video? Perhaps you'd like this podcast? To what extent is contemporary digital populism a form of semi-automated politics, networked communities of outrage and hope developing affinities for each other's causes because of encoded assumptions by platforms rather than articulations developed by political will?

## 5. Concluding Remarks

If the technospheric condition reduced the political to the technical, dulling our sense of political community and shared participation in our collective trajectory, the disruption caused by social media renders our contemporary platforms a veritable political playground. Laclau's discursive approach to populist politics complements ongoing understanding of populist movements – and politics more generally – as digital platforms mediate social relationships and dominate political communication. Laclau emphasises the role of discourse and language in shaping political identities and movements, increasing relevant in the age of tweets, posts and political activism often taking the form solely of sending messages. Laclau's understanding of populism as a discursive strategy that can be adopted by diverse political movements is particularly pertinent in the context of the fragile partisanship and conspiratorial elements of platform politics, and its flexibility as an approach may be able to adequately capture the algorithmic supplementation of rhetorical logics. Thinking technics alongside politics, however, raises the question of authenticity – does algorithmic interference make chains of equivalence easier to generate, or are they ties that will prove to be even weaker, given purpose-driven populist agents may no longer lay claim to be the primary cause of manufactured populist solidarities?

## Bibliography

Arendt, H. (1958) *The human condition*. Chicago: University of Chicago Press.

Chun, Wendy in Geert Lovink (2019) *Sad by design: on platform nihilism*. London: Pluto Books.

Couldry, N. (2020) *Media, voice, space and power*. London: Routledge.

Couldry, N. and Hepp, A. (2016) *The mediated construction of reality*. Cambridge: Polity.

Deuze, M. (2009) 'Media life', *Media Culture & Society*, 33 (1), pp. 137–148.

Durbin, P. T. (2000) Philosophy of technology: retrospective and prospective views', in Higgs, E., Light, A. and Strong, D. (eds) *Technology and the good life?* Chicago: University of Chicago Press.

Ellul, J. (1964) *The technological society*. New York: Vintage Books.

Fukuyama, F. (1992) *The end of history and the last man*. New York: Free Press.

Heath, D. quoted in Leslie David Simon, Javier Corrales and Donald R. Wolfensberger, *Democracy and the internet: allies or adversaries?* Washington, DC: Woodrow Wilson Canter Press (2002), pp. 5–6.

Heidegger, M. (1962 [1927]) *Being and time*, J. Macquarrie and E. Robinson (trans). Oxford: Basil Blackwell.

Kuhn, M., Schularick, M. and Steins, U. (2018) 'Research: how the financial crisis drastically increased wealth inequality in the US', *Harvard Business Review*, https://hbr.org/2018/09/research-how-the-financial-crisis-drasti cally-increased-wealth-inequality-in-the-u-s.

Laclau, E. (1990) *New reflections on the revolution of our time*. London and New York: Verso.

Laclau, E. (2005a) *On populist reason*. London: Verso Books.

Laclau, E. (2005b) 'Populism: what's in a name?', in Panizza, F. (ed.) *Populism and the mirror of democracy*. London: Verso Books.

Leopold, J. and Bell, M. P. (2017) 'News media and the racialization of protest: an analysis of Black Lives Matter articles', *Equality, Diversity and Inclusion*, (36) 8, pp. 720–735.

McTague, T. (2019) 'Jeremy Corbyn is like Donald Trump, not Boris Johnson', *The Atlantic*, US, https://www.theatlantic.com/international/archive/2019/11/jeremy-corbyn-like-donald-trump-not-boris-johnson/601957/ (accessed 5 January 2023).

Milkman, R. (2017) 'A new political generation: millennials and the post-2008 wave of protest', *American Sociological Review*, 82 (1), pp. 1–31.

Millman, O. (2019) 'Greta Thunberg condemns world leaders in emotional speech at UN', *The Guardian*, UK, https://www.theguardian.com/environment/2019/sep/23/greta-thunberg-speech-un-2019-address (accessed 5 January 2023).

Mouffe, C. (2018) *For a left populism*. London and New York: Verso.

Mumford, L. (2010 [1934]) *Technics and civilization*. Chicago: University of Chicago Press.

Oxfam (2013) A cautionary tale: the true cost of austerity and inequality in Europe, https://www-cdn.oxfam.org/s3fs-public/file_attachments/bp174-cautionary-tale-austerity-inequality-europe-120913-en_1_1.pdf.

Poster, M. (2001) *The information subject*. London: Routledge.

Rancière, J. (1999) *Disagreement: politics and philosophy*. Minnesota: University of Minnesota Press.

Ricoeur, P. (2007) *Reflections on the just*, David Pellauer (trans). Chicago, IL: University of Chicago Press.

Rosa, H. (2003) 'Social acceleration: ethical and political consequences of a desychronised high-speed society', *Constellations*, 10 (1), pp. 3–33.

Rosa, H. (2009) 'Social acceleration: ethical and political consequences of a desynchronized high-speed society', in Rosa, H. and Scheuerman, W. E. (eds) *High-speed society: social acceleration, power and modernity*. University Park: Pennsylvania State University Press.

Rosa, H. (2010) *Alienation and acceleration: towards a critical theory of late-modern temporality*. York: NSU Press.

Rosa, H. (2013) *Social acceleration: a new theory of modernity*. New York: Columbia University Press.

Simondon, G. (2020) See *individuation in light of notions of form and information*, Taylor Adkins (trans). Minneapolis and London: University of Minnesota Press.

Srnicek, N. (2017) *Platform capitalism*. Cambridge: Polity Press.

Stiegler, B. (1998) *Technics and time, vol. 1: The fault of Epithemeus*, George Collins and Richard Beardsworth (trans). Stanford, CA: Stanford University Press.

Stiegler, B. (2008) *Acting out*. Stanford, CA: Stanford University Press.
Stiegler, B. (2020) *Nanjing lectures (2016–2019)*. London: Open Humanities Press.
Watercutter, A. (2020) 'Doomscrolling is slowly eroding your mental health', https://www.wired.com/story/stop-doomscrolling/ (accessed 5 January 2023).
Wellman, B. and Haythornthwaite, C. (2002) *The internet in everyday life*. Oxford: Blackwell.

## Part III

## Populism and Time in Latin America

# 8

# Antagonism, Flexibility and the Surprising Resilience of Populism in Latin America

*María Esperanza Casullo*

The literature on populists in government usually presents a list of their alleged shortcomings, their tendency towards the personalisation of power and their antagonisation of adversaries (Mudde & Kaltwasser, 2017), their weak programmatic commitments, (Stankov, 2021) and their emotional discourses (Norris & Inglehart, 2019). However, a frame that focuses on these problematic characteristics loses sight of one relevant question: If populism is riddled with such obvious problems, why is populism in power so resilient? All the South American presidents of the most recent leftist wave (1998–2012) stayed in power for over a decade; this was no small feat in a region riddled with presidential crises. European populists have proven to be, at the very minimum, no less adept at staying in office than their non-populist counterparts. This chapter will attempt to explore the concept of 'populism resilience' and to analyse its causes. The explanation will focus on two features of populism: the flexibility of antagonism and the permanent mobilisation of supporters. Five leftist South American presidencies will be analysed: Hugo Chávez, Néstor and Cristina Kirchner, Evo Morales, Rafael Correa, and Fernando Lugo. All these had to face serious threats to their stability; four of them, however, were able to survive them and last in power. Populism was an important element in their resilience.

## 1. Introduction[1]

The literature on populists in government usually presents a list of their alleged shortcomings, their tendency towards the personalisation of power and their antagonisation of adversaries (Mudde & Kaltwasser, 2017), their weak programmatic commitments, (Stankov, 2021) and their emotional discourses

(Inglehart & Norris, 2019). Terms like mobilisation, performance and anti-elitism have come to be associated with populism in recent years. Resilience is not one of those terms, however. This chapter will make the case that it should be. Yes, populism is usually anti-elitist, mobilisational, and performative. It is also surprisingly resilient. Populists are adept at winning power and at staying there. It is hard to dislodge them from their seats once they have been elected.

That endurance has been explained by the supposed personal willingness of populists to push through authoritarian reforms (Levitsky & Ziblatt, 2019; Norris & Inglehart, 2019), which in turn is made possible by their personal and direct connection with the masses.

In this view, populism should be defined as a strategy for pursuing and sustaining political power. The direct relation with the masses is central. For Weyland (2001, p. 14), populists seek or exercise government power 'based on direct, unmediated, non-institutionalised support from large numbers of mostly unorganised followers'. Mobilisation and antagonism play an important role in the connection between leader and masses, according to Weyland (2017, p. 50), and the leader seeks to give 'extraordinary intensity' to their bond with the followers by 'attacking numerous enemies and mobilising the followers for heroic missions'. Populists do not seek to mobilise out of a sense of deep ideological commitment, since they 'avoid embracing a specific, well-defined ideology' (2017, p. 53). They do not seek to empower the people (even as they claim to do so). However, proponents of this 'strategic approach' do not offer an explanation as to why populists choose the populist path. Ultimately, it seems to be a matter of the individual morality of the leader; populists have no scruples about engaging in 'opportunistic calculations and manoeuvrings' (Weyland, 2017, p. 60). Within these explanations, populists stay in power because of their authoritarian personalities, which make them able to exploit the naivety of the institutionalised political actors and the gullibility of the masses.

Political analysis should be able to take the individual morality of the leaders into account. But, as Laclau noted, there is a danger of rendering the logic of populism impossible to understand if one defines populism as only a matter of immorality (of the leader) or irrationality (of the masses) (Laclau, 2005, p. 16). It becomes hard to explain the recent surge of populism solely in terms of the quality of individual leadership found in Latin America (and around the world). This chapter would argue that there are real strategic considerations behind the populists' calculations; the populist strategy is instrumental to staying in power in the face of threats.

Moreover, the unprecedented rise to power of populists is often matched with equally unprecedented threats to their political sustainability. This is even more notable given the fact that populist governments are usually denounced by the other political parties, media and intellectuals. Rather than being given free reign by unsuspecting adversaries, they face impeachment procedures, massive oppositional rallies, police uprisings, international pressures. Populist leaders are depicted by most of the mainstream media (Krämer & Holtz-Bacha, 2020) and traditional parties as irrational, buffoonish, unprepared, unfit to rule. They are usually considered to be always on the brink of falling. Yet they often find ways of persevering, and usually they are able to survive all of these; sometimes these setbacks strengthen their position rather than weaken it. Most populists are able to retain power while operating within the democratic framework and winning elections. They can accumulate political power, change the rules of the game and, in general, just *endure*. Silvio Berlusconi was considered an unserious politician yet he remade Italian politics in his own image. Donald Trump survived two impeachment trials even though he had never held a government position before. In South America one can look at former president Jair Bolsonaro, who was widely (and rightly) ridiculed for his parodic performative style (Mendonça & Caetano, 2021) and whose eccentric behaviour included refusing the COVID-19 vaccine on the grounds that it could turn a person into a *yacaré* (alligator). Bolsonaro was able to finish his four years in office against all odds, and, even though he lost his re-election bid against leftist former president Lula da Silva, he did so only narrowly. Moreover, he amassed substantial legislative and gubernatorial blocs even in defeat.

Why are populists in power so resilient? This question has not been adequately answered because it has never been formulated explicitly. Populists are seen as always at the verge of falling, as too irrational to endure, as perpetually on the verge of defeat. When they last, that is usually explained by their authoritarian tendencies. However, even if some populist governments end up transitioning into openly authoritarian regimes (like those of Nicolás Maduro in Venezuela or Viktor Orbán in Hungary), not all of them do. Some populists manage to remain popular, to win elections by large margins and stay in power with sufficient popular support. And, when they lose elections, they leave power; in some cases, just to come back to power at a later date.

The resilience of populism, thus, is an issue worthy of exploration. In fact, I would argue that it is one of the most pressing questions about this particular political phenomenon. In particular, the phenomenon of populist resilience should be explored to avoid democratic disenchantment. Many times, when supposedly irrational and unserious populists are able to remain in power, this gives way to the idea that a majority of the population is simply unfit for self-government. However, it's important to understand the roots of populist durability beyond the supposed ignorance of the masses.

In this chapter, I will try to explain the logic beneath the resilience of populist presidents. I will do so by comparing five South American left populist presidents, all belonging to the populist wave that swept the continent between 1998 and 2012. I have chosen this group of left-leaning presidents because they came to power roughly in the same period, because they shared some characteristics while in power, and because they governed for long periods of time, at least by the region's standards. That wave brought a number of remarkably durable populist presidencies. The presidents included here are Hugo Chávez (Venezuela 1999–2013), Néstor Kirchner and Cristina Fernández de Kirchner (Argentina 2003–2015),[2] Evo Morales (Bolivia 2006–2019), Rafael Correa (Ecuador 2007–2017) and Fernando Lugo (Paraguay 2008–2012). Two elements will be highlighted as key to populist resilience: the flexibility and adaptability of populist antagonism, and the ability to transform such flexibility into the rapid physical mobilisation of their followers in the public space in case of threats against the president. The inclusion of Fernando Lugo's example, whose term in office was cut short by impeachment, will strengthen the argument.

## 2. Conceptual Clarification

I define populism as a political strategy and mode of identification that is based on the relation between a leader and a mobilised people, who are connected by their sharing a common identity based on a *populist myth* (Casullo, 2019, 2020). The populist myth is a political discourse that makes sense of current social problems and feelings of social malaise by explaining them as being caused by the actions of a powerful and ruthless antagonist. In the populist myth, a dual hero (people/leader) is suffering because of the damage done to them by a dual antagonist (external villain/internal traitor). The people must become mobilised and follow the leader to overcome the villain, to redeem themselves and to achieve redemption.[3] Politics is thus depicted as a series of moral crises which require mobilisation and antagonism to be overcome.

The populist myth is structured around the notion of antagonism, which can be described as a political passion caused by the narration of shared social damage, a people comes to be defined as the collective of those who have been damaged by a common adversary. Unity is not simply predicated on a commonality such as class or age or ethnicity, only by the common antagonism towards an Other and the common loyalty to a leader. A people is, at its core, a heterogenous coalition that has been mobilised by a leader against a common adversary. Antagonism is thus essential to the very existence of a people, its existence is predicated on a common situational relation of opposition to such a degree that if the antagonism disappears, so would the people. However, one particularly advantageous feature of populism is that it does not require any *particular* form of antagonism. Unlike, for instance, Marxist antagonism, which is fixated on an 'objective' adversary, populists enjoy a large degree of latitude in choosing who to mobilise the people against at any given moment. The populist myth offers a formal template (a hero, a villain and a damage to be fixed through political action) that can be filled with almost any concrete political content; the antagonist can be defined as the IMF, or European Union bureaucrats, or big bankers, or China. The adversary can vary from today to tomorrow; the former ally can become a part of 'them' and vice versa. This creates a sense of situational flexibility that can be used to keep the antagonism alive and fresh over longer periods of time.

Antagonism and flexibility are connected with personalisation and mobilisation. These are personified both in the leader, who becomes the source of the myth and the embodiment of the common struggle against the elite, and in their adversaries, who are never characterised as abstract or impersonal groups, classes or processes, but are always presented as concrete *persons* with faces and names. The concrete personalisation of the antagonism in a leader and a villain, or a series of them, feeds into mobilisation. Unlike in more institutional, impersonal, 'modern' forms of political representation, the actual, physical mobilisation into public spaces is one key manifestation of the linkage between leader and followers. Canovan goes as far as defining a people as 'a mobilised public in which individuals have become engaged' (2005, p. 114). The people must remain willing to be mobilised in case of threats on the part of those defined as villains. The malleability and personalisation of antagonism and the physical mobilisation are two key elements in the formation of populist resilience.

## 3. What is Political Resilience?

The concept of 'regime resilience' was used by Tomsa (2017) to indicate the ability of a democratic regime to survive crises and challenges.[4] In this chapter I will concentrate on another type of resilience – the resilience of presidents. I propose to use the term 'presidential resilience'.

The political life of South America in the twentieth century was marked by truncated democratic projects, coups d'état, dictatorships and political violence. This changed after most of the region embraced democracy during the so-called 'third wave' of regime transitions in the 1980s. Since then, most of the countries of the region have remained democratic.[5] Instability, however, has not disappeared; rather, it has been displaced from the regime to the heads of government. South American presidents must govern in a context in which congressional impeachments, inter-power conflicts, threats of regional secession or social rebellions are the norm. Presidential tenures are often cut short due to forced resignations or impeachments.

Pérez Liñán (2007) has coined the term 'presidential crises' to describe the kind of threats that South American presidents routinely face (mostly impeachments). He argues that inter-power conflict and even replacement of the president do not necessarily cause open democratic backsliding. While it is comforting to know that the sort of instability that Pérez Liñán describes does not cause automatic authoritarian backsliding, it is far from a desirable outcome. Yet, given the structural instability, and as crises become routine in democratic regimes, the ability of presidents to navigate through them and just *survive* in power becomes key.

This capacity for survival can be called 'presidential resilience'. I define presidential resilience in a very simple way: as the ability of a given head of government to (a) fulfil their constitutional term to its maximum potential duration in the face of (b) credible threats to their hold on power. Presidential resilience has become a crucial requirement for South American presidents, and democratic stability at large.

Pérez Liñán (2007, p. 132) isolates one key variable that can explain the differential capacity to survive a presidential crisis. He focuses on the necessity for South American presidents to build partisan legislative majorities that can block impeachment attempts, even when they could be warranted; he calls this a 'legislative shield'. In this chapter I want to highlight another element, which could be called a 'street mobilisation shield'. The ability of populist presidents to mobilise a mass of supporters into the streets to defend them against a common antagonist in case of threat is one often ignored cause for their resilience in power.

Populism is a viable factor in creating presidential resilience in South America and, as such, it is a calculated strategy for presidents to foster and use. A populist strategy that nurtures antagonism but defines who the antagonist is in a situational and flexible way, and that uses that antagonism to keep their followers ready for mobilisation, is perfectly rational given the ever-present threats and challenges. The strategy, however, presents its own risks and drawbacks as well.

The starting point of the chapter is a simple empirical claim: South American populist presidents' hold on power is resilient once they are elected. Table 8.1 provides a succinct presentation of the duration of governments of left populist presidents of South America.

**Table 8.1** Duration of the presidencies of the South American populist wave

| Country | President | Dates | Years in power |
|---|---|---|---|
| Venezuela | Hugo Chávez | 1999–2013 | 14 |
| Argentina | Néstor and Cristina Kirchner | 2003–2015 | 12 |
| Bolivia | Evo Morales | 2006–2019 | 13 |
| Ecuador | Rafael Correa | 2007–2017 | 10 |
| Paraguay | Fernando Lugo | 2008–2012 | 4 |

The left populist wave started with the victory in 1998 of Chávez. A notable aspect of these four governments (Chávez, Kirchner, Morales, Correa) is their durability. With the exception of Lugo (which will be analysed as an important counter-case in the later sections) they all were able to complete their constitutional terms and they all lasted one decade or more in power. What is more, even when the tide started to recede after Lugo's impeachment in 2012 and Chávez's death in 2013, most of these leaders remained active, and in some cases their parties or themselves continued in power or won elections again after a short time outside of power. Chavismo still rules in Venezuela, if now as an openly authoritarian force. Morales was ousted by a coup d'état in 2019, but his party, the MAS, came back from repression to win the presidential elections in 2021. Cristina Fernández's Peronism was defeated in 2015, yet it won a new term in Argentina 2019, with her now as vice-president. Lugo was elected to the Paraguayan senate in 2013. These are stories of remarkable political resilience.

## 4. The Resilience of Populists in Power

With the exception of Lugo, all these left populists were able to hold on to power for a decade or more. That is a remarkable durability in South American politics. One only needs to put these populist governments in context to see how remarkable that period of stability was.

Chávez's accession to power in 1999 took place in what was considered at the time to be the most stable political system in South America. Venezuela had not had a military dictatorship since 1958, and it had been ruled by two parties, Acción Democrática (AD) and Comité de Organización Política Electoral Independiente (COPEI), in almost perfect bipartisanship for forty years. However, the apparent stability papered over fissures, which fuelled Chávez's rise. When Venezuela had to face the end of the oil-fuelled boom of the late 1970s, it embarked on harsh austerity measures that were backed by the two main parties. These caused explosive social protests (known as the 'Caracazo') and bloody state repression during the early 1990s. Chávez, then an officer in the army, attempted a coup d'état in 1992. While the attempt failed and he was sentenced to prison (and later pardoned), this helped build his popularity as an anti-system outsider.

Néstor and Cristina Kirchner's cycle of uninterrupted political hegemony lasted twelve years, even longer than what Juan Domingo Perón (1946–1955 and 1973–1974) achieved. Not by coincidence, another populist, Carlos Menem, came close to their mark, having governed for ten years (1989–1999). Non-populist presidents have proved less resilient in power. Raúl Alfonsin could not complete his time in office and had to step down in 1989, six months before the end of his term. The same happened to Fernando de la Rúa in 2001 after only two years in power. De la Rua was ousted by popular protests against austerity measures; the crisis that followed his fall from power framed the Kirchners' rise to power. Néstor Kirchner completed his four-year term, Cristina Kirchner finished her two terms in office (her husband died in 2010). The resilience of Peronism was supposed to be exhausted by 2015, when a long-time member of the Argentine economic elite, Mauricio Macri, conclusively defeated it and promised to vanquish it. However, to the surprise of many, he lost his re-election bid in 2019. Kirchnerism came back to power, with Cristina Fernández now as vice-president.

In Bolivia, Morales retains the title as the longest-serving president, as well as the one most voted for . Bolivia transitioned into democracy in 1982. Two constitutional presidents were forced to resign in the years before Morales' rise to power, former *de facto* president Hugo Banzer (elected in 1997, resigned in 2001) and Morales' immediate predecessor, Gonzalo Sánchez de Losada (resigned in 2003 after just one year in power in the midst of protests and social unrest). In contrast, Morales' Movimiento al Socialismo (MAS) has become the fundamental actor in Bolivian politics. Morales sought judicial approval for overstepping his term limits. He was deposed by a coup d'état in 2019 and had to flee into exile. However, the MAS won the presidency again in 2021.

The politics of Ecuador before Correa fits the same pattern. The presidential politics of Ecuador were famously turbulent before Correa's ascension. President Abdalá Bucaram resigned in 1997, only five months after being sworn in. Jamil Mahuad lasted two years in power but was forced to resign in 2000. Coronel Lucio Gutiérrez, himself a member of a group of armed forces officials that rebelled against Mahuad, was elected in 2002. He had to resign in 2005. Rafael Correa, then an economics professor, was elected in 2006.

He would go on to govern for twelve years; he was re-elected twice and stepped down at the end of his term in 2017; a remarkable feat of stability.

The basic fact is that South American populist presidents were able to accumulate and wield power for prolonged periods of time in a region in which presidential instability is the norm rather than the exception.[6] But this is only a fact, whose ultimate meaning can be debated. Objections can be raised to the idea that populism made them resilient. Maybe they remained in power for a long time in spite of populism, not due to it. Maybe they were just lucky. There are three common variations of this argument. Firstly, that the turn-of-the-century left populists were able to coast thanks to a 'tailwind' of high commodity prices. Secondly, that they came to power in the midst of severe political system crises, with a lack of opposition, so that they enjoyed easy political circumstances. Finally, that populism did not help them to last in power, rather it hindered their ability to remain in office – if they had been more moderate they might have lasted even longer or they might have built a more stable hegemony. I will answer each one of these objections in turn.

## 5. Objection 1: The 'Tailwind' of High Commodity Prices

A cycle of high commodity prices was a very common explanation of the relative success and stability of the populist governments of the turn of the century (Soler, 2020). A very simplified version of this explanation reads like this: the rise of China as a manufacturing powerhouse caused a surge in the global demand for raw materials, while the expansion of the urban middle classes in China strengthened the demand for staples such as soybeans, wheat, pork and beef. As commodities producers, South American countries were direct beneficiaries of this cycle. Chile with copper, Brazil, Argentina and Paraguay with beef and soybeans, Peru with silver, copper and zinc, Bolivia with natural gas for powering up the Brazilian factories, Venezuela and Ecuador with oil – all South American nations expanded their exports and grew their GDPs in the first decade of the century. These governments were able to use these windfall revenues for expanding social welfare, propping up wages and generally redistributing income towards their constituencies among the poor. In short, the argument states that the sudden 'tailwind' helped all governments – populists and non-populists alike; as such, it papered over the flaws of the populist ones.

Undoubtedly, the political landscape at the turn of the century cannot be comprehended without taking into account the export windfall. The first decade and a half saw improving social conditions. Between 2000 and 2008 poverty and inequality fell throughout the region, irrespective of the ideological orientation of the governments (López-Calva & Lustig, 2010, p. 1).

However, the (relatively) abundant resources could not be said to isolate politics completely. Firstly, because the cycle of high commodity prices was cut short by the 2008 and 2009 financial crisis, and yet these governments endured. Secondly, because the decision to use the higher revenues for redistribution was itself a political decision; in some countries the governing political parties chose not to distribute income downward. Thirdly, because in at least two regional cases the combination of high economic growth and presidential crises was notable.

Peru's economy is lauded as one of South America's biggest economic success stories, with economic growth averaging 6 per cent between 2002 and 2012 (Chacaltana, 2017), strong exports and a stable currency. However, its presidential politics have spiralled into ever-shorter cycles of presidential instability. Alberto Fujimori's decade of authoritarian rule ended in 2000 and was followed by a short provisional presidency. The following three elected presidents (Alejandro Toledo, Alan García and Ollanta Humala) were able to complete their times in office, but none of them could build anything resembling a political hegemony. (Alan García was later accused of corruption and ended up committing suicide.) Pedro Pablo Kukszinky was elected in 2016 and deposed by the Congress in 2018; since then, three provisional presidents have been appointed and removed in rapid succession. Pedro Castillo was elected in 2021, to be removed after only one year in power. At the time this chapter was being written, another provisional government was precariously clinging to power, with violent protests and repression engulfing the provinces.

Another important comparison is Paraguay. The commodity boom brought about the expansion of beef and soybean production. Paraguay's GDP grew at an average rate of 4.5 per cent between 2003 and 2008; it dropped with the global financial crisis but then grew 13 per cent in 2010 (Cruces et al., 2017, p. 363). Lugo was elected in 2008 with the promise of redistributing some of the growth into the poorest classes of the nation, and he might have, or should have, been able to capitalise on the robust post-crisis rebound. Yet, Lugo was impeached in 2012 and deposed after just a few days.

In sum, while a good economic performance can be considered a stabilising factor, by no means can it explain presidential resilience on its own. The economic cycle provides a set of challenges or a facilitating context for politics, and the construction of presidential resilience is a political phenomenon in itself.

## 6. Objection 2: Absence of Opposition

A second objection would be that, because these populist governments came to power amidst a widespread crisis of representation and among the electoral implosion of the established parties, they enjoyed a very favourable political context characterised by a lack of opposition. It is true that the rise of most left populists was facilitated by the delegitimation of the mainstream traditional parties, as they were compromised by their support of neoliberal adjustment packages during the 1990s. The reforms, which included privatisations, trade liberalisation and deregulation (in the most extreme case, Ecuador, they ended in the dollarisation of the economy) were implemented with bipartisan or even multiparty support. As the social costs and political unrest grew, the parties that had underwritten the reforms were brought down. The following vacuum created space into which outsiders (or people who successfully proclaimed they were so) could step in.

There is a correlation between the severity of the legitimacy crisis of the established parties and the degree of autonomy of the newly elected populist government. In countries such as Venezuela (Roberts, 2003) and Bolivia (Torre, 1997) the pre-existing parties were wiped out by a wave of popular rejection, including such stalwarts as AD and COPEI in Venezuela and the Movimiento Nacionalista Revolucionario (MNR) in Bolivia. In Venezuela, Bolivia and Ecuador, political outsiders were able to capitalise on the implosion of the political centre. Chávez was a former military man who had been in prison for attempting a coup, Morales was a coca grower and union organiser, and economics professor Rafael Correa was one of the public faces of the protests against the neoliberal policies of Lucio Gutiérrez. Their left populist governments were able to govern with relative freedom in the absence of organised opposition (Garay & Etchemendy, 2011). Chávez, Morales and Correa were able to write new constitutions and to reform the state with ease.

However, the absence of opposition that these populist governments faced was never complete. The speed with which the new governments attempted to implement political and social reforms was deeply worrisome to the economic, social and cultural elites who had often benefited from the neoliberal order and who felt that the electoral route was blocked due to their unpopularity. All the left populist governments were almost immediately denounced as anti-institutional and even undemocratic by diverse interest groups. Radical non-electoral measures were deemed justified in order to stop them, precisely because defeating them at the polls seemed impossible. So, all of these governments had to overcome serious non-electoral threats early in their tenures. Table 8.2 provides a list of the most salient threats early in their governments.

As one can see, all the left populist governments faced threats to their stability, in some cases even to their continuity and the physical safety of the leader. All were able to withstand these threats, with the sole exception of Paraguay. It is thus incorrect to state that they were able to coast on the inexistence of

**Table 8.2** Threats against left populists governments

| | Start of the presidency | Year of threat | Nature of threat | Outcome | Call to mobilisation |
|---|---|---|---|---|---|
| Hugo Chávez | 1999 | 2002 | Coup d'état, Chávez was imprisoned for two days, several foreign governments recognised the new administration | Survived | Yes |
| Néstor and Cristina Kirchner | 2003 (Néstor Kirchner) 2007 (Cristina Kirchner) | 2008 | Conflict with agricultural producers. Blockades and marches, defeat in Congress with the VP voting against his own government | Survived | Yes |
| Evo Morales | 2006 | 2007 | Eastern provinces attempt to secede – riots, skirmishes, several dead | Survived | Yes |
| Rafael Correa | 2006 | 2010 | Conflict with police – Correa is kidnapped in hospital – marches, skirmishes, several dead | Survived | Yes |
| Fernando Lugo | 2008 | 2012 | Impeachment | Fell | No |

political opposition. Rather, their resilience in the face of it should be better analysed.

## 7. Objection 3: The Call to Moderation

Most contemporary analyses of the leftist governments of South America at the turn of the millennium classified these as either 'populist' or 'moderate'.[7] Moderate leftist governments like the Chilean Concertacion, the Brazilian PT and the Uruguayan Frente Amplio were lauded as more stable, less antagonistic and more durable. The governments of the Chilean Concertación, the Brazilian Partido Trabalhista and the Uruguay Frente Amplio were seen as less personalistic, less mobilisatory and more technocratic in their style of governing. Supposedly, these traits helped them to build a broader base of support and hence to become less polarising. In the long run, moderation was supposed to be a better strategy for achieving resilience.

However, the fate of moderate leftist parties has not been so different from the so-called populists. The Concertación (a grand coalition composed of the

Socialist Party and the Christian Democrats based on their shared democratic opposition to Pinochet's dictatorship) defined Chilean politics for over two decades. Their leaders were moderates with impeccable technocratic credentials. They did not engage in mobilisational or antagonistic politics. They were a very successful case of left-leaning social-liberal governance. However, they were also engulfed by polarisation, and their agenda was progressively blocked starting with Michelle Bachelet's election in 2006. Bachelet's two governments (2006–2016 and 2014–2018) were hobbled by accusations of populism, Chavism and corruption (much to the surprise of the populist leftists of the other countries of the region). Neither the Socialist Party nor its partner the Christian Democratic party could develop an effective counter-strategy to Bachelet. The former Concertación dwindled and was not a relevant political player in the presidential elections of 2021, when leftist independent Gabriel Boric was elected and a right-wing populist, Felipe Kast, finished second.

The Uruguayan Frente Amplio governed Uruguay for a remarkable run of eighteen years (2002–2020). However, even though it developed the most institutionalised party structure of the region, it too faced strong opposition. Moreover, the opposing sectors were similar to those that mobilised against the left populism of Argentina. The main opposition to President Tabaré Vázquez's government in 2018 came from agricultural producers; they staged massive protests, which resembled the producers' blockades against Cristina Fernández de Kirchner's government in 2008.

The most relevant case is the Brazilian Partido Trabalhista (PT) – a leftist mass party built on the classic model, whose original leader and directive cadres were hardened from years of union organising in the metalwork factories of São Paulo, and through anti-dictatorship militancy. The PT climbed towards the presidency from the bottom up, gaining municipal and local elections before winning nationally; leader Lula da Silva ran for president three times before finally winning in 2004. His eight years in government were lauded by their moderation – the PT did not write a new constitution, did not seek to change property rights and implemented pro-market policies. It was a successful tenure: economic growth was impressive, fifty million Brazilians were lifted out of poverty, and Brazil was a stabilising influence for the entire South American region. When Lula's constitutional term came to an end, he did not try to force his way into a new term but came out in support of his former minister of economics, Dilma Rousseff.

Rousseff sought to court the powerful Brazilian industrial elite with even more pro-business policies. And yet, she was impeached on rather thin grounds in 2016 and forced out of government. Shortly after that, Lula da Silva, who had been hailed in international forums as a success story, was charged with corruption and served two years of prison time. The charges were ultimately thrown out by the Brazilian Supreme Court after it was discovered that the trial judge had fabricated evidence.

In sum, moderation and institutionalisation do not correlate with dramatically higher presidential resilience. Moderate President Bachelet's agenda was effectively blocked, President Rousseff was impeached and Lula da Silva was imprisoned, and the Frente Amplio faced very strong opposition from 2014 onwards. Leftism, not populism, seems to be the polarising element in South American politics.

## 8. Populist Antagonism, Mobilisation and Resilience

To recapitulate, three arguments have been presented so far. Firstly, that South American populist governments showed a remarkable degree of resilience, they all had the ability to win elections, wield power and survive serious threats to their stability. They were as resilient as the non-populist, moderate, institutional left governments, and in some cases even more so. I have tried to show that the resilience of populist governments cannot be explained only because of the high commodity prices of the time or by the relative absence of political opposition.

To isolate the source of this resilience into just one element or variable is probably impossible. The cycle of high commodity prices probably contributed to the stability of these governments, as did their coming into power amidst the vacuum caused by the delegitimation of the mainstream political parties in the face of the crisis of neoliberalism. However, these two elements cannot explain the outcomes fully. I argue that a populist antagonistic strategy was not a problem but rather a valuable tool in facilitating resilience. The search for consensus and the rejection of polarisation was not seen as a winning strategy necessarily in the context of those turbulent years. My argument is that the populist strategy of the personalisation of the hero (the leader) and the antagonisation of a villain played a part in the creation of resilience; that is, the ability to respond to a hostile political environment. The 'street mobilisation shield' was the key element in the ability to survive sudden and grave political threats, including impeachment, mass protests and attempts at sedition.

Lugo is a key case for establishing this comparison. Lugo's rise to power followed a similar pattern as that followed by Morales or Correa. A Catholic bishop with years of social activism in the leftist wing of the Catholic Church, Lugo was able to present himself as a political outsider with links to the poor. While in power, Lugo was close with the presidents of the left populist group, he appeared with them often and his discourse touched upon the same themes.

However, as I have argued elsewhere (Casullo, 2019, pp. 112–116), he was by far the less populist of the group. His discourse emphasised themes of humility, moderation and self-sacrifice, he did not personalise the antagonism with any concrete person or elite group. And, more importantly, he never called for his supporters to mobilise in his defence once the impeachment procedures started.

The ability to call one's supporters into the streets on very short notice is one of the most important elements in explaining the capacity to overcome a serious political crisis. Chávez's lieutenants called upon his supporters to not leave the city squares even as he was put in prison and foreign governments welcomed in the new administration. Morales also called upon his supporters to mobilise when the eastern Bolivian provinces threatened to secede in 2007. In 2008, the so-called *crisis del campo* involved massive marches and counter-marches, with hundreds of thousands mobilising against the government of Cristina Fernández de Kirchner; counter-mobilisations were immediately called to balance them. Néstor Kirchner personally attended one of the first counter-rallies, which had spontaneously mobilised, in the middle of the night and with no security.

The clearest example of the role played by mobilisation, however, is Correa's reaction to his kidnapping by members of the police. In 2010, Rafael Correa decided to go to where members of the police forces were staging a protest against wage reforms. Against the advice of his security team, Correa decided to attempt to speak with them personally; chaos ensued after his arrival, with pro-government and anti-government police forces clashing. The president's security team managed to get him into a military hospital, which in turn was surrounded by hostile police forces. In the few hours in which Correa's whereabouts were unknown, riots and clashes started in several Ecuadorian cities, with some anti-government groups taking over a TV station, for instance. Correa's response was to force all TV channels to broadcast the crisis for eight hours straight, and to give an impassioned plea from a balcony during which he highlighted the threat of violence against his life by tearing his shirt open. Following Correa's speech, a multitude came into the streets and marched towards the site of Correa's imprisonment; at least one person was killed in the clashes. Then, an elite military unit stormed the hospital and rescued Correa.

Lugo's reaction to the news of his impeachment was very different. He broadcast a short, recorded video message in which he said he would accept the results of the congressional procedures and would leave power if impeached. He did not call for mobilisation, and he did not present himself as physically endangered. The Congress voted for his dismissal, and he left promptly. It is not possible to assert whether he did not want to mobilise, or whether he judged this insufficient support, but there is no question that the absence of antagonism and mobilisation were an element in the fall in this case.

## 9. Conclusion

This chapter has presented a simple idea – that the constant but malleable antagonism of populism alongside its potential for mobilisation are effective tools in achieving presidential resilience. As such, populism is a perfectly rational political strategy belonging to the political toolkit of presidents concerned with their ability to survive threats to their power. Due to the turbulence and treachery of South American politics, there are many incentives to choose the populist path, as the technocratic 'moderate' one is no guarantee of a successful outcome. Politicians learn early on that polarisation will almost inevitably happen, especially in the case of governments that pursue leftist, or even moderately progressive, policies. If that is the case, it is better to be prepared to come out fighting from the outset.

South American leftist presidents are aware that they will face serious threats to their ability to govern at some point. Even moderate ones will have to show their mettle. If this is true, then, to be able to call upon the support of a mobilised public marching on the streets with the explicit commitment to defending the leader on an hour's notice is just as important as having a loyal block in Congress, and the populist strategy helps in this regard.

The goal of this chapter has never been to glorify, or even excuse, populist antagonistic and turbulent politics, but only to situate it within a framework that makes it possible to understand it as a rational, or at the very least effective, strategy of behaviour. This is important because, even though explaining populism by the immorality of leaders and/or the irrationality of the masses might be seductive, that really does not do much to advance the knowledge of the topic. It runs the risk of giving way to a kind of nihilism; while institutional and political incentives are within the reach of concerted action, individual morality and collective rationality seem much harder to alter.

The idea, then, is merely to shed light on the fact that there is an inherent rationality to them. Any rational political behaviour ultimately relates to incentives and contexts, and this cannot be changed simply by appealing to individual morality. And, conversely, if the leader's decision to keep their followers mobilised is a rational one, so is the follower's decision to heed their leader's call in times of crisis. For it is not irrational to decide to participate in a collective effort to sustain a deeply held narrative of threat, survival and collective resilience. It can be an unsuccessful quest, or even a defeated one. But, at the end of the day, is that not also what politics is about?

## Notes

1. The idea of a 'street shield' for presidents presented in this chapter was born out of a conversation with my friend and colleague Andrés Malamud, a professor at the University of Lisbon. Any flaws in the argument, however, are all mine.
2. I will treat Néstor Kirchner's (president from 2003 to 2007) and Cristina Fernández de Kirchner's tenures (2007–2015) as just one presidency. There was no functional difference between the two; Néstor and Cristina met in college, married in their early twenties, developed their political careers in close consultation, and governed as a functional unit until Néstor Kirchner's death in 2010.
3. 'Populist myths belong to the class of political myths, but they are unique in that the commonality between all of those who form the "us" is anchored in the common feature of having been recently wronged by a nefarious elite. Hence, the temporal organisation of all populist myths follows the same structure, there is a people who in the past was wronged by a nefarious "them"; it suffers in the present, but, aided by a redeemer, it will be vindicated in the future' (Casullo, 2020, p. 29).
4. The study of regime resilience is not a common topic in Latin America (Remmer, 1992), even as democracy has shown to be remarkably resilient in the last forty years.
5. With some exceptions, most notably Perú in the 1990s, Venezuela after 2013, Bolivia between 2019 and 2021.
6. The examples presented so far have been left populists, but there are some impressive examples of right populism resilience. I mentioned earlier the case of the Argentine Peronist Carlos Menem (1989–1999). A more recent case was the Colombian presidency of Alvaro Uribe (2002–2010). Both Menem and Uribe were forbidden from seeking re-election under their respective constitutions; both of them were able to write new ones and win a second term in power.
7. Levitsky and Roberts (2011, p. 11), 'Indeed, many recent analyses converge around the idea that there are "two Lefts" in the region (…) Thus, the "radical" or "wrong" Left is said to be characterized by personalistic leadership, statist economic policies, and more autocratic rule, whereas the "moderate" or "right" Left is said to be institutionalized, market-oriented, and democratic.'

## References

Canovan, M. (2005) *The people*. Cambridge: Polity.
Casullo, M. E. (2019) *¿Por qué funciona el populismo?* Siglo XXI Editores.
Casullo, M. E. (2020) 'Populism and myth', in Eklundh, E. and Knott, A. (eds) *The populist manifesto*. London: Rowman & Littlefield, pp. 25–38.
Chacaltana, J. (2017) 'Peru, 2002–2012, growth, structural change and formalization', *CEPAL Review*, 2016(119), pp. 45–64. DOI: 10.18356/78b19d57-en.
Cruces, G., Fields, G. S., Jaume, D. and Viollaz, M. (2017) *Growth, employment and poverty in Latin America*. Oxford: Oxford University Press. DOI: 10.1093/oso/9780198801085.003.0019.
Garay, C. and Etchemendy, S. (2011) 'Left populism in comparative perspective, 2003–2009', in *The resurgence of the Latin American left*. Baltimore, MD: Johns Hopkins University Press, pp. 283–305.
Krämer, B. and Holtz Bacha, C. (2020) *Perspectives on populism and the media*. Baden Baden: Nomos Verlag.
Laclau, E. (2005) *On populist reason*. London: Verso.
Levitsky, S. and Roberts, K. M. (2011) *The resurgence of the Latin American left*. Baltimore, MD: Johns Hopkins University Press.
Levitsky, S. and Ziblatt, D. (2019) *How democracies die*. New York: Broadway Books.
López-Calva, L. and Lustig, N. (2010) *Declining inequality in Latin America*. Washington DC: UNDP and Brookings Institution Press.
Mendonça, R. F. and Caetano, R. D. (2021) 'Populism as parody, the visual self-presentation of Jair Bolsonaro on Instagram', *The International Journal of Press/Politics*, 26 (1), pp. 210–235.
Mudde, C. and Kaltwasser, C. R. (2017) *Populism: a very short introduction*. Oxford: Oxford University Press.
Norris, P. and Inglehart, R. (2019) *Cultural backlash, Trump, Brexit, and authoritarian populism*. Cambridge: Cambridge University Press.
Pérez Liñán, A. (2007) 'Building a legislative shield, the institutional determinants of impeachment', in *Presidential impeachment and the new political instability in Latin America*. Cambridge: Cambridge University Press, pp. 132–175.
Remmer, K. L. (1992) 'The process of democratization in Latin America', *Studies in Comparative International Development*, 27 (4), pp. 3–24. DOI: 10.1007/bf02687137.
Roberts, K. M. (2003) 'Social correlates of party system demise and populist resurgence in Venezuela', *Latin American Politics and Society*, 45 (03), pp. 35–57. DOI: 10.1111/j.1548-2456.2003.tb00249.x.

Soler, L. (2020) 'Populismo del siglo XXI en América Latina', *Estado & Comunes, Revista de Políticas y Problemas Públicos*, 1 (10), pp. 17–36. DOI: 10.37228/estado_comunes.v1.n10.2020.146.

Stankov, P. (2021) *The political economy of populism, an introduction*. London: Routledge.

Tomsa, D. (2017) 'Regime resilience and presidential politics in Indonesia', *Contemporary Politics*, 24 (3), pp. 266–285. DOI: 10.1080/13569775.2017.1413502.

Torre, J. C. (1997) 'El lanzamiento político de las reformas estructurales en América Latina', *Política y Gestión*, 4 (2), pp. 471–498.

Weyland, K. (2001) 'Clarifying a contested concept: populism in the study of Latin American Politics', *Comparative Politics*, 34 (1), pp. 1–22.

Weyland, K. (2017) 'Populism: a political-strategic approach', in Kaltwasser, C. R. et al. (eds) *The Oxford handbook of populism*. Oxford: Oxford University Press, pp. 48–73.

# 9

# Rupture, Institutionalisation and Tension: About Populist Temporality in Latin America

*Paula Biglieri and Gloria Perelló*

Amidst the global political context in which populism had become a key word, the Foundation of Urgent Spanish declared populism its word of the year in 2016. This was unsurprising given Spanish is the most widespread language in Latin America, a region that has a long tradition of populist politics and was at that point ending a renewed populist wave that had even impacted in Spain with the rise of Podemos. Spanish-speaking people could increasingly hear the term being used in different public spaces: in the media, 'political analysts' used the term in the most uncritical and pejorative way to label any political experience that distanced itself from the model of a neoliberal-oriented representative democracy; politicians started using it as an insult to degrade their opponents; and within academia, students, professors and researchers witnessed how it became (once again, as it had been before in the mid-twentieth century with the period of classical populisms) the predominant issue in debates in the humanities and social sciences, particularly in political science and political theory.

Latin American scholarship has a long tradition of studying populism. Many researchers have addressed a variety of its dimensions. However, little has been said about the dimension of temporality. Thus, in advancing the connection between populism and temporality, the analysis is based on Latin American cases (in particular, the last populist wave of the late twentieth and early twenty-first centuries), which may prove translatable to other contexts. We use Ernesto Laclau and Chantal Mouffe (1985) as a theoretical framework, especially their accounts of hegemony and antagonism, alongside Laclau's (2005) understanding of populism. In what follows, our argumentative strategy will be: first, to briefly map the diverse interventions made by Latin American scholars to present a general review of the tradition on populist studies in the region. Second, after discussing the notion of temporality involved in radical political thought, we explore how the notion of change in Latin American populisms is linked to a rupturist moment related to temporal dislocation. Third, we address how temporal dislocation needs a supplement of spatialisation and what kind of spatialisation is involved in populism. Finally, we develop the idea that there is an ineradicable tension between time and space or, in other words, between rupture and institutionality. This is where 'the heart' of populist politics lies and we explore the different aspects that arise from it.

## 1. (Latin American) Scholarship on Populism

Latin American scholars have historically engaged in the worldwide polemics about populism. In fact, if we do a minimum review, we find that the early interventions of Latin American academics contributed to forge a field of debate mostly dominated by condemnatory readings, a trend initiated in the US academy by Hofstadter's work and other modernisation theorists of the Cold War period (see Stavrakakis, 2017a). The early works of the Italian-Argentine Gino Germani (1956) and his disciple Torcuato Di Tella (1965) were inscribed in this sense: studying the case of Peronism from sociological modernisation's approach deemed populism to be a deviation from the 'rationally correct' (that is, Western-prescribed) social and political path of liberal- and market-oriented development and, as a consequence, had to be avoided. From a left-wing perspective, Latin American scholars introduced a sophistication into the predominance of class-based interpretations that had initially equated populism with Bonapartism or with the fascist experiences (of the 1920s and 1930s in Italy and Germany), and they understood populism as the expression of an inter-class alliance that did not match the worker-led class struggle. For Miguel Murmis and Juan Carlos Portantiero (1971) this inter-class alliance was not irrational, but a pragmatic 'deviation': although it distracted the working class from its main anti-capitalist goal, they regarded Peronism to have fulfilled its most immediate demands. Later on, Portantiero shifted position when writing with Emilio de Ípola (1981). In attempting to differentiate populism from socialism, they insisted that populisms were a 'betrayal' of the popular class struggles because they had transformed the working class into a national-statist force tied to capitalism.

More recently and bringing this overview up to date with the current discussion, Slavoj Žižek (2006) through the sieve of psychoanalysis returned to the initial simplistic interpretation that assimilated populism to fascism. More precisely, he insisted that it had a 'long-term proto-fascist tendency' inasmuch as it always projects the constitutive antagonism of any social being onto a positive identity whose elimination would bring absent fullness back. Éric Fassin (2017) also subscribed to this viewpoint, warning the left not to fall under the 'fascist seduction' of populisms. Contesting Mouffe's (2018) position (who advocated a left populist strategy in Western Europe as a challenge to the ascendant right), Fassin affirmed that populism always brings about the worst right-wing authoritarian elements, dissolving the multiple pluralities into the homogeneous unity that is the people. For both Žižek and Fassin, populism can only be placed on the fascist extreme right. Žižek and Fassin have generated responses from Latin American scholars. Using psychoanalysis, Jorge Alemán (2016, 2019) offered the opposite reading: it is not just that populisms are not a form of fascism, but 'right-wing populism' is an impossibility. Moreover, populism can only have an emancipatory orientation because, in facing the uninterrupted and totalising neoliberal circuit, it attempts to install a circuit-break (the people) that would enable the establishment of frontier effects through the articulation of a variety of elements that never cancel the difference. Following Alemán, two Latin American women, Paula Biglieri and Luciana Cadahia (2021), also asserted that populism has an emancipatory dimension as it is constitutively traversed by the egalitarian logic of the people. It is the attachment of the qualifier 'right-wing' to populism that facilitates its confusion with populism. Instead, they insist that populism and fascism are entirely different phenomena, wherein the former articulates differences that construct an heterogeneous people, while the latter homogenises them in an attempt to collapse them into a people-as-one. In this way, Alemán, and Biglieri and Cadahia, also distanced themselves from those Essex School scholars with whom they hold close theoretical positions, such as Mouffe (2018), Yannis Stavrakakis (2017b, Stavrakakis & Katsambekis 2015, Stavrakakis et al., 2017c) and Oliver Marchart (2018), for whom populism can have orientations of both the left and right.

Latin American scholars have held views that cut against the grain on a number of issues. Feminists had a say, Mercedes Barros and Martínez (2020), Malena Nijensohn (2019, 2022), Biglieri (2020), Biglieri and Cadahia (2021) – participating in a large debate on populism and feminism that included authors such as Jenny Gunnarsson-Payne (2020) and Elżbieta Korolczuk (Gunnarsson-Payne & Korolczuk, 2021) – questioned the long-held view that populism and feminism are incompatible with each other and discussed to what extent is 'feminist populism' or a 'populist feminism' possible. Against the widely held view that populisms are the other side of institutions, a set of Latin American scholars explored the link between populism and republicanism. Carlos M. Vilas (2009) described populism as a practical republicanism which gives priority to the welfare of the people rather than to private interests and privileges, materialising it in rights and public regulations. Eduardo Rinesi and Matías Muraca (2010) went further, affirming that populism is the form through which republicanism has developed in Latin America. Valeria Coronel and Luciana Cadahia (2018) have explored what kind of institutions populisms generate, considering that once in power they attempt to construct counter-hegemonic institutions that include the irruption of popular forces within their institutional arrangements. Researchers have also questioned another widespread opinion: that populism holds an exclusively national dimension. The debate around the possibility of a transnational populism has had few voices; namely: De Cleen et al. (2019), Mark Devenney (2020) or Luis Blengino (2019). Blengino, a Latin American, differentiated reactionary populisms (nationalist and xenophobic authoritarianism) from the emancipatory ones, whose main characteristic is their transnational dimension because, for emancipatory populisms, there is no possibility of defeating local oligarchies without also embracing the international context as a frame for their struggle. Another crucial aspect of debates has been the ontological status of populism. Ernesto Laclau (2005), the Latin American initiator of the Essex School, has been the main protagonist of this debate, and has argued that populism is a constitutive dimension of politics. The position in favour of an ontological reading of populism can be found in Biglieri and Gloria Perelló (2020), Biglieri and Cadahia (2021), as well as in Oliver Marchart (2018); while it has been rejected by Benjamin Arditi (2003, 2005), also from Latin America, who proposes to discard the term, and Devenney (2020). Finally, we turn to another two Latin American women, Senda Sferco (2015) and María José Rossi (2021), who have worked on the relation between populism and the baroque through rhetorical analysis. Rossi affirms that Latin American populism should be better named baroque populism because of its metaphoric richness born from the creative vitality of its communities which is elusive to univocal meaning, domestication or one-dimensional reduction. Sferco compares populism with the baroque, considering that while the baroque articulates heterogeneous elements through allegory, her case study of Peronism does so through metaphor. Then, by introducing the notion of 'temporalities' from Giacomo Marramao, Sferco distances her analysis from Laclau by de-metaphorising Peronism by bringing it closer to the baroque. In passing, Sferco also addressed the neglected issue of populist temporality, although it shares affinities with Samuele Mazzolini's (2020) critique of Laclau's populist temporality.

This overview of the Latin American literature on populism, while not claiming to be exhaustive, reveals the richness of the variety of works in this field, while at the same time showing the absence of works on the temporal dimension. This is the point we will address below.

## 2. The Attraction of Temporal Dislocation

The French Revolution shaped the Jacobin notion of change that would prevail over radical political thought for two centuries: the idea of emancipation linked to an event, the revolution conceived as a cut that clearly establishes a before and an after, and that opens up a new historical moment as an absolute beginning. Šumič characterises this as 'a messianic redemption from historical time' (2004, p. 184). Marxism and the different threads of socialism during the nineteenth and twentieth centuries followed this model of political change, until it was abandoned after the collapse of real socialist experiences, their totalitarian drift, the fall of the Berlin Wall and the deconstruction of Marxism (see Laclau & Mouffe, 1985; Laclau, 1990). At that point, conservative academics cheered what they considered the end of historical temporality with the definitive triumph of capitalism in its neoliberal version (see Fukuyama, 1992). This was presented as the counterpart to the historical defeat of Marxism alongside its prediction of the end of history through the arrival of a fully reconciled society. On the other side, left theorists began to think about what would be coming for the left 'after the deluge' (Paramio, 1988). The discussion soon shifted to that of mourning. Initiated by Jacques Derrida (1993), this reached a high point with the 2003 special issue of *Parallax* in which thinkers as diverse as Wendy Brown, Martin Jay, Julia Kristeva and Arnaud Spire, Rado Riha, Yannis Stavrakakis, Alain Badiou and Benjamin Arditi gathered under the title 'Mourning Revolution'. The hovering question was how to think about change, and whether it was still possible, now that a 'once and for all' transformation was unavailable. 'Mourning revolution' brought about the cancellation of the utopia of a time to come which would bring the closure of any kind of oppression and, consequently, complete emancipation. The result was a paralysing and overwhelming neoliberal 'presentism: a diluted and expanded present absorbing and dissolving in itself both past and future' (Hartog, quoted in Traverso, 2016, pp. 7–8). If the possibility of a horizon of change was cancelled because a collective disconnection from neoliberalism was considered impossible, all the symbolic legacies of social and political struggles aimed at creating a different order were also cancelled as futile past attempts. All that remained was a kind of absolute present, a never-ending loop that returns us to the same place of a dead-end present. In such a context of no imagination for the future, there were no attempts of changes capable of recreating any emancipatory idea, not even the so-called 'velvet revolutions' in Eastern Europe after the Soviet breakdown, nor the Arab revolutions in 2011, both of which ended up being swallowed by presentism. Hence Traverso's diagnosis:

In short, the turn of the twenty-first century coincided with the transition from the 'principle of hope' to the 'principle of responsibility.' The 'principle of hope' inspired the battles of the past century, from Petrograd in 1917 to Managua in 1979, passing through Barcelona in 1936 and Paris and Prague in 1968. It haunted also its most terrible moments and encouraged resistance movements in Nazi Europe. The 'principle of responsibility' appeared when the future darkened, when we discovered that revolutions had generated totalitarian monsters, when ecology made us aware of the dangers menacing the planet and we began to think about the kind of world we will give to future generations. (Traverso, 2016, p. 6)

However, beyond the generalised disheartenment and resignation implicit in the appearance of the 'principle of resignation' mostly in the Global North, at the turn of the twenty-first century a reactivation of the 'principle of hope' was already under way in Latin America, with its tradition of popular struggles under the sign of populism. We are referring to the new series of populist governments in the region that started when Hugo Chávez was elected as the president of Venezuela in 1999, Néstor Kirchner in Argentina in 2003 (succeeded by his wife Cristina Fernández de Kirchner in 2007), Evo Morales in Bolivia in 2006 and Rafael Correa in Ecuador in 2006, and which brought about a renewed hope in politics as a (collective) practice to struggle for emancipation and change people's life.[1] Thus, the 'principle of hope' can be reinterpreted in Margaret Canovan's terms as 'the redemptive face of democracy' (1999, p. 10); which, in turn, refers to Michael Oakeshott's (1996) 'politics of faith' – the style that considers politics the terrain to make extraordinary things happen to change governments and people's lives through the mobilisation of popular enthusiasm.[2] The question is: When is the 'principle of hope' unleashed? This is the point at which populist temporality enters the scene: the temporal dislocation enables a subjective shift away from one of subordination (Laclau & Mouffe, 1985, pp. 136–137). In populist terms it means the moment that allows 'the passage from the underdog (a variety of subordinated non-politicised and non-articulated differential positions) to the people (a political subjectivity of articulated differences through leadership and organisation) as a site of antagonism' (Biglieri, 2023).[3]

The first aspect we can point out about populist temporality is that the emergence of new populist formations is usually related to a moment of reactivation that makes explicit the constitutive dislocation of any social space. Edmund Husserl initially coined the pair reactivation and sedimentation, although we will follow Laclau's reformulation (1990). Sedimentation refers to naturalised practices whose initial moment of institution has been obscured, while reactivation is the moment when such practices are called into question and the original, forgotten link becomes visible again. For Husserl, reactivation is a philosophical matter, since the task of phenomenological intervention is to reactivate the original meaning that lies at the root of sedimented practices; for Laclau, on the contrary, it is a political task. This is because reactivation reveals the contingent character of all 'objectivity' insofar as it reveals that those sedimented practices arose because one decision prevailed when others were also available. Thus, any moment of reactivation contains a kind of re-foundational ethos that suspends order as its sedimented practices have been called into question and paused.

Neoliberal 'presentism' was suspended in Latin America with the arrival of Chávez, and the arrival of a new series of populist governments. In Venezuela, Argentina, Bolivia and Ecuador, their rise was preceded by a widespread questioning of the neoliberal model that affected the whole sociopolitical and economic arrangements that had prevailed until that point through its presentation as the only possible reality. Let us see the examples. In Venezuela it was the breakdown of the elite amalgamated around the 'Fixed Point Pact', which had regulated for decades the cohabitation between two dominating political parties which were supported by numerous institutions – the armed forces, the Catholic hierarchy, the main trade union confederation and the largest business sector organisation. These elites embraced the neoliberal agenda (at least since the economic crisis arrived with the abrupt fall of the international crude oil prices in the 1970s) and were met by a response in February 1989, with the event known as *Caracazo* (named after Caracas, Venezuela's capital). A riot that started in Caracas quickly spread out to the whole country because of price rises in public transport and oil. Mass popular pillaging ensued, and the government-decreed curfew and crackdown led to hundreds of deaths. The social space became divided into the elite of the 'Fixed Point Pact' and the underdog, whose discontent found its expression years later, first in February 1992 when Chávez (then an unknown young military major) led a failed coup d'état but was eventually elected president in 1999. In Argentina it was the interruption of neoliberal routines organised around the 'Convertibility Law' of 1991 that fixed the peso to the US dollar. The debt crisis unleashed in December 2001 pushed the government to restrict access to salaries and savings, accelerating levels of unemployment and poverty which provoked ongoing and widespread social discontent involving attacks on banks, looting in supermarkets, and the disregard of the decreed state of siege as people took to the streets with a variety of demands that converged in the slogan 'everybody has to leave, no one must remain' and the creation of popular assemblies. In this way the formation of two places of enunciation – 'us, the ordinary neighbours or people' in relation to 'them, the elites' – took place. Fernando de la Rua eventually resigned in December 2001 and five further presidents were consecutively named within ten days. Social demonstrations continued and the dichotomisation of social space provided the ground from which Kirchner built his leadership after becoming president in 2003. In Bolivia the reactivation of the neoliberal sedimented practices came along with the so-called 'Rebel cycle' in 2000 and 2005. The peculiarity of Bolivia was that the neoliberal arrangements included a distinctive element – the 'fight against drug dealing' – to the extent that the United States gave financial aid and approval of the IMF goals conditional on not only the implementation of austerity but also to progress in coca leaf eradication. The defence of the coca leaf was the nodal point from which the whole indigenous peasant movement broke out, resulting in the 'Rebel cycle' that was the antagonistic expression of the social space division between those above (the US and its local allies, the national government and the traditional oligarchies) and those below (the indigenous peasants). The symbolic defence of the coca leaf converged into a national sovereignty issue, through the incorporation of demands to protect threats to livelihoods and natural resources alongside accusations of racism and exclusion. The peasants' practices of resistance – including road blocks, demonstrations, hunger strikes and even direct clashes with security forces resulting in peasant deaths – disabled the reproduction of neoliberal practices leading to the 2005 election of Evo Morales, the main cocalero leader. In Ecuador, sedimented practices were reactivated through the protest known as the 'revolution of the bandits', which took place mainly in the city of Quito in April 2005 and overthrew President Lucio Gutiérrez. 'Bandit' was the derogatory name the government bestowed on the protestors, but it was semantically appropriated by them. Gutiérrez, the third successive president removed from office, was a military man who secured office by forging an alliance between the 'Pachakutik Movement' (the electoral branch of the indigenous movement) and the 'Popular Democratic Movement', a left-wing party representing students and teaching unions – but, once in office, formed a cabinet that continued with the neoliberal orthodoxy and aligned with the Colombian Plan of the Washington-Bogota axis.[4] The massive demonstration in Quito, which started with the demand 'Lucio (Gutiérrez) has to leave', easily slipped into 'everybody has to leave' and, as in Argentina's crisis in 2001, provoked a dichotomisation of the social space into two: 'the corrupt politicians' versus 'the common people', or 'the *partidocracia*' versus 'the people'. This was the terrain in which Rafael Correa, a young economist opposing neoliberalism, won the presidential election in 2006.

All these examples reveal that neoliberal presentism was called into question, undermining the claim that it was the only reality available. In addition, they departed from traditional Marxist-informed left schemas that inserted these struggles into the 'historically necessary' class struggles and analysis. Instead, they should be understood as effects of dislocation which interrupted the continuity of sedimented (neoliberal) practices, revealing their contingency and, in doing so, opened up new possibilities for the future. The suspension of neoliberal presentism demonstrated that any order with its sedimentations was disputable, and many possible futures were available. The suspension of any given order is what Laclau called 'the very form of temporality' (1990, p. 41). These events opened a time for imagining the future, reactivating the 'principle of hope' which was subjectively expressed with joy at the detachment from what was supposedly an inexorable destiny, although it also implied the vertigo and the fear that uncertainty provokes with the loss of established references and the struggle on the streets. In short, participating in direct actions such as pan-banging, debating politics in neighbourhood assemblies, disobeying the state of siege, rejecting established authorities, and so on, were all dislocatory events that can be summarised in two temporal phrases: the anonymous graffiti that appeared on the streets of Buenos Aires, 'let it come what never was'; and, Morales' phrase, 'this is when'.

However, temporality needs the supplement of spatiality. We are capable of recognising these events in their whole dislocatory dimension, only in relation to the spatial hegemonies they shook. In Laclau's terms, 'the very form of temporality' can only be identified insofar as it has effects in a spatial structure. Thus, the commotion of the established hierarchies' status due to the unmaking of assigned places and the creation of new ones is what retroactively allows us to say that those were dislocatory events. In all the aforementioned cases, what retroactively allows us to indicate that we are facing a rupture that gives rise to populism is the unmaking of the place of the underdog (disperse subordinated subjectivities) and the creation of two new places that put into question the designation between those at the top and those at the bottom: first, the people (who emerge from their heterogeneity as a political subject) and, second, the place of the – populist – leader (who links together different particular demands into a chain of equivalence through their name). This produces the widespread politicisation of the social space, divided into two antagonistic places of enunciation (the people versus the oligarchy, the oppressor, and so on).

At this point it is worth mentioning that if we look at the classical Latin American populisms, those of the early and mid-twentieth century, we also find that they were preceded by moments of reactivation: the Mexican Revolution as the prelude of Cardenism, Varguism emerging out of the Prestes Column and the revolution of the 1930s in Brazil, and the 17 October 1945 events that led to Peronism in Argentina. However, the way in which the space of the popular field was structured differs. The emergence of classical populism brought into 'the public arena largely virgin masses with a weak degree of corporate organisation and identity' (Laclau, 2013, p. 16). Then, the organisations (national trade unions, militant neighbourhood formations) that assisted the formation of the people were themselves in the process of formation. In contrast, 'the new populisms are based on much more structured civil societies and much more autonomous social actors in their collective action' (Laclau, 2013, p. 16) – such as unemployed workers' movements (*piqueteros*), human rights organisations or indigenous trade unions (*cocaleros*), and so on. Thus, this time the creation of both the people and the leader 'is verified through social agents whose original identity was constituted outside the populist chain of equivalence and whose autonomy cannot be renounced' (Laclau, 2013, p. 17). This is the achievement of the political task of reactivation: the creation of a popular field forging the relationship between the emerging leader and the people. The task of the constitution of a populism is successful as long as it manages to make what had been declared impossible (from within the sedimented order) seem possible.

## 3. After Temporality: Spatialisation

The inscription of a new people under the name of a leader (Chavism, Kirchnerism, and so on) entails a re-foundational ethos but not in the way the traditional left has proclaimed it. We find at least two differences: there are no attempts within the populist re-foundational ethos to declare a clear break and the inauguration of an absolute beginning, nor to announce a post-political 'reconciled society' completely free of antagonisms.

Regarding the first aspect, populisms build their legitimacy through the creation of a chronological spatialisation placing themselves within a series connecting the past, the present and the future. Although they claim to be 'the new', born from the temporal rupture and the suspension of a certain spatial distribution, they always construct a narrative that situates themselves in relation to the history of their home country and, more broadly, Latin America, with a particular focus on inscribing themselves as part of the history of the tradition of popular struggles. We find no attempt to achieve a *tabula rasa* as a starting point from which to build a future anew, but to situate themselves as the heirs of past struggles of 'those from below' that were defeated or did not reach their full realisation. Subaltern social sectors, marginal historical characters, events and antagonisms are brought from the past to the present and are reinscribed, reinterpreted and launched into the future. As a consequence, sites of memory are established through new commemorative holidays, monuments, museums and spaces of political significance while there is a reformulation of the dominant Latin American historiographical discourses traditionally hegemonised by the nineteenth-century liberal-conservative tradition. Ordinary people, workers, peasants, slaves, indigenous, blacks, mestizos, mulattos, and so on, alongside marginalised popular leaders of independence struggles and prior antagonists of the old conservative–liberal–oligarchic regimes such as Juana Azurduy, Manuel Dorrego, Mariano Moreno, Tupac Amaru, Tupac Katari, Manuela Sáenz Aizpuru or Eloy Alfaro – all of these are repositioned in the historical narrative alongside central heroes like Simón Bolivar, José de San Martín or Manuel Belgrano. They are all reassumed as part of the current struggles to mend the damage of the past and build a future order different from the present of shame and injustice. Thus, they take up a series that continues with the popular struggles and popular leaders of the twentieth century (adding Augusto Sandino, Emiliano Zapata, Juan Domingo Perón, Ernesto Che Guevara, Salvador Allende, amongst others to this sequence), which they themselves take on in the present to redeem the oppressed, to reverse defeats and to reshape a future of hope. A clear example of this construction is the repetitive appealing to the Bolivarian political project of the 'Great Latin American Homeland', a truncated political project of regional unity that left an indelible trace in the popular imaginary, and that has been defended by all the region's different populist leaders throughout its history. The 'Great Latin American Homeland' disseminated the idea that it is only through solidarity among the region's oppressed peoples and through antagonisms with their local oligarchies that this optimistic future will be secured – an idea articulated from Perón to Chávez.

The populist re-foundational ethos implies an updated renewal of the historical traces informing the popular imaginary. Even the constituent processes followed this logic: the legitimacy of contemporary radical institutional change was based on grievances of the past and the present, whereby the reparation of the latter would begin to address the damage of the former. Emancipation from the yoke of 'those above' necessarily implies an egalitarian push that repudiates that imposed spatial distribution of the past. So it was with Peronism's 1949 constitution, which dismantled oligarchic rule and enshrined social and labour rights and political legal equality for women. And in the last populist period, the 1999 constitution that inaugurated the Bolivarian Republic of Venezuela included forms of political participation encouraging the direct involvement of the people (including the removal of all public officers through referendum) and guaranteed social and economic rights, to health, education, social security and beyond. Ecuador's 2008 constitution furthermore established its general orientation under the principle of *Sumak Kawsay* – 'Good Living' in *Quechua*. As with Bolivia's constitution of 2009, these new foundational texts aimed at dismantling the 'colonial state',[5] while including the indigenous as equal members of the people. Through these re-foundational texts, Ecuador and Bolivia became pluri-national states. Here, it is worth drawing a contrast with the 'ethno-national populisms' of the Global North. These uphold the fantasy of the people-as-one protected by a state that aims to return to a mythical, original and uncontaminated race or nationality, while pluri-national states assume the heterogeneity of the people by recognising the existence of diverse nations, cultures and languages – all to be equally included and respected in their autonomy within the communitarian space.

Populisms also avoid implementations of a post-political order. This entails the repressive spatialisation of politics, which 'sought to transcend politics through the creation of conflict-free societies fulfilling a universal conception of the "true human interest", thereby eliminating social conflict and the need of politics' (Schwartz, quoted in Stavrakakis, 2011, p. 2). Nor do they attempt to avoid any spatialisation, aestheticising the moment of reactivation which they would remain fascinated by even within contexts of temporal dislocation. Although they hold an anti-institutionalist impulse, populisms are not 'pure' rupture as their goals exceed merely breaking with the status quo. They also feature a counter-hegemonic will that seeks to institutionally translate the moment of reactivation from which the people and its leader emerged. Here, there is an effort to spatialise the event but without a claim to a totality free of antagonisms and politics. As Valeria Coronel and Luciana Cadahia (2018) affirm, populism aims to build an institutionality that can account for the irruption of the popular masses into politics and, at the same time, 'keep the figure of an empowered people alive' (2018, p. 77). This is where the 'heart' of populist politics lies: in the irresoluble tension between time and space or, in other words, between rupture and institutionality. On the one hand, populisms need to give a response to the moment of reactivation with an institutionalising effort capable of creating a distribution of spaces different from the previous order that entail new practices of sedimentation. And, on the other hand, they need to appeal to an almost permanent popular mobilisation to keep something of the moment of reactivation alive. To have the people out on the streets expressing support for the leader and, where applicable, the government is the way the people is kept active, allowing the circulation of new demands and bestowing legitimacy on the new institutional arrangements. If a populist leader wants to remain popular, s/he necessarily needs to operate within this tension. Populist virtuosity is to ensure that the repetition implied by spatialisation does not drown enthusiasm and hope. Thus, bringing about palpable changes to everyday life becomes an almost permanent populist imperative.

We can see how populist spatialisation works through three spatial metaphors that are most widely deployed in social structuration (Stavrakakis, 2011): above/below, exclusion/inclusion, public/private. Mid-twentieth-century classical populisms called into question the spatialisation of oligarchic regimes as they broke with their institutionalisation of spaces. Under oligarchic regimes, while in the public sphere each property owner was declared a free citizen, in the private sphere a very different spatialisation ensued. Here, the underdog was at the mercy of all the patron owned: land, factory, peasants, workers, maids, butlers, even wife and children. This was the distribution that classical populisms interrupted, through a whole set of laws and institutions. For instance, Peronism extended rights such that the state encroached into domains the oligarchy previously regarded as untouchable. Thus, we find the development of labour rights with the creation of labour courts as a branch of the judicial power (setting public mediation between capital and labour), regulatory statutes (ordinances regulating the activities of peasantry, industry or trade) and mandatory collective labour agreements (deals between companies and trade union representatives, concerning aspects such as wages, amount of working hours, overtime, decent working conditions, severance pay, minimum wage, supplementary annual salary, paid holidays, right to strike, the extension of the pension system coverage). All of this new institutionality along with the massive unionisation promoted by the state enabled a change in the correlation of forces between those above and those below. This extension of rights also enabled the inclusion of women into politics, overturning their prior exclusion, through a bill enabling women's suffrage, which led to women deputies entering National Congress. With the last populist wave at the turn of the millennium, it was the neoliberal spatialisation which was called into question. These populisms sought to reinstate the primacy of the logics of public space, collective organisation and solidarity – core features of classical populisms that had been discarded by neoliberalism. This strengthened the state through intervention in the private sphere: regulating markets, imposing progressive regulation of incomes, pushing up wages and wealth distribution, reversing austerity measures while developing social policies, supporting unions, nationalising private-public services companies (for instance, Bolivia's natural resources were nationalised, including gas, the country's main source of income, while Argentina's retirement and pension system was nationalised returning to the public solidarity system), and investments in public systems of education, health and housing, and so on. However, the demands regarding equality that supported the respatialisation went beyond the elements associated with classical populisms. For instance, the chains of equivalence that constituted the people were extended in Bolivia and Ecuador to large majorities such as the indigenous, previously subordinated but now participating in the process of policy-making as a political subjectivity. And in Argentina, the extension absorbed the demands of a diversity of minority political subjectivities such as the LGBTI+ movement that was then included as equal part of the people, through bills such as 'egalitarian marriage' and 'gender identity'.[6] All of this indicates a more heterogeneous and complex weave in the construction of the people and, therefore, in structuring the antagonism between 'those above, oppressors' and 'those below, oppressed'.

Two further aspects of spatialisation present in both classical and recent populisms are offered as a way of conclusion. Firstly, although the state is a fundamental space for the inscription of demands, the prevalence of the idea of the 'Great Latin American Homeland' shows that populist spatialisation is not exclusively confined to the nation-state. The oppressors–oppressed dichotomisation has its international correlate that is translated into regional institutions that claim to defend the people's sovereignty as a demand for equality amongst nations. This is what was at the basis of the transnational populist politics developed during the last populist period in which the institutional production aimed at creating horizontal spaces of participation that would dispute power with those international institutions dominated by the US, which have historically reproduced the above–below dichotomy in which Latin American countries clearly have a subordinate position. Thus, the Bolivarian Alternative for the Americas (ALBA) in 2004, the Union of South American Nations (UNASUR) in 2008 and the Community of Latin American and Caribbean States (CELAC) in 2010 were created.[7] Secondly, within nation-states the new spatialisation had an impact on geographical locations as the people increasingly appropriated emblematic public spaces for its mobilisation (as with Plaza de Mayo in Buenos Aires, or Plaza Grande del Palacio de Carondelet in Quito). This new popular approach to spatialisation was reinforced by the way 'those from below' accessed places from which they were previously excluded (holiday destinations, leisure or recreational facilities, and so on) bringing the populist antagonism to the ground, body to body, displacing the oligarchy to other geographical spaces.

## 4. Conclusion

We have explored the moment of the populist rupture, its consequent supplementary institutionalisation and the irresoluble tension between both, which is nothing other than the impossibility of the complete domestication of time by space. We have pointed out that this is where the 'heart' of populist politics and the clue of populist virtuosity lies, to keep something of the moment of reactivation alive while spatialising it. However, there is still one last aspect of this tension to highlight.

We have also affirmed that the rupture that gives rise to populism is the one that enables a new spatialisation with the unmaking of the place of the underdog and the creation of two places – the people and its leader. However, if the moment of the populist irruption cannot be totally resolved through a passage to spatialisation, it means that the creation of the people and its leader can never exhaustively absorb the rupturist moment – there are always remainders; more precisely, remainders of subordination as the underdog cannot be totally translated into the people. This tension can also be interpreted as the gap between the moment of the promise and the moment of fulfilling it, which also can be formulated as the gap between the underdog and the people. It is the impossibility of the people to completely overlap the underdog that makes the people a political subjectivity that is always lacking something. And it is what condemns the people to the permanent task of struggling against oppression, which at one point never dies out – the future for populisms, as a result, is always and necessarily open. Populism always requires new demands to revalidate and re-legitimise both the leadership and its actions; it needs to bring about changes that actually can be tangible for the concrete life of the people, and thus entails constant attempts at re-spatialisation, which ultimately sustains its democratic dimension.

## Notes

1. In this respect we explicitly refuse to call this populist period a 'pink tide' because it implies a metaphysics of full presence and also some sort of contempt: as if these governments were not 'leftist' enough to match the complete status of 'red', then they were labelled just 'pink', a 'washed-out' version of the left, and they do not recognise them as political formations with their own characteristics.
2. Oakeshott affirmed that modern politics is criss-crossed by two styles – faith and scepticism – which do not have a dialectical solution and are condemned to inhabit a perpetual *concordia discors*. In turn, 'politics of scepticism' considers that the most that politics can achieve is gradual adjustments through basic minimum schemes of engagement. Any party, government or movement is constituted by these irreconcilable and ineliminable styles. Canovan brought these two styles to the terrain of representative democracy to study populism. She referred to two constitutive and opposing faces of democracy: the redemptive face (politics of faith) and the pragmatic face

(politics of scepticism). The pragmatic face of democracy is characterised by the slogan 'ballots, not bullets' as 'a system of processing conflicts without killing one another' (1999, pp. 9–10). And as Oakeshott previously did, Canovan considers that both faces cannot exist without one another although there is no possibility of reconciliation between them. The gap between one face and the other would allow the emergence of populism.
3. Building 'the people' is one of the main features of populism. Following Laclau we can summarise its constitutive aspects as follows: (a) the experience of a lack; (b) the inscription of that lack as a demand; (c) the primacy of the logic of equivalence between diverse demands over the logic of difference, giving rise to the subjectivity called the 'people' (the plebs that claim to be the only legitimate populus, i.e., that part claiming representation of the whole); (d) the antagonistic dichotomisation of social space into two overdetermined places of enunciation – the people (those below) versus the enemies of the people (those above); and (e) the emergence of a leader.
4. The Colombian Plan was a political agreement between the US and Colombia through which the US government provided military and financial aid to eliminate drug dealing cartels and the left-wing insurrectional guerrilla group called *FARC*. The plan did not match their goals, and subsequently brought about the creation of paramilitary forces, human rights violations, the killing of peasants and popular leaders, massive migrations, and so on.
5. The notion of the 'colonial state' comes from the influence of the *Katarista* movement (named after Tupac Katari, the Aymara leader of the 1781 indigenous revolt against the Spanish colony) that emerged in the 1970s among Aymara students. They interpreted the history of Bolivia as a movement from the Spanish colonial domination to another type of colonialism – an internal one – which ruled through the white or mestizos republican Bolivian elites that dominated the indigenous.
6. It established that any trans person could register his/her personal identification with the name and elected sex, it also ordered to include all the medical treatments of adaptation to gender expression in the Mandatory Medical Programme, what guaranteed those practices in the whole health system, either public or private. This law aims to not pathologise transgender people.
7. These regional institutions displaced the Organisation of American States (dominated by the US) and the Ibero-American Summits (promoted by Spain). For instance, in 2008 UNASUR played a leading role in stopping the civilian coup d'état that threatened Evo Morales in Bolivia. The urgent conclave of the presidents of UNASUR in Santiago de Chile backed Morales, isolating the insurrection against the central government of the

right-wing governors of the Media Luna (the richest areas of Bolivia), which found themselves with no support within the region. The counter-example is the support given by the OAS in 2019 to the civilian coup d'état that could then displace Morales and took Jeanine Áñez to the presidency, backed by the military and police forces and the right-wing political sectors of Bolivia.

## References

Alemán, J. (2016) *Horizontes neoliberales de la subjetividad*. Buenos Aires: Grama Ediciones.

Alemán, J. (2019) *Capitalismo. Crimen perfecto o emancipación*. Buenos Aires: Ned Ediciones.

Arditi, B. (2003) 'Populism, or, politics at the edges of democracy', *Contemporary Politics*, 9 (1), pp. 17–31.

Arditi, B. (2005) 'Populism as spectre of democracy. A response to Canovan', *Political Studies*, 52, pp. 135–146.

Barros, M. and Martínez, N. (2020) 'Let's not talk about it: feminism and populism in Argentina', *Baltic Worlds*, 13 (1), pp. 77–84.

Biglieri, P. (2020) 'Ni Una Menos – not one woman less: how feminism could become a popular struggle', *Baltic Worlds*, 13 (1), 77–84.

Biglieri, P. (2023) 'Peronism and its legacy', in Stavrakakis, Y. and Katsambekis, G. (eds) *Elgar research handbook on populism*. Edward Elgar, forthcoming.

Biglieri, P. and Cadahia, L. (2021) *Seven essays on populism*. Cambridge: Polity Books.

Biglieri, P. and Perelló, G. (2020) 'Populism', in Stavrakakis, Y. (ed.) *Routledge handbook of psychoanalytic political theory*. London: Routledge, pp. 330–340.

Blengino, L. (2019) '¿Qué hay de nuevo, viejo? Populismo transnacional, nacionalismos autoritarios y neoliberalismo global', paper delivered at the Fascism? Populism? Democracy? conference, International Consortium of Critical Theory Programs, University of Brighton.

Canovan, M. (1999) 'Trust the people! Populism and the two faces of democracy', *Political Studies*, XLVII (1), pp. 2–16.

Coronel, V. and Cadahia, L. (2018) 'Populismo republicano: más allá de "Estado versus pueblo"', *Nueva Sociedad*, http://nuso.org/articulo/populismo-republicano-mas-alla-de-estado-versus-pueblo/.

De Cleen, B., Moffitt, B., Panayotu, P. and Stavrakakis, Y. (2019) 'The potentials and difficulties of transnational populism: the case of the Democracy in Europe Movement 2025 (DIEM25)', *Political Studies*, pp. 1–21.

De Ípola, E. and Portantiero, J. C. (1981) 'Lo nacional popular y los populismos realmente existentes', *Nueva Sociedad*, 54, pp. 5–6.

Derrida, J. (1993) *Spectres of Marx. The state of the debt, the work of mourning and the new international.* London: Routledge Classics.

Devenney, M. (2020) *Towards an improper politics.* Edinburgh: Edinburgh University Press.

Di Tella, T. (1965) 'Populism and reform in Latin America', in Véliz, C. (ed) *Obstacles to change in Latin America.* Oxford: Oxford University Press.

Fassin, É. (2017) *Populismo de izquierdas y neoliberalismo.* Barcelona: Herder.

Fukuyama, F. (1992) *The end of history and the last man.* New York: Macmillan.

Germani, G. (1956) *Política y sociedad en una época de transición.* Buenos Aires: Ediciones Paidós.

Gunnarsson-Payne, J. (2020) 'Women as "the people": reflections on the black protests as a counterforce against right-wing and authoritarian populism', *Baltic Worlds*, 13 (1), pp. 6–20.

Gunnarsson-Payne J. and Korolczuk, E. (2021) 'Antigenuspolitik-från globala diskurser till lokala strategier'. Lund: Studenlitteratur, pp. 195–208.

Gunnarsson-Payne, J. and Tornhill, S. (2021c) 'The enemy's enemy: feminism at the crossroads of neoliberal co-optation and anti-gender conservatism', *Journal of Political Ideologies*, https://doi.org/10.1080/13569317.2021.1921937.

Laclau, E. (1990) *New reflections on the revolution of our time.* London and New York: Verso.

Laclau, E. (2005) *On populist reason.* London and New York: Verso.

Laclau, E. (2013) 'Argentina: anotaciones preliminares sobre los umbrales de la política', *Revista Debates y Combates*, 5, pp. 7–18.

Laclau, E. and Mouffe, C. (1985) *Hegemony and socialist strategy: towards a radical democratic politics.* London and New York: Verso.

Marchart, O. (2018) *Thinking antagonism. Political ontology after Laclau.* Edinburgh: Edinburgh University Press.

Mazzolini, S. (2020) 'Populismo y hegemonía entre espacio y tiempo', in Ema, J. E. and Ingala, E. (eds) *Populismo y hegemonía.* Madrid: Lengua de Trapo, pp. 21–36.

Mouffe, C. (2018) *For a left populism.* London and New York: Verso.

Murmis, M. and Portantiero, J. C. (1971) *Estudios sobre los orígenes del peronismo.* Buenos Aires: Siglo XXI.

Nijensohn, M. (2019) *La razón feminista. Políticas de la calle, pluralismo y articulación.* Buenos Aires: Cuarenta Ríos.

Nijensohn, M. (2022) 'Precarity and counter-hegemonic articulation: from the massification of feminisms toward a radical and plural feminism', *International Feminist Journal of Politics*, 24 (1), pp. 133–152.

Oakeshott, M. (1996) *The politics of faith and the politics of scepticism.* New Haven, CT and London: Yale University Press.

*Parallax* (2003) 'Mourning Revolution', *Parallax*, 2 (2).
Paramio, L. (1988) *Tras el diluvio. La izquierda ante el fin de siglo*. Buenos Aires: Siglo XXI.
Rinesi, E. and Muraca, M. (2010) 'Populismo y república. Algunos apuntes sobre un debate actual', in *Si este no es el pueblo. Hegemonía, populismo y democracia*, Buenos Aires: Universidad Nacional de General Sarmiento, pp. 59–73.
Rossi, M. J. (2021) 'Populismo neobarroco: una lectura alternativa al capitalismo tecnofeudal', *Hercritia. Cátedra Internacional de Hermenéutica Crítica*, Buenos Aires, https://www.catedradehermeneutica.org/wp-content/uploads/2021/09/09_Populismo-neobarroco_MARIA-JOSE-Rossi.pdf?fbclid=IwAR2OOeJrkz2OqAOg2kXcG9S7_Y4FZRiXpIpzqgucW1Ehx18XEyfB1saGyp8.
Sferco, S. (2015) '¿Las metáforas tienen un límite? Temporalidad, barroco y peronismo', *Pléyade* (16), pp. 215–234, http://www.revistapleyade.cl/index.php/OJS/issue/view/12.
Stavrakakis, Y. (2011) 'The radical act: towards a spatial critique', *Planning Theory*, pp. 1–24.
Stavrakakis, Y. (2017a) 'How did populism become a pejorative concept? And why is this important today? A genealogy of double hermeneutics', *Populismus* Working Papers No 6.
Stavrakakis, Y. (2017b) 'Discourse theory in populism research. Three challenges and a dilemma', *Journal of Language and Politics*, 16 (4), pp. 523–534.
Stavrakakis, Y. and Katsambekis, G. (2015) 'El populismo de izquierda en la periferia europea: el caso de Syriza', *Revista Debates y Combates*, 5 (7), pp. 153–192.
Stavrakakis, Y., Katsambekis, G., Nikisianis, N., Kioupkiolis, A. and Siomos, T. (2017c) 'Extreme right-wing populism in Europe: revisiting a reified association', *Critical Discourse Studies*, 14 (4), pp. 420–439.
Šumič, J. (2004) 'Anachronism of emancipation or fidelity to politics', in Critchley, S. and Marchart, O. (eds) *Laclau: a critical reader*. London: Routledge, pp. 182–198.
Traverso, E. (2016) *Left-wing melancholia. Marxism, history and memory*. New York: Columbia University Press.
Vilas, C. M. (2009) 'Populismo y democracia en América Latina: convergencias y disonancias', http://cmvilas.com.ar/index.php/articulos/15-populismos/15-populismo-y-democracia-en-america-latina-convergencias-y-disonancias.
Žižek, S. (2006) 'Against the populist temptation', *Critical Inquiry*, 32 (3), pp. 551–574.

# 10

# Populism and Constitutionalism in Brazil: An Enduring or Transitional Relationship in Time?

*Eleonora Mesquita Ceia*

## 1. Introduction

The implementation of populism is not homogenous among South American countries, such that populism in this particular region has many variations. Yet, they are similarly determined by episodes of political and social transition – for instance, the crisis of political traditional elites and the appearance of new political actors – along with other variables such as economic instability.

Brazil serves as a prime case study for the populism-constitutionalism nexus. Since the classical populism of Getúlio Vargas in the 1930s until the far-right authoritarian populism of Jair Bolsonaro, all populist experiences in Brazil have been linked to important changes in society. In consequence, their duration depends on the political and economic circumstances associated with the social transition, which exposes the temporality of populism. However, the emergence of populist regimes and their use of the constitution appears to persist over time.

The constitution occupies an important place in the rhetoric and practices of populist regimes. Populism considers that institutions prevent, due to their formalism and elitism, the direct exercise of democracy by the people. Therefore, it defends a constitutionalism that critically exposes the flaws of representative liberal democracy. However, in certain cases, this constitutional project becomes illiberal, when it aims to defend only the will of one cohesive majority, rather than the plural and political participation by all members and different groups in society.

The purpose of this chapter is to answer the question of whether a populist constitutionalism is a permanent element of Brazilian political history. Brazil has experienced several particular populist governments: some with more marked populist features than others; some exposing a reactionary antagonism while others a mitigated one. This empirical variation has generated a complex relationship between populism and constitutionalism in Brazilian history, and calls into question the opposition between populism and liberal constitutionalism advocated in populism studies.

The constitutional projects of Brazilian populist governments have not always sought to undermine liberal-democratic constitutionalism, while at the same time aiming to transform institutions and public policies. On the contrary, there are examples of populist constitutional projects in Brazilian history that reinforce the pillars of liberal democracy, showing no hostility to the principles of constitutional democracy, such as division of powers, pluralism and minorities' rights. There are even cases of a constitutional turn against populist governments and leaders (Lula and Dilma Rousseff are prominent examples), which contradicts the standard view of a populist turn against the constitution. This overall picture illustrates an ambiguity between populism and constitutionalism in Brazilian political history.

In terms of methodology, a qualitative approach is adopted, in order to explore the temporal relation between populism and constitutionalism in Brazil, based on bibliographic and documentary research, in addition to online news materials. This chapter will be organised as follows: after the introduction, I will make a brief overview of populism in Brazilian political history. Then, I will critically analyse the political-strategic approach to populism considering the relevant literature and the Brazilian experience, in which populism is historically associated with crises and related socioeconomic factors. The next section will explain the connection between populism and constitutionalism and the differentiation between liberal-democratic constitutionalism and populist constitutionalism. After that, the relationship between populism, constitutionalism and time in Brazil will be discussed as the central problem of the chapter.

In conclusion, I will argue that in the Brazilian case, due to the distinct experiences of populist governments, the relationship between constitutionalism and populism is one of complexity. This refutes the view that populist constitutionalism is an enduring temporal and unamendable element of Brazilian political history and, more broadly, challenges the view within populism studies that populism is committed to opposing liberal-democratic constitutionalism.

## 2. Populism in Brazilian Political History

For a better understanding of the populist experience in Brazil, this section provides an outline of Brazilian political history, in particular the evolution of its constitution, which displays the fundamental periods of crisis and transitions in Brazilian political history. Then, the concept of populism in Latin America will be analysed, focusing on the Brazilian experience, in which populism is historically associated with crises and other socioeconomic factors. Here the political-strategic approach of populism will be critically assessed considering the relevant literature.

The analysis of populism in Brazil will be focused on four specific episodes: the classical populism of Getúlio Vargas; the neopopulism of Fernando Collor de Mello; the moderate populism of Luiz Inácio Lula da Silva and Dilma Rousseff; and the far-right populism of Jair Bolsonaro. This selection is justified, because these cases illustrate the diverse dimensions of populism in Brazilian political history over time.

*2.1 Brazilian Political History*

Brazil has a colonial past. For centuries (1500–1822) it was the main colony of Portugal, and under Portuguese rule Brazil developed a political-economic system based on political patronage, privatism, personalism, massive land concentration, slavery and racism. After independence, which peculiarly lacked popular engagement (Comparato, 2017), the first constitution was adopted in 1824, establishing a confessional monarchy under a unitary state structure ruled by an emperor. Initially, the constituent assembly held important debates between liberals, conservatives and abolitionists, but overall this document truly reflected the centralising and authoritarian political will imposed by the emperor Pedro I (Bonavides & Andrade, 1991).

The abolition of slavery, formally effected in 1888, was a gradual, negotiated and late process, which imparted only a formal freedom to the victims, rather than a real social and ethnic integration. This resulted in the social exclusion of the black population within a context of developing industrial capitalism and paid employment (Ribeiro, 2020).

The Constitutional Charter of 1824 had a long duration until 1891, when it was replaced by the first Republican Constitution of Brazil. The defining feature of the republic was the end of the monarchy, and it maintained 'a political privatist regime without popular democracy' (Comparato, 2017, p. 147). As with independence, the instauration of the republic (1889) was a political process that did not involve the participation of the people. Initiated by the military, with the support of elites, the 'Old Republic' (1889–1930), so called by its opponents for perpetuating the political dominance of the traditional oligarchies, was an unstable period characterised by civil unrest and an acute financial crisis.

In attesting to the permanent role of the armed forces in political affairs, the 1930 Revolution ended the Old Republic, with the prominence of the military and the support of the elites. The Revolution established the 'Vargas Age' (1930–1945), which introduced elemental changes in the social, economic and political order (Young, 1964). Firstly, it presented the state as the key actor in promoting national industrialisation through state economic interventionism. Secondly, certain social groups, such as the business sector, the middle class and the urban workers, achieved political prominence. Conflicts of interest among these different social forces were dealt with by Getúlio Vargas through a state nationalist discourse, political manipulation and, if necessary, repression (Weffort, 2003).

Whereas the 1891 constitution 'had clearly an elitist and abstract character' (Comparato, 2017, p. 157), the 1934 constitution advanced social and labour rights. It kept the presidential system of government, inaugurated by the 1891 constitution which remains today, and defines the concentration of power in the person of the president of the republic. The 1937 constitution launched the dictatorial regime of Vargas, with provisions regarding censorship, the dissolution of the National Congress, the declaration of the state of emergency and the suspension of political liberties. In 1945, Vargas fell from power through a smooth transition negotiated with the elites and the military, which included a broad amnesty to those state agents responsible for torture and homicides perpetrated during the dictatorial regime (Bonavides & Andrade, 1991).

After the end of the Vargas Age, the alliance between conservatives and liberals (large landowners and business elite) achieved stability, assisted by the continuous presence of the armed forces in political affairs. A new constitution was enacted in 1946 which marked the re-democratisation period. Vargas returned to power for his third administration (1951–1954), which had a mixed policy framework: conservative and nationalist concerning the monopoly over oil resources (in 1953 Petrobras was created); while expansionist through social welfare policies, such as the extension of labour legislation and increases in the minimum wage and pensions. The opposition demanded his resignation based on their suspicion of a return to dictatorship. In 1954 Vargas committed suicide to avoid being overthrown again by the military (Bethell, 2018, pp. 181–182).

The Cuban Revolution of 1959 directly impacted the political landscape in Brazil and in 1961 Janio Quadros, a charismatic and conservative politician, became president with support from an ideologically eclectic mass formed by the urban middle class, the economic elite, trade unions and the armed forces. Janismo was an experience of mass populism based on a strong anti-corruption and anti-elite discourse. Yet, due to political ineptitude and the loss of support from important sectors, Quadros resigned after only eight months in office (Bethell, 2018, pp. 184–185).

The vice-president, João Goulart (1961–1964), assumed power and implemented 'basic reforms', namely land reform, the valorisation of public education, the legalisation of the Brazilian Communist Party and the nationalisation of strategic industrial sectors, among others. It was a time of an 'unusually high degree of popular politicisation and mobilisation' in Brazil (Bethell, 2018, p. 186). This raised a radical opposition from the economic elite, the military and the US government. As a consequence, in 1964 a civil military coup took place, ending the era of classical populism in Brazilian politics (Bethell, 2018, p. 187). The 1967 constitution alongside the 1969 Constitutional Amendment defined the authoritarian regime that lasted more than twenty years (Comparato, 2017).

The same solution implemented after the Vargas dictatorship, based on political agreements and amnesty, was used for the transition to democracy in the late 1980s. Despite its core elements of citizens' participation and the guarantee of fundamental rights, the current 1988 constitution is the result of a negotiated transition to democracy. It reflects a widespread political agreement among the various (even opposing) political and social forces present in the constituent assembly (Vieira, 2018). The text is extensive (containing 250 articles) and rigid, although there have been successive amendments. Since its enactment, the constitution has already been amended 128 times. This picture of constant constitutional changes can be explained by the necessity of accommodating the interests of the different social forces throughout the years under the large political pact of the 1988 constitution.

The term crisis expresses a crucial moment that demands an ultimate decision linked to an exceptional historic transitional phase (Koselleck & Richter, 2006). It is noteworthy that throughout Brazilian political history, key crisis situations, for instance the abolition of slavery, the proclamation of the republic and the re-democratisation at the end of the 1980s, were decided under gradual and negotiated processes between political and economic elites, without effective popular participation.

In this respect, two final observations are in order. First, the exclusion of the people from crucial political events in Brazilian history does not mean a passivity of the various social actors. Throughout Brazilian history there have been fundamental experiences of popular revolt and resistance against oppression and authoritarianism. However, they have been deleted from the collective memory by a culture of oblivion and silence. Some important examples are the political and legal struggle of black abolitionists, as well as the collective and organised resistance of black people during and after slavery (D'Salete, 2022).

In this context, the Quilombo of Palmares deserves special mention, which scholars regard as an African state in colonial Brazil (Lara, 2021). Further examples are the massive workers' strikes at the beginning of the twentieth century and the armed struggle against the military regime of 1964–1985.

Secondly, the historic political marginalisation of the social masses justifies the relevance of investigating the populist experience in Brazil. That's because populism in Latin America can be understood as a phenomenon that incorporates the people into the political process, as will be analysed below.

## 2.2 Populism in Latin America

Recently scholars have seemed to come to an agreement on a minimal concept of populism that encompasses three basic elements: the antagonism between the people and the elite; the exclusive promotion of the will of the people through politics; and populist leaders as the only ones able to manifest the true will of the people because of the direct bond they share. The nature of the antagonism, as well as the content of the ideas of 'people' and 'elite', may vary according to the ideological approach the populist leader adopts (Bertomeu & Saffon, 2022).

Populism in Latin America is a concept that encompasses various meanings interconnected to the region's historical experiences. Different experiences regarding the populist phenomenon have emerged over time, prompting diverse theoretical positions to explain these experiences. Yet, a political approach to the concept with emphasis on the discursive and institutional elements of populism has been consolidated over the years.

Latin-American populism has many variations: classical, left-wing revolutionary, neoliberal, and far-right nationalist. Political and social transition episodes determine which of these are adopted. For instance, it is the crisis of traditional political elites and the appearance of new political actors and variables of economic force or instability. The cases of classical populism in the decade of 1930s are the governments of Getúlio Vargas and Juan Domingo Perón in Brazil and Argentina. Both arose after the 1929 financial crisis prompting a decline in agricultural exports. They employed a state nationalist discourse to neutralise the conflicts of interest among different social forces, namely the social reforms demanded by the working class and the economic elites' interests (Gonzales, 2007).

Scholars have interpreted classical populism differently, emphasising it (i) as the result of social transition in the context of rapid industrialisation and urbanisation, which promoted the bond between the masses and their charismatic leader; (ii) as the product of the specific 'process of development of the capitalist relations of production in the countries of the region' (Ianni, 1991, p. 9); and (iii) through the discursive bond between the leader and the people, highlighting it as both a historical phenomenon and political category (Laclau, 1977). This discursive element focuses on the central reference of 'the people' and the antagonistic discourse which produces emotions and identities that divide the society between the people and its enemies (Morán, 2021).

In the 1980s and 1990s, a new wave of populism emerged in Latin America that differed considerably from classical populism, since it favoured the adoption of neoliberal reforms. Examples of 'neopopulism' include the administrations of Carlos Salinas de Gortari in Mexico and Alberto Fujimori in Peru. The neoliberal reforms consisted of trade liberalisation, state reform, privatisation, and labor market flexibilisation (Weyland, 2001).

These neopopulist experiences shifted attention away from aligning populism with any specific economic policy agenda, generating continuity with the previous experiences of classical populism. For this reason, analysts of populism started to prioritise the political dimension of the phenomenon that encloses the concentration of power in the leader and his/her capacity to emotionally mobilise the masses (Morán, 2021).

In the first decade of the 2000s the 'pink tide' emerged as a left-wing populist response in Latin America. Although these varied, all critiqued and antagonised neoliberalism (Silva, 2022, p. 8). In Brazil, Lula (2003–2010) performed a moderate populism based on antagonism towards neoliberalism, but which was conciliatory and reinforced liberal-democratic structures. At the same time, a revolutionary populism more radically opposed to neoliberalism emerged in Venezuela, Bolivia and Ecuador. This was a populism linked to 'twenty-first-century socialism'. The radical populism of Hugo Chávez, Evo Morales and Rafael Correa was based on the antagonism between the people and the traditional elites, based on the sociopolitical inclusion of traditionally excluded sectors, and the promotion of economic policies oriented towards social justice (Torre, 2013).

These developments prompted a conceptual redefinition, whereby populism was conceived as a political strategy based on a personalistic and charismatic leader with the ability to mobilise voters (Weyland, 2001, 2003). This view explains the historical persistence of populism in Latin America by a particular political culture and institutional structure characterised by patronage, presidentialism, irrationality, corruption and institutional weakness (Roberts, 2008) – all of which reveals the pejorative nature of this 'political strategic' approach to populism (Morán, 2021).

As an alternative understanding, populism is not merely a demagogic political strategy used by charismatic leaders to manipulate the masses and thus maintain popular support. Rather populism is a political logic that forges a collective identity, 'the people' as a political subject. This is emphasised by the ideational and discursive approaches to populism. According to the ideational approach populism can assume different ideological contents, so that is useful in order to analyse populist leaders and governments from different ideological dimensions, such as the Brazilian case.

Laclau (2005) theorises populism as a political category derived from the discursive bond between the leader and the people based on the central reference to 'the people' and the antagonistic discourse that forges a popular identity. Populism as a political logic entails a context of social crisis composed of unmet demands of different groups of individuals by the traditional institutional forces. The role of the populist leader is to unify these different social groups into a cohesive political subject, 'the people', through the perception of a common enemy, 'the elite'. This political dynamic 'does not necessarily result in populist governments' (Silva, 2022, p. 2).

The result is the creation of a popular identity, which starts to question the constituted powers and oppose the people against the formal institutions. Thus, populism places the people, rather than the institutions, as the central actor of political relations. That's because the people is able to break with the status quo and at the same time act as a force of reconstruction through the articulation of an 'equivalence of demands' that leads to unification (Reano, 2012).

The populist leader is the one capable of mobilising citizens through a dichotomous discourse, which places the people as its core element. The content of the terms 'the people' and 'the elite' is constructed. Consequently, it may vary according to the political struggle or ideological content the discourse is bound to. Thus, the populist leader may mobilise the masses in a reactionary or emancipatory manner. In effect, according to Laclau, the concept of populism is not connected to any specific political orientation, ideological strand or social groups (Feres Júnior et al., 2023). On that account, Laclau's definition is ideal to study Brazilian populism and its multiple empirical variations.

Moreover, Laclau offers a definition of populism that challenges the scholarship that considers populism to be a threat to democracy, since in his view populism succeeds in including into politics the social actors erstwhile excluded from the political process. In short, it questions the dominant order and, as a consequence, enhances democracy and significant social changes. In accordance with this view, the persistence of populist governments in Latin America strengthens popular participation in politics in opposition to governments that maintain institutional structures at the service of the traditional elites (Laclau, 2005). This approach best explains the different populist experiences in Brazilian political history, as will be shown in the following section.

## 2.3 Populism in Brazil

The first main experience of populism in Brazil was the government of Getúlio Vargas in the 1930s, which arose out of the financial crisis of 1929 causing agricultural exports to decline (Comparato, 2017). The crisis of the oligarchical system led to the adoption of import substitution industrialisation in order to foster economic development. Varguism transformed dominant features of the political scene, integrating the working class, and broadening the social basis of the state through a strong developmental economic policy and the expansion of social rights. As seen before, the exclusion of the popular classes from the political process was a central characteristic of the political landscape prior to the 1930 Revolution. In short, the classical populism of Vargas reflected the 'political emergence of the "popular classes"' (Weffort, 2003, p. 93).

Vargas played the role of an arbiter of social conflicts in trying to conciliate between the social reforms and the interests of economic elites. Weffort (2003) regards Vargas as an articulator of heterogeneous groups who secured his political project through the manipulation of both masses and elites. This interpretation of Varguism as a movement based on manipulation, which entails the passivity of the masses, warrants criticism. It does not examine the political complexity inherent within all populisms. Simultaneously, it neglects that Varguism forged a power structure for both dominant groups and the popular sectors that had emerged due to processes of urbanisation and industrialisation (Groppo, 2009).

In the 1980s and 1990s, Latin America faced a severe economic recession. As a solution a consensus was reached among national elites and international financial institutions in favour of austerity fiscal policies and subsequently a group of politicians declared themselves committed to implementing a neoliberal agenda.

In this context a new variation of populism emerged in Latin America, which differed from classical populism. This 'neopopulism' combined the populist logic with neoliberal economic reforms, which consisted of trade liberalisation, state reform, privatisation and labor market flexibilisation. It also undermined organised social movements, unions and the public sector (Comparato, 2017).

The compatibility between populism and neoliberalism is a controversial one in the literature. On the one hand, the structuralist approach argues that populism and neoliberalism are incompatible concepts. Because neoliberalism is unpopular, it is inimical to populist economic policies. On the other hand, the political-strategic approach to populism considers some affinity between populism and neoliberalism. In common, they presuppose low levels of institutionalisation. Moreover, neoliberal reforms can benefit neopopulist leaders: the privatisation of public companies favours essential business sectors, and labor market flexibilisation weakens the working class. It is beneficial for the market and populist leaders when representing the dominant political class (Weyland, 2003).

Brazil's example of neopopulism was the government of Fernando Collor de Mello (1990–1992), a member of a traditional oligarchical family. He was the first directly elected president after the end of the civil-military dictatorship and 'the closest thing to a right-wing populist that Brazil had ever had' (Edwards, 2010, p. 208). He utilised the direct relation with the disorganised mass of individuals, political charisma and an anti-corruption discourse, in order to implement neoliberal economic reforms. During the 1989 presidential campaign he was framed as 'the Maharajas hunter' (Andrade, 2021, p. 347).

At first, the strategies and goals of neopopulism and neoliberalism matched. Neoliberalism required the concentration of power in the populist president to remove any opposition to economic reforms. In turn, the promotion of such reforms could help Collor to strengthen the social basis of government support, since the reforms were responding to hyperinflation, and the economic crisis this induced (Weyland, 2003). However, this strategy left structural problems unaddressed, such as socioeconomic inequality, poverty and unemployment, leading to a rapid loss of popular and elite support. In 1992 the lower house of the National Congress opened an impeachment process against Collor for corruption, but he resigned to prevent his removal from office (Comparato, 2017).

Another meaningful episode related to the inclusion of popular masses in Brazilian political history was the victory of Luiz Inácio Lula da Silva (2003–2010) in the presidential elections of 2002, when he became Brazil's first president from a working-class background (Comparato, 2017). Previously, Lula had stood in three presidential elections (1989, 1994 and 1998). With popular support, heavily affected by the economic and social crisis caused by neoliberal policies, his government began in 2003 based on a broad political coalition formed by left and centre parties. At the end of the campaign Lula had publicly undertook the commitment to preserve the orthodox macroeconomic policies of the previous neoliberal government. In fact, the strategy was to present a moderate political programme to be implemented by his government, if elected. This was already indicated in Lula's 2002 campaign slogan 'Brazil, a country for all' (Andrade, 2021, p. 344). Lula's administration gained an international reputation through its redistributive economic policies and inclusive social policies, which improved the living conditions of the popular classes, without fully departing from neoliberalism.

Lula was re-elected in 2006 mostly through the support of the working poor, which had benefited from the social inclusion programmes of his first mandate. This re-election adopted a clear antagonist discourse, with the campaign slogan: 'Lula again, with the power of the people' (Andrade, 2021, p. 346). This government's policy framework blended developmentalism with neoliberalism, which did not break the reproduction of structural inequality. As Andrade (2021, p. 356) argues, 'In his government, the dominant classes [...] benefited from structural macroeconomic policies, while [...] the benefits for the working class were short term, selective, restricted and assistentialist.'

In 2022 Lula won the presidential elections with a tight majority of 50.8 per cent of the vote against Jair Bolsonaro, which proves that Lulaism survived despite years of persecution and demoralisation for both Lula and the *Partido dos Trabalhadores* (PT, Workers' Party) mainly due to Operation Car Wash. In his inauguration speech in Brasília, on 1 January 2023, he relaunched the 2022 conciliatory tone promising 'to govern for everyone, looking forward to our shining future, not our past'. And in opposition to the friend-foe logic of his predecessor, Lula stated 'a country permanently at war is no good for anyone, neither is a family living in disharmony. It's time to rebuild our ties with friends and family, broken by hate speech and the spreading of lies' (Marshall, 2023).

Lula does not consider himself as a populist leader. In 2008 he stated, 'I like to be called popular and [it] offends me to be mistaken by being populist' (Reano, 2012, p. 59). This view was shared by leftist intellectuals during his first mandate. According to this view, Lula's trade union biography is a practice of tutelage incompatible with populism. Lula's figure was seldom and marginally connected to populism until the 2006 re-election campaign. In 2005 the *Mensalão* case began, in which high-level members of the PT were investigated and later convicted of corruption and bribery. After this, Lula started to adopt an antagonist discourse against the elites that tried to overthrow him based on false corruption claims (Zicman de Barros & Lago, 2022, pp. 52–55).

Among scholars, the characterisation of Lula as a populist leader is disputed. On the one hand, there is the perception that Lula has been a pragmatic rather than a populist president (Edwards, 2010). Indeed, his conciliatory discourse in both the 2002 and 2022 campaigns, as well as his conformity with the neoliberal agenda once in power, demonstrate the absence of confrontation, which Laclau views as central to populism.

On the other hand, some authors reject that this distances Lula from populism. They argue that Lulism is based on social conciliation between proletariat and bourgeoisie, which led to the disorganisation and depoliticisation of the working classes. 'Delivering material improvements to the poor without active engagement, Lulism reinforced a passive political actor' (Andrade, 2021, p. 357). In this respect, Lulism would approximate to Varguism regarding the manipulation of the politically disorganised masses in order to secure power. Lula and Vargas would have committed the same mistake, namely a 'limited, compromising and depoliticized populism' (Zicman de Barros & Lago, 2022, p. 53).

Silva (2022) argues that Lula's speeches use the discursive elements of populism, namely people-centrism and anti-elitism. His discourse stressed the antagonism between rich and poor, workers and employers. However, this view is too simplistic as it neglects issues such as Lula's avoidance of the antagonist logic of populism in its relationship with the legislative and judiciary and in the formulation of public policies. Lula rather provided the strengthening of liberal institutions and combined left-wing policies (such as affirmative actions and social welfare programmes) with state-sponsored programmes for agrobusiness and other economic elites.

Hence, Lula introduced a new model of left-wing populism, 'as representative of interests "from below" while advancing a political project that protected and nurtured interests "from above" – a populist ambiguity' (Andrade, 2021, p. 338). In fact, this ambiguity can be considered distinctive of populism since it is a logic not committed to one specific ideological content, according to both the ideational and discursive approaches.

Lula thus can be regarded as a moderate populist leader: he resorted to a populist discourse, but once in power he did not continue the populist logic of polarisation in implementing institutional reforms and public policies. His successor, Dilma Rousseff, similarly adopted Lula's strategy of left-wing moderate populism.

Dilma Rousseff (2010–2016), a member of the armed struggle against the former military dictatorship, was the first woman to be elected president in Brazil. Transgressions, namely radical changes that break with the status quo, are indeed a characteristic feature of populism. Lula as the first president from a working-class background is yet another example (Zicman de Barros & Lago, 2022, p. 88). Like Lula, Dilma adopted in her discourse the antagonism between workers and the upper classes, but to a lesser extent.

Rousseff adopted expansionary economic policies in her first term, based on income redistribution and wage rises as a response to the economic crisis. This displeased the economic elites, which had representatives in Rousseff's political coalition. Her second term was characterised by austere economic policies, which proved unsuccessful, due to government faults, a lack of legislative support to implement the necessary fiscal reforms and the adverse international context (Meyer, 2021, pp. 76–77).

This resulted in a severe political crisis, materialised by the 2013 massive protests ('June Journeys'), which originally had a leftist claim to the improvement of public services but later were co-opted by the right-wing conservative middle classes with the support of corporate media. The opposition against Rousseff was exacerbated by the growing political movement to remove Rousseff from power, due to Operation Car Wash (Andrade, 2021, p. 358). During her time as president, Rousseff had never interfered in the investigations carried out by the Federal Police and the Public Prosecutor's Office.

Operation Car Wash was a massive corruption investigation, characterised by the intense politicisation of the judiciary, which started to gain mainstream media attention from 2014. Sérgio Moro, who was the leading judge of Operation Car Wash, perpetrated several abuses against constitutional principles, which selectively harmed the Workers' Party. He violated the constitutional principles of presumption of innocence and of reasonable process through long periods of pre-trial detention and the denial of *habeas corpus*. Moreover, he argued for the importance of public opinion in supporting the judicial function regarding the investigation of white-collar crimes, so he favoured the public disclosure of investigations through a close collaboration with the mainstream media. However, in practice, this publicity proved to be selective (Camargo & Vieira, 2016).

When he was investigating ex-president Lula for alleged unlawful enrichment acts, Moro authorised wiretapping measures and illegally divulged a conversation between Lula and Rousseff regarding his nomination as her minister, a position that would secure him immunity. Furthermore, days before the first round of the 2018 elections, Moro publicised a collaboration agreement testimony of a former PT politician against Lula, without providing evidence. Lula was accused of bribery and money laundering, in exchange for a beach flat.

Lula's condemnation by Moro, which was ratified by the Fourth Regional Appellate Court, prompted widespread criticism. There was no evidence that Lula received the property, nor that he benefited a construction company with Petrobras oil contracts. In April 2018 Lula was arrested after the Federal Supreme Court (STF) decreed the imprisonment constitutional ahead of a final ruling, breaching the constitutional principle of presumption of innocence. In 2020 the STF reversed its stance and subsequently Lula was freed.

Lula's imprisonment for 580 days prevented him from being a candidate in the 2018 presidential elections, which he was leading according to the polls. In 2021 Lula's condemnation was declared unlawful by the STF, based on Moro's incompetence and suspected collusion. The grave legacy of Operation Car Wash was the construction of public enemies, namely left-wing corrupt politicians, alongside exacerbating political polarisation. Later Moro became Bolsonaro's first Minister of Justice (Meyer, 2021, pp. 91–97).

The last years of Rousseff's first mandate can be regarded as the starting point of Brazil's constitutional erosion (Meyer, 2021). The 2013 'June Journeys' were followed by a series of events that culminated in Bolsonaro's electoral victory in 2018: the refusal of Aécio Neves to recognise his defeat in 2014 presidential elections; the consolidation of the highly politicised and abusive Operation Car Wash; and the 2016 judicial-parliamentary coup.

Rousseff was the second president to face impeachment in Brazil. The main accusation against her was related to the adoption of executive decrees that surpassed the debt ceiling established by law. However, the relevant legislation expressly allows supplementations, absolving Rousseff from any unconstitutional act that could justify impeachment. Nevertheless, at that time she had limited parliamentary support and low approval ratings. The Chamber of Deputies Speaker, Eduardo Cunha, authorised the impeachment process, notably acting on behalf of his private political interests. Soon after, Cunha was accused of intervening in Operation Car Wash and suspended from his legislative activities by the STF. Likewise, Michel Temer, Rousseff's vice-president, faced investigations into the same Operation. During the impeachment process he turned against Rousseff and left the political coalition that supported her government. The absence of offences that could justify Rousseff's removal became clear when she was impeached, but without the imposition of the eight-year ineligibility sanction stipulated by the 1988 constitution. In conclusion, the constitutional rules regarding the impeachment process were abused to the benefit of shadowy political interests, with the awareness of the National Congress and the STF. The latter supervised the entire process (Meyer, 2021, pp. 206–208).

Rousseff's impeachment is correctly characterised as a coup because it removed an elected government and substituted it with another without new elections. In her case the impeachment was distorted and operated as a vote of no confidence specific to the parliamentary system. In presidential systems, however, the lack of parliamentary support or popular approval are not causes to overthrow an elected president (Hoffmann, 2016). Moreover, the complicity between the judiciary and the corporate media helped to create the narrative that the whole process was legitimate according to the rule of law. After Rousseff's condemnation by the Federal Senate, Temer substituted her and in his short unpopular presidency he introduced the ultra-neoliberal agenda that was later continued by Jair Bolsonaro. Operation Car Wash is an example of the constitution (tenuously) turning against both Lula and Rousseff. This turns on its head the accusation that populism is anti-constitutionalism: in this instance, it was the constitution that turned on the moderate left populism of Lula and Rousseff.

Bolsonarism brought an authoritarian and neoliberal populism to power in Brazil. It is connected to the emergence of a new right, as a conservative reaction to the progressive social achievements implemented during the Workers' Party administrations of 2003–2016. Hostility to the PT was widespread within the middle classes, mainly fuelled by the selective anti-corruption discourse of Operation Car Wash. This movement increased after the 2013 mass protests, informed by an anti-politics, anti-party and anti-corruption perspective, which gained more traction between 2014 and 2015 when a severe financial crisis hit Brazil's economy. The loss of income and jobs, as consequences of the intense economic internationalisation, generated resentment towards incumbent politics. Popular mobilisation is a necessary ingredient for the PT to succeed, and this was compromised, opening a space for the authoritarian populist discourse of Jair Bolsonaro, facilitating his rise to power in 2019 (Rocha & Solano, 2021).

Bolsonaro managed to mobilise different social actors through a discourse focused on the opposition between 'the people' and 'the elite'. Bolsanoro's 'people' was restricted to religious and conservative groups opposed to minorities' policies, the upper and middle classes who embraced neoliberalism and the military, while his 'elite' comprised 'corrupt left politicians' and plural groups deemed contrary to the majority (Silva, 2022, pp. 10–11). He introduced a nationalist, ultraconservative, religious and neoliberal politics. Moreover, with Bolsonaro's administration the active participation of the military in Brazilian politics re-emerged for the first time after re-democratisation (Meyer, 2021). The number of military persons employed in bureaucratic positions of the federal executive branch increased significantly in comparison to previous administrations (Feres Júnior et al., 2023).

Bolsonaro's disastrous management of COVID-19 was characterised by denial and opposition to basic preventive measures. He also opposed establishing social protection programmes despite the tragic socioeconomic context of the pandemic (Brum, 2021). The chaotic response of Bolsonaro's administration to the pandemic induced complaints and derision nationally and internationally. Furthermore, his government was characterised by low economic growth and high levels of inflation, unemployment and hunger, after years of social development (Meyerfeld, 2022). As a result, Bolsonaro lost the presidential elections of 2022 to Luiz Inácio Lula da Silva.

Since its inception, Bolsonaro's administration has been conflictual with entities regarded as enemies of the people, for instance, the traditional press, international institutions, scientists and intellectuals, but especially the STF.

His populist strategy was to limit the Court's powers and control them. For this purpose, Bolsonaro appointed loyalists as Justices and made use of intimidation and threats. As a response the STF has opened inquiries into Bolsonaro and his allies, to investigate the dissemination of fake news and personal attacks against the Court's Justices and the organisation of anti-democratic acts. It led to a conflictual relationship between the federal government and the STF throughout Bolsonaro's administration.

This antagonism radicalised and became violent on 8 January 2023 when thousands of Bolsonaro supporters organised riots in Brasília and stormed the STF, the National Congress and the Planalto Palace (Buschschlüter, 2023). This anti-democratic event was motivated by false claims over election fraud and the refusal to accept the result of the presidential election. During his government Bolsonaro has continuously discredited the legitimacy of elections in Brazil by disseminating fake news on the safety of the national electronic voting system (Nicas et al., 2022).

From the analysis in this section, one can conclude that populism has been a continuous feature of the governments spanning Brazil's republican history. The Vargas Age of the mid-twentieth century launched populism into Brazilian politics, and implemented substantial changes in the social, economic and political order. In the re-democratisation period since the 1980s, diverse populist projects have been carried out: from Collor's neopopulism, which introduced the neoliberal agenda; through the moderate populisms of Luiz Inácio Lula da Silva and Dilma Rousseff and their promotion of inclusive social policies; and onto the far-right populism of Jair Bolsonaro and the social regression it achieved. But does this mean that there has been an enduring relationship between populism and constitutionalism in Brazil? This temporal relation is examined in the next section.

## 3. Populism, Constitutionalism and Time in Brazil

This section provides an analysis of the connection between populism and constitutionalism and the differentiation between liberal-democratic constitutionalism and populist constitutionalism. After that, the relationship between populism, constitutionalism and time in Brazil is examined, in order to assess whether it is possible to affirm the existence of a permanent 'populist' constitutionalism considering the different historical experiences of populism in Brazil.

Laclau's theory is the best suited to examine the cases of Getúlio Vargas, Fernando Collor de Mello, Luiz Inácio Lula da Silva, Dilma Rousseff and Jair Bolsonaro as populist leaders, because of their distinctive ideological orientations. All these particular experiences emerged within the context of a social crisis that highlighted a process of equivalence among unmet demands of different social actors produced by the antagonism pointed out in the populist leader's discourse.

In its various manifestations, populism can effectively offer an answer to socioeconomic or existential vulnerabilities (Zicman de Barros & Lago, 2022, p. 75). With Vargas, 'the people' was the worker class and 'the elite', the traditional dominant classes. In Collor's discourse the antagonism was between the middle and business classes and the traditional corrupt elite. With Lula and Rousseff, 'the people' was the individuals marginalised because of their class, gender or ethnic identities, whereas 'the elite' was the upper classes associated with the neoliberal project. Lastly, Bolsonaro based his government on the antagonism between resentful conservative groups (the middle class and evangelicals) pitched against the Workers' Party progressive social administrations and 'corrupt leftists' (Silva, 2022, p. 6).

However, there are some difficulties regarding Bolsonaro's case. His speeches lack what Laclau regards as populism's core, namely central reference to 'the people'. Instead, it is anti-left and anti-corruption elements that prevail. In addition, the reactionary content of Bolsonarism discourse against minorities' rights contrasts to Laclau's democratic and inclusive perspective (Feres Júnior et al., 2023). Collor's discourse was similarly focused on anti-corruption, and devoid of appeals to 'the people'. Nevertheless, in each case the populist leader was capable of mobilising the masses through a dichotomous discourse. This means that the 'Team Populism' database ranks Collor and Bolsonaro as the most populist leaders in Brazil after Getúlio Vargas (Hawkins et al., 2019).

## 3.1 Populism and Constitutionalism

The relationship with constitutionalism is a crucial issue for populism. The centrality of the invocation of 'the people' within its antagonistic discourse seeks to justify uses or misuses of constitutional law to achieve the political goals of populist leaders and regimes. Populist constitutionalism refers to the constitutional approach of populism, which identifies constituent power with popular will as the primary source of legitimacy (Blokker, 2021).

Moreover, populism has a close connection with constitutionalism concerning mechanisms of constitutional change. Indeed, populism aims to transform the institutions (Zicman de Barros & Lago, 2022, p. 66). The advent of a new constitution or constitutional amendments, which symbolise a constitutional rupture with the traditional constitutional order, can be useful instruments for populist leaders to achieve their objectives, for instance to secure power in their favour and dismantle the current political system linked to the corrupt elite (Landau, 2018). When populist leaders do not succeed in changing the constitution, for instance, due to a lack of support by the legislative majority, they try to 'capture' the constitutional courts, the ultimate interpreters of the constitutional text (Mudde, 2013).

Many commentators oppose populist constitutionalism to liberal-democratic constitutionalism since it blames the formality and elitism of institutions as an impediment to the direct connection between the people and democracy. In that sense, populist constitutionalism critically exposes the contradictions of liberal-democratic constitutionalism. Liberal democracy, which is just one of the existing models of democracy, combines the majoritarian principle with essential values of liberalism, such as the protection of minorities' rights, plural political competition and the separation of powers. Populism does not necessarily follow this specific concept of democracy. In turn, populism is aligned with the classical version of democracy that underlines majority rule and popular sovereignty. For this reason, populist discourse can be qualified as illiberal, but not anti-democratic (Mudde, 2013), which may solve partially the difficulty of accommodating Bolsonarism to Laclau's definition of populism, as explained above.

In particular, populist constitutionalism challenges pillars of liberal constitutionalism, such as the rule of law and the separation of powers. That is because populism considers that institutions don't exclusively represent the sovereign will of the people, but rather only the populist leader does. Consequently, populist constitutionalism argues in favour of the concentration of powers in the figure of the president, in order to put into affect the will of the people (Blokker, 2019).

Populist constitutionalism argues that the inherent contradiction of liberal-democratic constitutionalism is that between the rule of law and majority rule. It is because the majority should be protected against the tyranny of the minorities and not the opposite. Hence, there is also an antagonism between the majority and the non-elected institutions, for example the Judiciary, and especially constitutional courts due to their counter-majoritarian nature. Therefore, populist constitutionalism is committed to challenging the authority of constitutional courts, or the attempt to exercise control over them.

In this regard, populist constitutionalism is connected to Laclau's differentiation between populism and institutionalism. Under Laclau's view (2005) in a liberal democracy the demands of the different social groups or classes are discussed and decided inside the institutions. This hampers the ability of citizens to mobilise and build among themselves bonds and articulated claims ('the equivalence of demands'). In other words, the institutional way of doing politics blocks the exercise of democracy directly by the people. On the contrary, under populism the leader mobilises the social masses through a discourse that places 'the people' at the centre of the populist political (and constitutional) project, by including into the political decision-making those masses previously marginalised from politics.

Bolivian populist constitutionalism under Evo Morales serves as an empirical example of how populism can resort to institutions as core elements of a constitution, but at the same time not discarding the criticism against them. The 2009 Constitution of the Plurinational State of Bolivia provides that the Pluri-National Constitutional Court is composed of judges elected by universal suffrage on the basis of pluri-nationality, including representatives of the rural native indigenous system (articles 197 II and 198). In addition, the candidacies for the constitutional court are proposed by organised civil society and the nations and rural native indigenous peoples (article 199 II). In short, populist constitutionalism can manage to enhance political popular participation inside institutions.

In any event, the relationship between constitutionalism and populism needs to be carefully analysed, taking into account the political and ideological specificities of each populist government. Depending on these specific features, some may perform against the constitution, but others may not (Bugaric & Tushnet, 2020).

### 3.2 Is Populist Constitutionalism Permanent in Brazil?

Time influences the structure and the content of constitutions. Constitutional changes (replacement, revision and amendments) reflect the political struggle of a certain period in history. In particular, constitutional amendments may indicate two different scenarios. According to the 'conservative approach', which argues for the protection of constitutional supremacy from a transitory majority, constitutional amendments create instability over time as a fundamental feature of a specific constitutional order. Whereas the 'progressive approach', which regards the constitution as a 'living body', understands that constitutional amendments prove the adaptability of the constitutional text to socioeconomic developments, crises and political clashes (Fabbrizi, 2022, pp. 8–9).

As explained above populist constitutionalism refers to the constitutional approach of populism, which places 'the people' at the centre of the constitutional project, grounded on the role of an antagonistic discourse within a context of crisis. The concept of 'the people' can vary extensively and denote any content designated by the populist discourse; for example, the workers, the middle class, the poor, or conservative and religious segments of the society.

Populist leaders resort to the constitution through different ways and mechanisms; for instance, by disputing constitutional interpretations in their discourse; by calling a constituent assembly, plebiscite and referendum; by proposing or enacting constitutional amendments, for example, to change term limits, introduce presidential re-election and reduce the powers of controlling organs; and by packing the constitutional court. In particular, Latin American populist constitutionalism is seen as a form of constitutionalism that blends 'empowering and constraining clauses', 'popular mobilization through constitutional change' and 'uneven implementation of constitutions through institutional capture' (Bertomeu & Saffon, 2022, p. 140).

By increasing power concentration and weakening control bodies, populist leaders can limit impairments to the implementation of their popular policies and goals. Popular mobilisation is a key feature of Latin American populist constitutionalism. Because of the critical perspective of populism towards institutions, the populist constitutional approach fosters mechanisms of popular participation outside of periodic elections. Furthermore, an active popular mobilisation shows that the populist leader personifies and executes people's will. However, Latin American populist constitutionalism has an ambivalent relation with democracy. On the one hand, it promotes the inclusion of popular classes in the political process, but, on the other, it seeks to extend the president's powers at the cost of accountability rules and the checks and balances principle (Bertomeu & Saffon, 2022).

Based on this description of Latin American populist constitutionalism the cases of Getúlio Vargas, Fernando Collor de Mello, Luiz Inácio Lula da Silva, Dilma Rousseff and Jair Bolsonaro will be evaluated in order to establish whether a populist constitutionalism is a permanent phenomenon in Brazil's political and legal landscape.

Bertomeu and Saffon argue that 'in Latin America, constitutions are so crucial for populism that the image of populist presidents with the constitution in their pocket is frequently invoked' (2022, p. 138). This exemplifies the case of Vargas. After the 1930 Revolution, Vargas assumed power, established the provisional government and called the constituent assembly and general elections. The 1934 constitution, the first Varguist constitution, instituted an interventionist and social state. Vargas was elected to rule until 1938, but due to the antagonistic political scene repression began through banning the Communist Party. By 1936, Vargas had decreed a state of war and the next year witnessed a coup d'état and the 1937 constitution.

This second Varguist constitution had authoritarian characteristics. It provided that constitutional amendment proposals could be submitted to national plebiscite in certain cases (article 174 paragraph 4), even stipulating that its own text would be approved by national plebiscite, although Vargas never summoned this (article 187). Using constitutional amendments, Vargas extended the state of siege and the deepening of political persecution. Furthermore, the 1937 constitution provided the dissolution of the National Congress (article 178) and the power of the President of the Republic to render null and void decisions of the STF in constitutionality control matters (article 96). Lastly, Vargas legislated by decree over all subjects of federal competence (article 180), but selectively regarding redistributive policies and labour and union law. To sum up, Vargas put into effect a full populist constitutionalism during his two first governments (1934–1945).

Likewise, his third mandate (1951–1954) showed a populist political project based on legislation and institutional reforms that enhanced labour rights and national industry. In brief, the experience of Varguism with constitutionalism, ended by the military dictatorship, managed to fuse political inclusion, socioeconomic reforms and concentration of powers.

In contrast, Fernando Collor de Mello (1990–1992) failed to strategically use the constitution to implement his political project and goals. His base in the National Congress was very weak (Bethell, 2018, p. 189). Collor failed to initiate constitutional amendments or launch referenda during his rule. There have been just three popular consultations in Brazil's political history: in 1963 a plebiscite regarding the continuity of the parliamentary system, adopted after João Goulart took office; in 1993 a plebiscite, called by the 1988 constituent assembly, to decide the form and system of government; and the 2005 referendum regarding the prohibition of firearms. Only two constitutional amendments were enacted during Collor's administration which related to the implementation of the 1993 plebiscite, and rules regarding the salaries of state and local legislative representatives.

Collor made extensive use of provisional measures in order to implement his neoliberal economic policies. Article 62 of the 1988 constitution states that the president may adopt provisional measures, in relevant and urgent cases, with an immediate force of law and subsequently submit them to the National Congress. Nevertheless, regarding power concentration through institutional capture, Collor appointed his cousin as Justice of the STF, but this was the only important institutional nomination.

There were no constitutional programmes to challenge liberal-democratic constitutionalism under the moderate populist governments of Lula and Rousseff. Despite using an antagonistic discourse, which qualifies them as populist leaders, their governments were pragmatic and respectful to liberal institutions, the promotion of pluralism and social inclusion programmes (Silva, 2022). There were no constitutional changes aiming to concentrate power and institutional capture. Although Rousseff proposed a 'small constituent assembly' specifically created to promote political reform in response to the 2013 'June Journeys', it lacked public support (Meyer, 2021, p. 229).

There was no interference with political nominations. Since his first tenure Lula began the tradition of nominating the Prosecutor General from a list provided by the National Association of Federal Prosecutors (Meyer, 2021, p. 99). Rousseff also adopted this clear deference to the Public Prosecutor's Office. In fact, the autonomy of the judicial system was enhanced during Workers' Party administrations (Meyer, 2021, p. 104). In short, Lula and Rousseff adopted a mitigated antagonism, promoting conflicts and confrontations inherent to the political debate within liberal democracy. Lula's political relationship with elites, based on agreements and consensus, demonstrates this (Zicman de Barros & Lago, 2022, pp. 84–88).

In contrast, Bolsonaro resorted to the constitution regularly to perpetuate a reactionary antagonism aimed at eliminating enemies (Zicman de Barros & Lago, 2022, pp. 79–84). Bolsonaro's populist constitutionalism reinforced traditional forms of social domination (machismo and racism, for example), while weakening the autonomy of control institutions.

Bolsonaro attempted to launch his populist constitutional project via constitutional reform proposals including: reducing the legal age for criminal responsibility; the return of the printed vote ballot; increasing the number of justices in the STF; and reducing the mandatory retirement age of STF justices from 75 to 70 years. None of these proposals succeeded: they are either still pending or were rejected by the National Congress. Furthermore, the vice-president and leader of Bolsonaro's government in the Chamber of Deputies spoke out in favour of a plebiscite for a new constitution.

Bolsonaro appointed two conservative Justices to the STF. One, Justice André Mendonça, is a Presbyterian pastor, whose nomination fulfilled Bolsonaro's promise to appoint a 'terribly evangelical' Justice to the STF (RFI, 2021). Bolsonaro's appointment of Prosecutor General – whose responsibilities include opening inquiries to investigate and file complaints against high authorities, including the president – was also strategic. In 2019 he appointed Augusto Aras who was reappointed in 2021. In both cases Aras' name was not in the top three of the National Association of Federal Prosecutors' triple list. While not compulsory, it is customary for the president to nominate one among the three on that list, which Bolsonaro ignored twice. Aras reciprocated by showing leniency towards the president, in refusing to open inquiries, and asking the STF to drop cases against him.

Bolsonaro distorted the meaning of constitutional provisions. Article 142 of the 1988 constitution is notorious, stating that the Brazilian Armed Forces, under the supreme authority of the president, is responsible for the defence of the country, guarantor of constitutional powers, and, on the initiative of any of these, of law and order. According to the STF and National Congress, this provision does not confer power to the Armed Forces to act as a 'moderating power'. However, Bolsonaro has always distorted the meaning of article 142, claiming constitutional power to request military intervention in order to solve any conflict between the three branches, or to restore internal order.

Finally, Bolsonaro legislated selectively by decree regarding the interests of his reactionary agenda; for instance, deregulating gun ownership, granting presidential amnesty to political allies and military police officers sentenced for homicide, and the promotion of mining activities in the Amazon. He also proposed laws against indigenous land rights, and the deregulation of pesticides, which failed.

In fact, since inauguration Bolsonaro faced difficulties implementing constitutional and legal reforms due to a lack of support in the National Congress and STF resistance to Bolsonaro's authoritarian populist advances. Therefore, key features of Brazil's constitutionalism prevented Bolsonaro's populist constitutional project, especially coalitional presidentialism and the 1988 constitution's rigidity protected by a constitutional review system – which proved solid under attack.

The most important conclusion to draw from this analysis is that a 'populist constitutionalism' has not been a persistent feature of Brazilian politics since the 1980s. Different populist projects have defined this recent period of Brazilian republican history. These have taken different ideological patterns and emerged in moments of disruption that entail swift changes in political, social and economic environments. Indeed, populist governments have emerged as a response to social unrest and crisis. In short, populism has often challenged long-term ideas, interactions and actors in Brazilian politics. However, this does not mean that different populist leaders have consistently targeted constitutional reforms when in office. When all populist governments are taken into account there have been significant cases – the governments of Collor, Lula and Rousseff – that have not sought constitutional reform and have, rather, reinforced the values and institutions of liberal constitutionalism. Any simplistic binary pitting a populist constitutionalism versus a liberal constitutionalism is undermined by Brazil's history.

## 4. Conclusion

Populism has proved an ongoing phenomenon in Latin American countries – a historically unstable region with several periods of political and economic crises and social unrest. Due to the serious problem of structural inequality, its vulnerable population is most affected by these crises. According to Laclau, populism requires a scenario of crisis, in which demands of certain social groups are not met by the state. This has been particularly evident throughout Latin American political history.

Under Laclau's view, within crises those from different social segments are connected via unmet demands, are mobilised by a personalistic and charismatic political figure through an antagonistic discourse that interpellates those previously excluded from politics and re-situates them at the heart of a new politics. However, Laclau's account of populism is weak on the question of populist governments, namely populist leaders in power and the implementation of their political and constitutional project. In this regard, the comparative analysis presented here of the temporal relationship between Brazilian populist governments and constitutionalism contributes to the theoretical debate regarding the populism-constitutionalism correlation.

The idea of 'populist constitutionalism' is based on an anti-elitist critique of liberal-democratic constitutionalism, in particular the failure of liberal-democratic institutions to represent the will of the people, as the sovereign political subject. Only the populist leader's decisions are legitimate due to the direct bond maintained with the people. Yet, the variety of Brazilian populist governments through history and their different constitutional relations contradict any simplistic view on the relationship between populism and constitutionalism. In Brazil's political history one cannot detect a clear distinction between liberal-democratic constitutionalism and populist constitutionalism. That's because among its various populist governments, some have confronted liberal-democratic constitutionalism, whereas others have reinforced its principles and institutions.

In Brazilian political history the main cases of populist leaders are Getúlio Vargas, Fernando Collor de Mello, Luiz Inácio Lula da Silva, Dilma Rousseff and Jair Bolsonaro. Some were more 'populist' than others. In fact, 'populism is a matter of degree' (Zicman de Barros & Lago, 2022, p. 90). Apart from their ideological and style differences (the social welfare populism of Vargas; the neopopulism of Collor; the moderate populism of Lula and Rousseff; and the far-right authoritarian populism of Bolsonaro), all these governments emerged in periods of economic, social or political crisis and had in common intrinsic features of Latin American populism: the antagonistic discourse that divides society between the people and the elite through a political leadership.

The cases of Collor, Lula and Rousseff illustrate firstly that the dynamics of populist discourse do not necessarily result in populist governments according to Laclau's understanding. Secondly, these experiences dispute the claim that by definition populist governments implement populist constitutionalism.

Collor, Lula and Rousseff did not put into effect a populist constitutional project once they assumed the presidency. In inter-institutional relations and in the formulation of public policies their governments protected the rule of law and the rights of minorities, while shunning power concentration.

Lula and Rousseff turn the claim that populists attack the constitution on its head, as it was the institutional framework that was mobilised against their presidencies. Both faced constitutional abuses perpetrated by institutions and the judicial system via Operation Car Wash and the 2016 impeachment process. Their experiences indicate, instead, the intricate and ambiguous relationship between populism and constitutionalism in Brazil's recent history.

In contrast, Vargas and Bolsonaro represent notorious cases of 'populist constitutionalism'. Once in power both put in practice a government oriented by the populist dynamic of antagonism and polarisation. They pursued constitutional change, institutional capture and selective implementation of constitutional rights and programmes, in order to promote the political mobilisation of the people or their voters, while concentrating power to the detriment of the legislative and judiciary.

Taking into consideration these different historical instances of populism and how their relationship with the constitution manifests ambiguously in time, one clear conclusion to draw is that it is impossible to speak of a permanent populist constitutionalism in Brazil. Populism emerges in periods of economic, social or political crisis, but not all experiences fall in line with the standard approach to 'populist constitutionalism' – which insists that populist leaders capture the constitution and undermine the rule of law, minorities' rights and separation of powers. Of the populist governments investigated herein, it is the ones that also display authoritarian features – those of Vargas and Bolsonaro – that have reformed the constitution. So, more accurately, it is not populism but, rather, authoritarian populism that can be aligned with any 'constitutional populism'. Lastly, another notable conclusion is that populist advances against the constitution and liberal institutions are hampered by a lack of popular support. The failure of Bolsonaro's attempt to capture the constitution confirms this. It was popular support for the constitution of 1988 that hindered the authoritarian advances of Bolsonaro.

## References

Andrade, D. (2021) 'Populism from above and below: the path to regression in Brazil', in Scoones, I., Edelman, M., Borras Jr., S. M., Forero, L. F., Hall, R., Wolford, W. and White, B. (eds) *Authoritarian populism and the rural world*. London and New York: Routledge, pp. 338–364.

Bertomeu, J. F. G. and Saffon, M. P. (2022) 'The mix of Latin American populist constitutionalism', *Law & Ethics of Human Rights*, 16 (1), pp. 137–165. DOI: https://doi.org/10.1515/lehr-2022-2001.

Bethell, L. (2018) *Brazil: essays on history and politics*. London: Institute of Latin American Studies.

Blokker, P. (2019) 'Populism as a constitutional project', *International Journal of Constitutional Law*, 17 (2), pp. 535–553. DOI: 10.1093/icon/moz028.

Blokker, P. (2021) 'Populism, constituent power and constitutional imagination', in Belov, M. (ed.) *Between constitutional imagination, normative entrenchment and political reality*. Cambridge: Intersentia, pp. 149–169.

Bonavides, P. and Andrade, P. de (1991) (3rd edn) *História constitucional do Brasil*. Rio de Janeiro: Paz e Terra.

Brum, E. (2021) *Study finds that Brazil's Jair Bolsonaro carried out an 'institutional strategy to spread the coronavirus*. Available at: english.elpais.com/americas/2021-01-29/study-finds-that-brazils-jair-bolsonaro-carried-out-an-institutional-strategy-to-spread-the-coronavirus.html (accessed 10 January 2023).

Bugaric, B. and Tushnet, M. (2020) 'Populism and constitutionalism: an essay on definitions and their implications', *Harvard Public Law* Working Paper No. 20-17. DOI: http://dx.doi.org/10.2139/ssrn.3581660.

Buschschlüter, V. (2023) *Brazil Congress storming: how did we get there?* Available at https://www.bbc.com/news/world-latin-america-64206220 (accessed 13 January 2023).

Camargo, M. L. and Vieira, J. R. (2016) 'O impeachment e a instrumentalização do poder Judiciário pelas mãos do juiz Sergio Moro', in Proner, C., Cittadino, G., Tenenbaum, M. and Ramos Filho, W (orgs) *A resistência ao golpe de 2016*. Bauru: Canal 6, pp. 297–302.

Comparato, F. K. (2017) *A oligarquia brasileira: visão histórica*. São Paulo: Contracorrente.

D'Salete, M. (2022) *Mukanda Tiodora*. São Paulo: Veneta, 2022.

Edwards, S. (2010) *Left behind: Latin America and the false promise of populism*. Chicago: University of Chicago Press.

Fabbrizi, V. (2022) 'Conservation, progress, and change. How time affects politics and democracy', *Trauma and Memory*, 10 (2), pp. 148–159. DOI: 10.12869/TM2022-2-02.

Feres Júnior, J., Cavassana, F. and Gagliardi, J. (2023) 'Is Jair Bolsonaro a classic populist?', *Globalizations*, 20 (1), pp. 60–75.

Gonzales, O. (2007) 'Los orígenes del populismo latinoamericano. Una mirada diferente', *Cuadernos del CENDES*, 24 (66), pp. 75–104.

Groppo, A. J. (2009) *The two princes: Juan D. Perón and Getulio Vargas: a comparative study of Latin American populism*. Villa María: Eduvim.

Hawkins, K. A., Aguilar, R., Castanho Silva, B., Jenne, E. K., Kocijan, B. and Rovira Kaltwasser, C. (2019) *Global populism database*. Harvard Dataverse, V2. DOI: https://doi.org/10.7910/DVN/LFTQEZ.

Hoffmann, F. (2016) 'Alguns pensamentos sobre (e do) Brasil', in Proner, C., Cittadino, G., Tenenbaum, M. and Ramos Filho, W (orgs) *A resistência ao golpe de 2016*. Bauru: Canal 6, pp. 126–128.

Ianni, O. (1991) (2nd edn) *A Formação do Estado Populista na América Latina*. Rio de Janeiro: Civilização Brasileira.

Koselleck, R. and Richter, M. W. (2006) 'Crisis', *Journal of the History of Ideas*, 67 (2), pp. 357–400.

Laclau, E. (1977) *Politics and ideology in Marxist theory: capitalism, fascism and populism*. London: NLB.

Laclau, E. (2005) *La razón populista*. Buenos Aires: Fondo de Cultura Económica.

Landau, D. (2018) 'Populist constitutions', *University of Chicago Law Review*, 85 (2), pp. 521–544.

Lara, S. H. (2021) *Palmares & Cucaú: O Aprendizado da Dominação*. São Paulo: Edusp.

Marshall, E. (2023) *Lula promises to govern for all in tearful final inauguration speech*. Available at https://brazilian.report/liveblog/2023/01/01/lula-tearful-inauguration-speech/ (accessed 7 February 2023).

Meyer, E. P. N. (2021) *Constitutional erosion in Brazil*. Oxford: Hart.

Meyerfeld, B. (2022) *Brazil: widespread hunger will be one of Jair Bolsonaro's legacies*. Available at lemonde.fr/en/economy/article/2022/10/01/brazil-widespread-hunger-will-be-one-of-jair-bolsonaro-s-legacies_5998742_19.html (accessed 13 January 2023).

Morán, S. (2021) 'El populismo o los populismos. Actualidad y Particularidades del concepto en América Latina', *América Latina Hoy*, 87, pp. 29–44. DOI: https://doi.org/10.14201/alh.22677.

Mudde, C. (2013) *Are populists friends or foes of constitutionalism?* Available at: fljs.org/sites/default/files/migrated/publications/Mudde_0.pdf (accessed 21 December 2022).

Nicas, J., Milhorance, F. and Ionova, A. (2022) *How Bolsonaro built the myth of stolen elections in Brazil*. Available at nytimes.com/interactive/2022/10/25/world/americas/brazil-bolsonaro-misinformation.html (accessed 13 January 2023).

Reano, A. (2012) '"Los populismos realmente existentes" repensar la relación entre populismo y democracia a partir de dos experiencias latinoamericanas contemporáneas', *Pensamento Plural*, 10, pp. 59–88.

RFI (2021) *Brazil Senate approves Bolsonaro-backed pastor for Supreme Court*. Available at rfi.fr/en/brazil-senate-approves-bolsonaro-backed-pastor-for-supreme-court (accessed 18 January 2023).

Ribeiro, A. L. R. C. (2020) *Racismo estrutural e aquisição da propriedade: uma ilustração da cidade de São Paulo*. São Paulo: Contracorrente.

Roberts, K. M. (2008) 'El resurgimiento del populismo latinoamericano', in Torre, C. de la and Peruzzotti, E. (eds) *El retorno del pueblo: Populismo y nuevas democracias en América Latina*. Quito: FLACSO, pp. 55–73.

Rocha, C. and Solano, E. (2021) 'A ascensão de Bolsonaro e as classes populares', in Avritzer, L., Kerche, F. and Marona, M. (orgs) *Governo Bolsonaro: retrocesso democrático e degradação política*. Belo Horizonte: Autêntica, pp. 21–34.

Silva, M. G. (2022) 'Populism in the XXI century in Brazil: a dangerous ambiguity', *Genealogy*, 6 (36), pp. 1–18. DOI: https://doi.org/10.3390/genealogy6020036.

Torre, C. de la (2013) 'In the name of the people: democratization, popular organizations, and populism in Venezuela, Bolivia and Ecuador', *Revista Europea de Estudios Latinoamericanos y Del Caribe*, 95, pp. 27–48.

Vieira, O. V. (2018) *A batalha dos poderes: Da transição democrática ao mal-estar constitucional*. São Paulo: Companhia das Letras.

Weffort, F. C. (2003) (5th edn) *O populismo na política brasileira*. Rio de Janeiro: Paz e Terra.

Weyland, K. (2001) 'Clarifying a contested concept: populism in the study of Latin American politics', *Comparative Politics*, 34 (1), pp. 1–22. DOI: https://doi.org/10.2307/422412.

Weyland, K. (2003) 'Neopopulism and neoliberalism in Latin America: how much affinity?', *Third World Quarterly*, 24 (6), pp. 1095–1115.

Young, J. (1964) 'Military aspects of the 1930 Brazilian Revolution', *Hispanic American Historical Review*, 44 (2), pp. 180–196. DOI: https://doi.org/10.1215/00182168-44.2.180.

Zicman de Barros, T. and Lago, M. (2022) *Do que falamos quando falamos de populismo*. São Paulo: Companhia das Letras.

# 11

# Conclusion: Time for More? Populism's Prospects

*Andy Knott*

This concluding chapter speculates on the future of populist politics. Futurology was a regular feature of accounts on populism produced in the second half of the twentieth century. These were informed by the prevailing ideas of modernisation and developmentalism, and they insisted that populism was a temporary political phenomenon as different nations moved from one stage of development to another. Once a suitably mature stage had be reached, populism will fall by the wayside. This concluding chapter draws on two different models indicating not populism's disappearance from the political stage but, rather, its future potential. The two models are the populisation thesis and the cyclical approach, and these are laid out in the following section. They are then applied to the recent history of populism in Europe and Latin America, to establish each model's fit with political developments of the present and recent past, but also to provide a framework for populism's prospects as this century's politics continues to take shape.

This question of the future of populism can be traced back to one of its earliest recorded episodes. Historians regard the People's Party as one of populism's first iterations, prompting the first recorded coinage of the term. The consolidation of monopoly capitalism in the US, and its widespread rejection by farmers, workers and beyond was the context within which the party achieved its rapid rise. Beyond this economic backdrop, there was a further prompt for the party's emergence and consolidation in the 1890s, which informed its ideological programme. This was the publication and widespread dissemination of the utopian novel *Looking Backward 2000–1887*. Edward Bellamy's book became only the second novel to sell a million copies after *Uncle Tom's Cabin* (1852). Published in 1888, it rapidly became a best-seller that 'embodied the *Zeitgeist*' (Beaumont, 2007, p. viii), inspiring numerous societies to form across the land with the view of attending lectures and discussion groups. These considered its social and political ideals, which went on to inspire and provide much of the content for the People's Party pioneering 1892 election manifesto.

## 1. Populism's Future: From Content to Form

The intricate detail Bellamy projects onto the future society at the turn of the millennium provides a helpful contrast to the focus of the remainder of this concluding chapter. Now, we shift from content to form in order not to consider any ideological populist content but, rather, the prospects for populism as a form of politics.

Before delving into the future potential of and prospects for populism, consider a brief recap on populism's recent past and present from the vantage point of 2023. Over the past decade, the signifier populism has exploded, such that there is even talk of 'populism studies' (see, for instance, De Cleen & Glynos, 2021). These authors have dismissed the inflation of this signifier as 'populist hype' (Glynos & Mondon, 2016; De Cleen et al., 2018). In focusing on populism as a signifier (see also Dean & Maiguashca, 2020), these authors have sought to differentiate between populism as a signifier and alternatives to this – they conceive populism to be a 'logic', whereas others deem it as a 'phenomenon'. Their aim is to address the loose and persistent talk or resort to the signifier 'populism' – a 'bucket' or catch-all term into which all the aberrant and malevolent political developments of recent years can be thrown into – which in their view rarely meets populist practice, or logic. In sum, theirs is a familiar academic exercise: to restrict the way in which the term is used to a more clearly and carefully demarcated form. Their intervention and identification of the 'populist hype' is a welcome development for two reasons. In the first place, the hysterical reaction aimed at 'populism' and its excessive deployment by so many political commentators – whether they be electoral representatives, academics or journalists – has been an overfamiliar feature of the past decade. And, second, the intervention introduces a useful analytic distinction between the signifier 'populism' and populism as a phenomenon.[1] This analytic distinction enables populism to be differentiated from other (sometimes related but distinct) political phenomena, such as nationalism or socialism.

This chapter then considers the future/s of populism via an understanding of populism *per se* as a form – and not a content, ideology, vision, and so on – and that this consideration is of populism as a phenomenon, as opposed to the multiple usages that commentators attach to the signifier 'populism'. What does it mean to say that populism is a form and a phenomenon? It means that certain claims are made about the appearance of populism, alongside its disappearance and non-appearance. To say that populism appears, disappears and fails to appear is to attach the practice of populism to certain conditions. In other words, populism is contextual: within certain contexts, it has widespread prevalence, while other contexts are defined by the absence or marginalisation of populism.

With this theoretical and analytical groundwork conducted, attention now turns to analysing two different models speculating about the future of populism. Both insist that populism is a contextual phenomenon but provide markedly different accounts of populism's prospects. The first model is that of 'populisation' as developed by Simon Tormey in Chapter 5 of this collection. The second 'cyclical' model has been hinted at in the foregoing analysis, and particularly in the previous paragraph, but will be fleshed out once the 'populisation' thesis has been summarised.

## 2. Tormey and the 'Populisation' of Politics

In 'Populisation: Populism – Temporary Dysfunction or Modernity's Revenge' (Chapter 5 in this volume), Simon Tormey offers a bold diagnosis not only of contemporary politics, but also for its future. To say that politics has been 'populised' means to say that populism is with us, will continue to be with us, and that politics will display the populist form in the twenty-first century's future decades. Precisely *how* this occurs isn't elaborated, which is not altogether surprising given the speculative nature of future-gazing, but to offer three different (but not mutually exclusive) modes it could take the form of greater intensity (populism marginalises other practices of politics), wider geographic extension (it occurs in more places across the world) and, finally, longer duration (it proves to be a persistent, 'resilient'[2] or even permanent feature of politics).

As his title indicates, the historical context Tormey aligns populisation with is late modernity. Within this context, five dominant tendencies are isolated that contribute to the populisation of politics. These dominant tendencies are: the decline of traditional authority structures; the rise of individualisation; the growth of bureaucracy and its complexification; the intensification of globalisation; and the emergence of a new media ecology. Tormey arrives at this through an investigation into the 'ontology' (being and meaning) of populism, and insists that populism 'must mean something, be something. This meaning is ... located in the trends and tendencies of contemporary society (2024, p. 123).' The methodology adopted in identifying the trends and tendencies that have consolidated populism on the political scene is defined as a 'sociological approach'. This is in keeping with the 'contextual' approach advocated in this chapter and seeks to ground populism as a substantial feature – even a phenomenon – of political life. This differs from those commentators who treat populism as a species of language or rhetoric ('the people versus the elite') that can be picked up and discarded by politicians on a whim in any convenient circumstance.

The five identified tendencies are themselves a symptom of the intensifying crisis of the historical model that democracy has arrived at in late modernity. This model of electoral representation (Rosanvallon, 2008) has come increasingly under challenge (see Tormey, 2015) and has generated a proliferating register of democratic grievances. Such grievances and the intensifying crisis of the broader electoral-representative model mean that, for Tormey, populism is no longer an exception or a disruption to the normal state of affairs. Perhaps it is a harbinger that the electoral-representative model has entered into a crisis mode. These dominant tendencies when combined with the wider ennui – crisis, grievances, deficit – ensure that 'populism becomes the new normal', which is another way of saying 'populisation'. Tormey has thus diagnosed wider contextual, cultural symptoms in late modernity to account for populism's increasing prevalence, and its prospects:

> Our culture is more brusque, less thoughtful, more given to immediacy, visuality. It is by extension more affective and emotive in tone and content. The ontology of populism is thus located in the ontology of late modernity itself. (Tormey, 2024, p. 000).

The combination of these tendencies and the democratic deficits generate the short-term affective response of blaming elites, prompting the search for alternatives to 'normal politics'. This leads in turn to the search for outsiders, a role well served by populists. The particular understanding of crisis Tormey isolates is one that is chronic, rather than acute, and this habituation explains the role of crisis as the background to the populisation of politics. We could additionally name this 'perma-populism', whereby populism is neither an aberration nor a departure from a norm but a new permanent presence that can be read off the culmination of trends and tendencies generated under the conditions of late modernity.

### 3. Populism's Cyclicality

The second proposed model to understand populism's potential in the future shares two core features with the populisation model proposed by Tormey.

In the first place, in emphasising the linkage between the increasing prominence of populism and the historical context of crisis, it is in keeping with the 'sociological approach' of Tormey – or what I'd rather refer to as an understanding of populism as a phenomenon. And this overlap informs the second shared feature, namely that populism is not some ephemeral element of politics that can be taken up and discarded on a whim by politicians. As opposed to this view that treats populism as a species of rhetoric or language, the cyclical view of populism treats it as a substantial phenomenon – or a phenomenon of substance. In other words, populism is a valid response to distinctive contextual conditions that generate a range of demands – demands made by (growing numbers or groups of) people who increasingly urge politicians to implement these demands. The substantiality of these demands and depth of the crisis in which they are made means that populism is something other than the anti-populist view that dismisses it as a temporary outburst and aberration that, once normality and grown-up politics returns, is destined for the dustbin of history.

The cyclical view insists that populism is, in the first place, contextual and a substantial phenomenon and, secondly, that analytically there is a need to distinguish populism from its Others. To the first point, the linkage between populism and the context of crisis is widespread throughout the literature on populism, although this linkage is notably absent from, marginal to or inconsistent within most of its leading 'approaches' (Mudde, 2004, 2017; Mudde & Kaltwasser, 2017; Weyland, 2001, 2017; Ostiguy, 2017). To link populism with crisis is to suggest that crisis situations are the breeding ground of populism. It is also to indicate that contexts absent of crisis or crises will inhibit the flourishing, spread and persistence of populism. While crisis is its breeding ground, there is no automatic, necessary relation between populism and crisis. The crisis needs to be articulated such that it resonates widely, and this resonance facilitates the construction of a populist people or, in Laura Grattan's words, 'peopling' (Grattan, 2016) – the emergence, consolidation and increasing prominence of the people as a potent political actor coalescing behind an alternative political project. This construction of a populist people will necessarily also forge a social chasm or frontier and, in doing so, will construct the establishment, elite or some related signifier on the other side of that frontier. Another way of saying this is that the crisis needs to be of substance, and broadly felt and experienced by significant sectors of the population in order for the 'peopling' process to occur. This insistence on linking contextuality and substantial phenomenality to populism shares affinity with the economic notions of supply and demand that Cas Mudde and Cristóbal Rovira Kaltwasser (2017) align with populism. Populism becomes a substantial phenomenon within a context where both significant change is demanded from social sectors, and these are gathered together under the sign of the people through the supply or articulation of an alternative political project by a populist leader (or some other populist actor). These notions of supply and demand have the additional benefit of enabling analysts to identify whether there has been an over- or under-supply of particular populist projects. For instance, within Europe, the US and beyond, the past decade has witnessed the overwhelming prominence of right-populist projects impacting upon more 'mainstream' politics. Although these territories have experienced left-populisms, they have been more limited, raising the possibility of their under-supply.

One major cause of misunderstanding of the approach to populism outlined here – which insists that populism is a phenomenon and contextual – can be accounted for through an analysis of the notion of discourse. Discourse has been widely deployed of late within the academy and it's worth highlighting the different methodologies and understandings of two of the schools associated with discourse, namely the 'Lancaster School' and the 'Essex School'. To simplify the key distinction, the Lancaster School is associated with Critical Discourse Analysis (CDA) which seeks to analyse language – through speeches, texts, and so on – and to do so using a range of quantitative, qualitative and other methods (Fairclough, 2006, 2010, 2014; Wodak, 2015; Wodak & Meyer, 2015). The Essex School, by contrast, insists that discourse is not (just) language. Building on the work of Ernesto Laclau (and, in turn, Michel Foucault), the Essex School uses discourse to undermine the distinction between language and materiality (Laclau & Mouffe, 1985; Laclau, 1990, 1996, 2005; Howarth, 2000). Discourse as understood by Laclau and the Essex School, then, would incorporate both language and materiality, and this combination lends itself to the approach situating populism contextually, as advocated in this chapter. While the Laclauian approach is more widely practised within populism studies, the methods associated with the Lancaster School also feature (Hawkins, 2009, 2010).

While the notion of crisis continues to be interrogated in academia (see, for instance, Koeselleck, 1988; Roitman, 2014), it is used in a quite specific manner in the cyclical account through its alignment with the notion of hegemony. The crisis that is the feeding ground for populism is a hegemonic one. This entails the breakdown of an extant hegemony. When there is hegemonic breakdown, three broad alternatives are available: the extant hegemony recovers from its crisis and continues to exert its dominance over society; a rival hegemonic formation emerges and replaces it; and, finally, neither of these first two options pertain, and the crisis persists as differing political projects compete to become hegemonic but fail to embed themselves. This is what Gramsci described as 'the old is dying, but the new cannot be born' (1971; Fraser, 2019) – and it is only when an alternative hegemonic formation

CONCLUSION: TIME FOR MORE? POPULISM'S PROSPECTS    241

embeds itself that the crisis is finally averted. Populism has a far wider scope for prevalence in this third and final scenario.

This consideration of hegemonic formations is a useful entry point to the second core attribute of the cyclical account: analytically, populism exists alongside specific Others. Within Mudde's 'ideational' approach that conceives of populism as a 'thin-centred ideology', its Others are alternative ideologies, such as socialism, liberalism and conservatism (Mudde, 2004; Mudde & Kaltwasser, 2017; see also Freeden, 1996, 2017). Within populism studies, the clear rival to ideationalism is what's increasingly become known as the 'discursive-performative' approach (Moffitt, 2020; Moffitt et al., 2021). This discursive-performative approach hasn't been too forthcoming in specifying Others of populism. The most obvious example offered is that of anti-populism (Stavrakakis, 2014; Stavrakakis et al., 2018). The cyclical account requires a further Other of populism to anti-populism, which elsewhere I've designated as non-populism (Knott, 2020, 2022). This notion of non-populism is pivotal to the cyclical account, as it identifies contexts within which populism struggles to take hold. Contexts of non-populism should equally be understood as ones of hegemonic calm, in which a hegemonic formation lacks rival political projects, enabling it to propel its project forward and consolidate itself as a hegemonic formation. Within the hegemonic calm of non-populism, the populist appeal falls flat largely because there is sufficient support behind the establishment, and the peopling process of constructing a people against the establishment lacks broad resonance and fails to take hold.

While this analytic triplet of populism, anti-populism and non-populism has not been named elsewhere in the literature on populism, equivalent analyses and different signifiers operate with such a cyclical framework. Throughout the 1990s and 2000s, for instance, Chantal Mouffe (1993, 2000, 2005, 2013) developed the notion of post-politics to account for the constriction of political projects and the marginalisation of the crucial agonistic element of politics during those decades. It is post-politics itself that has become sidelined in Mouffe's more recent texts, as the space is deemed fertile to advocate alternative political projects, with calls 'for a left populism' (2018) and the movement 'towards a green democratic revolution' (2022). Mouffe's prior identification of post-politics and recent intervention behind political projects maps onto the non-populism/populism distinction raised here. Similarly, in the work of Ernesto Laclau, there are two core contrasts that share affinities with this distinction. The first is Laclau's contrast between 'the political' (which he also aligns with populism) and administration, for which Laclau relies on the motto from Saint-Simon whereby 'the government of men is replaced by the administration of things'. The second contrast relates to the two logics that are crucial to Laclau's theory: logics of equivalence and difference. While there are crucial differences between these two contrasts, there are distinct affinities between Laclau's notions of 'the political' and equivalential logics on the one hand, and administration and differential logics on the other hand. These, in turn, align with the distinction between populism and non-populism raised here. In addition, many of the leading contributions to populism studies clearly situate populism within the context of crisis (Moffitt, 2015, 2016; Stavrakakis, 2014; Stavrakakis et al., 2017; Casullo, 2020) and such contextualisation at the very least promises an acceptance of the cyclical account offered here.

In contrast to the singular future of the populisation thesis offered by Tormey, the cyclical account points towards different potential futures for populism. Put simply, populism could persist if a new hegemonic formation fails to embed itself and either a populist challenge or rival populist projects retain political prominence, or it could be marginalised through the consolidation of such a framework as it wards off populist challenges and succeeds in bringing a period of protracted hegemonic calm into being. One of the heuristic benefits of both the populisation thesis and the cyclical account is that they offer analytical frames built from past and present populist experiences to inform future analyses of populism.

## 4. The Models' Application to Continental Histories of Populism

While both models can be applied to different continental histories of populism, their heuristic fertility will only become apparent through the populist experiences of the future. In offering a frame through which the future(s) of populism can be analysed, they are necessarily speculative and their research potential is bound up with the fate of populism into the 2020s and beyond. When analysed alongside past and present populist episodes, however, different continental trajectories promise heuristic potential for each model.

The twenty-first-century Latin American experience with populism points towards the populisation thesis. The new millennium commenced with the coinage of the moniker 'the pink tide' to account for the return of populism through first multiple and widespread crises and then the emergence and consolidation of populist presidencies, including Chavez, Correa, Morales, Lula and the Kirchners. The pink tide itself was directly preceded by what became known within the literature during the 1990s as 'neopopulism', a new assemblage of populism and neoliberalism (Weyland, 1999, 2001). The pink tide was a direct response to the politics of neopopulism. As Casullo (2024, pp. 169–87) outlines in this collection, the pink tide itself proved remarkably resilient but spawned new but different rival populist projects, most prominently Jair Bolsonaro. In Brazil, Bolsonaro's presidency prompted Lula's return, while in Argentina Christina Fernández de Kirchner became vice-president in 2019. Lula and Kirchner are just a part of a wider turn to the left and/or populism across the continent in recent years. All of this activity points towards populism becoming the 'new normal' in South America, such that we could speak about the permanence of populism, or even 'perma-populism', as the continent's distinctive and persistent form of politics. Such terminology is very much in keeping with the populisation thesis offered by Tormey.

The twentieth-century populist experience in South America, however, was more in keeping with the cyclical model. There was an explosion of populist projects in the middle of that century, with Peronism as the exemplar, but the practice spread throughout the continent. These episodes were interrupted by a series of non-populist projects, in which the people and democracy were truncated, and military dictatorships were installed and remained until the century's closing decades. It is in Europe – more especially, Western Europe – that the cyclical model maps onto the recent history and present of populism. There is growing acceptance that Europe's post-war history has been defined by two successive political projects or, to adopt the terminology of this chapter, two successive hegemonic formations. The first goes under various names including 'the post-war consensus', Keynesianism, 'the historic compromise' and social democracy, and lasted at least until the 1970s. It was then replaced by what I'll term neoliberal financialised globalisation, which began with Margaret Thatcher and Ronald Reagan, before then spreading in Europe, and also elsewhere via the Washington Consensus. The 2008 financial crisis was the moment in which the onward march of this hegemonic formation entered into difficulty.

The solidity (or calm) of these two hegemonic formations made it difficult for populism to flourish for (at least) a generation, but the key question is what happened when they were beset with crisis and the hegemonic formation began to break down. In terms of the shift from the post-war consensus to neoliberal financialised globalisation, few accounts find a role for populism in this transition. The notion of 'authoritarian populism' developed by Stuart Hall (1983, 1988a, 1988b) is somewhat of an outlier. During the 1970s, there was no such thing as 'populism studies' or 'populist hype', and populism was very much a marginal, obscure pursuit within academies in the Global North. This may explain the reluctance to align populism with the shift between hegemonic formations, but a more likely explanation is that populist actors themselves were absent. In other words, the shift was not brought about through an antagonism between the people and the establishment, but rather was achieved through other means. The same cannot be said for the breakdown of the hegemonic formation of neoliberal financialised globalisation that has occurred since 2008. In the past fifteen years, populism has been dictionaries' 'word of the year', and both populism studies and the populist hype have been widespread. While commentators frequently predict the demise of populism and the return of serious politics, it too has proved a persistent feature of the past decade's politics. This might point towards its permanence on the stage of the Global North and give succour to the populisation thesis but, equally, it might point towards a protracted interregnum before the success of a new hegemonic formation, its consolidation and a future period of hegemonic calm and non-populism – in line with the cyclical account. Several rival political projects have emerged in Europe (and beyond) during the past fifteen years – with the nationalist challenge to the globalisation prong of the neoliberal financialised globalisation trident most prominent – but, as yet, few commentators have insisted that we've entered into a new stable period of calm, in line with the consolidation of a hegemonic formation. Some of the recent nationalist challengers have eschewed the populist form, whereas others have embraced it fully. In sum, from within a protracted crisis and extended hegemonic breakdown, we lack the vantage point to identify whether a new hegemonic formation will be achieved, when or even if it will do so, and what its 'flavour' will be (or, put differently, what contents it will display).

The chronicity and protraction of the crisis experienced in Europe may also point towards Latin America as serving as the harbinger for a more widely held politics. The extent and resilience of the pink tide alongside the successive and continuing episodes with populism suggest it as 'the new normal' of politics, in keeping with the populisation thesis – and even to its travelling geographically to other continents such as Europe. Equally, however, it might transpire that the cycle turns again, and Europe returns to the non-populism and calm of a new hegemonic formation which travels elsewhere.

Both scenarios feature in what remains the most significant theoretical contribution to our understanding of populism, namely the work of Ernesto Laclau. Through the two contrasts of the political versus administration and the logics of equivalence and difference, this chapter has already aligned Laclau with the cyclical account. At the same time, the populisation thesis can locate theoretical resources within his account. This is perhaps most prevalent in the closing sentence of *On Populist Reason* before that text's 'Concluding Remarks' in which Laclau directly engages with his contemporaries. In this final paragraph, it is speculated that:

> Perhaps what is dawning as a possibility in our political experience is something radically different from what postmodern prophets of the 'end of politics' are announcing: the arrival at a fully political era, because the dissolution of the marks of certainty does not give the political game any aprioristic necessary terrain but, rather, the possibility of constantly redefining the terrain itself. (Laclau, 2005, p. 222)

This dual possibility in Laclau alongside the two models enumerated in this chapter offer alternative analyses of populism's potential to the dominant account that prevails throughout academia, journalism and representative politics. This dominant account articulates an anti-populist projection of the future for politics. It insists that populism is a temporary aberration, and that normal, adult politics will resume once the public has awakened from its deviant departure. This dominant anti-populist account of populism's future has a long history, and it can be traced back at least as far as the developmentalist and modernisation theories of the later twentieth century (Germani, 1978; Di Tella, 1965). These accounts insisted that history went through stages, and that populism was a temporary sign highlighting difficulties in the passage from one stage to the next – difficulties that, in time, would be superseded such that the stagist model could continue on its merry way. The latest iteration of the anti-populist position is yet to learn the lesson that the analyses of Germani and Di Tella now reveal – that populism has returned and has remained and, once it disappears, its potential to return remains.

### Notes

1. This chapter uses the term phenomenon to distinguish populism as a phenomenon from populism as a signifier. Populism's phenomenality is used alongside the analytic understanding of populism as a form that occurs in specific contexts. Other contributors to the debate prefer to use other terms to distinguish the signifier populism from something else, usually a logic. For a fuller elaboration, see Knott (2022).
2. See Chapter 8 of this collection.

### References

Beaumont, M. (2007) 'Introduction' to Edward Bellamy *Looking backward 2000–1887*. Oxford: Oxford University Press.

Bellamy, E. (2007) *Looking backward 2000–1887*. Oxford: Oxford University Press.

Casullo, M. (2020) 'Populism and myth', in Eklundh, E. and Knott, A. (eds) *The populist manifesto*. London: Rowman and Littlefield, pp. 25–38.

Casullo, M. (2024) 'Antagonism, flexibility and the surprising resilience of populism in Latin America', in Knott, A. (ed.) *Populism and time: temporalities of a disruptive politics*. Edinburgh: Edinburgh University Press, chapter 8, this volume, pp. 169–87.

Dean, J. and Maiguashca, B. (2020) 'Did somebody say populism? Towards a renewal and reorientation of populism studies', *Journal of Political Ideologies*, 25 (1), pp. 11–27.

De Cleen, B. and Glynos, J. (2021) 'Beyond populism studies', *Journal of Language and Politics*, 20 (1), pp. 178–195.

De Cleen, B., Glynos, J. and Mondon, A. (2018) 'Critical research on populism: nine rules of engagement', *Organization*, 25 (5), pp. 649–661.

Di Tella, T. (1965) 'Populism and reform in Latin America', in Veliz, C. (ed.) *Obstacles to change in Latin America*. London: Oxford University Press.

Fairclough, N. (2006) *Language and globalization*. London: Routledge.

Fairclough, N. (2010) *Critical discourse analysis: the critical study of language*. London: Routledge.

Fairclough, N. (2014) *Language and power*. London: Routledge.

Fraser, N. (2019) *The old is dying and the new cannot be born*. London: Verso.

Freeden, M. (1996) *Ideologies and political theory: a conceptual approach*. Oxford: Oxford University Press.

Freeden, M. (2017) 'After the Brexit referendum: revisiting populism as an ideology', *Journal of Political Ideologies*, 22 (1), pp. 1–11.

Germani, G. (1978) *Authoritarianism, fascism and national populism*. London: Routledge.

Glynos, J. and Mondon, A. (2016) 'The political logic of populist hype: the case of right-wing populism's "meteoric rise" and its relation to the status quo', *Populismus* Working Papers No. 4.

Gramsci, A. (1971) *Selections from the prison notebooks*. London: Lawrence and Wishart.

Grattan, L. (2016) *Populism's power: radical grassroots democracy in America*. Oxford: Oxford University Press.

Hall, S. (1983) 'The great moving right show', in Hall, S. and Jacques, M. (eds) *The politics of Thatcherism*. London: Lawrence and Wishart.

Hall, S. (1988a) 'Popular-democratic vs authoritarian populism: two ways of "taking democracy seriously"', in *The hard road to renewal: Thatcherism and the crisis of the left*. London: Verso, pp. 123–149.

Hall, S. (1988b) 'Authoritarian populism: a reply to Jessop et al.', in *The*

*hard road to renewal: Thatcherism and the crisis of the left*. London: Verso, pp. 150–160.
Hawkins, K. (2009) 'Is Chávez populist? Measuring populist discourse in comparative perspective', *Comparative Political Studies*, 42 (8), pp. 1040–1067.
Hawkins, K. (2010) *Venezuela's Chavismo and populism in comparative perspective*. Cambridge: Cambridge University Press.
Howarth, D. (2000) *Discourse*. Buckingham: Open University Press.
Knott, A. (2020) 'Populism: the politics of a definition', in Eklundh, E. and Knott, A. (eds) *The populist manifesto*. London: Rowman and Littlefield, pp. 9–24.
Knott, A. (2022) 'Theory after practice: revisiting populism and hegemony', *Journal for the Study of Radicalism*, 16 (2), pp. 39–56.
Koeselleck, R. (1988) *Critique and crisis: enlightenment and the pathogenesis of modern society*. Cambridge, MA: The MIT Press.
Laclau, E. (1990) *New reflections on the revolution of our time*. London: Verso.
Laclau, E. (1996) *Emancipation(s)*. London: Verso.
Laclau, E. (2005) *On populist reason*. London: Verso.
Laclau E. and Mouffe, C. (1985) *Hegemony and socialist strategy: towards a radical democratic politics*. London: Verso.
Moffitt, B. (2015) 'How to perform crisis: a model for understanding the role of crisis in contemporary populism', *Government and Opposition*, 50 (2), pp. 189–217.
Moffitt, B. (2016) *The global rise of populism: performance, political style, and representation*. Stanford, CA: Stanford University Press.
Moffitt, B. (2020) *Populism*. Cambridge: Polity.
Moffitt, B., Ostiguy, P. and Panizza, F. (2021) *Populism in global perspective: a performative and discursive approach*. London: Routledge.
Mouffe, C. (1993) *The return of the political*. London: Verso.
Mouffe, C. (2000) *The democratic paradox*. London: Verso.
Mouffe, C. (2005) *On the political*. London: Verso.
Mouffe, C. (2013) *Agonistics: thinking the world politically*. London: Verso.
Mouffe, C. (2018) *For a left populism*. London: Verso.
Mouffe, C. (2022) *Towards a green democratic revolution*. London: Verso.
Mudde, C. (2004) 'The populist zeitgeist', *Government and Opposition*, 39 (4), pp. 541–563.
Mudde, C. (2017) 'Populism: an ideational approach', in Rovira Kaltwasser, C., Taggart, P., Ochoa Espejo, P. and Ostiguy, P. (eds) *The Oxford handbook of populism*. Oxford: Oxford University Press, pp. 27–47.
Mudde, C. and Kaltwasser, C. (2017) *Populism: a very short introduction*. Oxford: Oxford University Press.

Ostiguy, P. (2017) 'Populism: a socio-cultural approach', in Rovira Kaltwasser, C., Taggart, P., Ochoa Espejo, P. and Ostiguy, P. (eds) *The Oxford handbook of populism*. Oxford: Oxford University Press, pp. 73–97.

Roitman, J. (2014) *Anti-crisis*. Durham, NC: Duke University Press.

Rosanvallon, P. (2008) *Counter-democracy: politics in an age of distrust*. Cambridge: Cambridge University Press.

Stavrakakis, Y. (2014) 'The return of "the people": populism and anti-populism in the shadow of the European crisis', *Constellations*, 23 (4), pp. 505–517.

Stavrakakis, Y., Katsambekis, G., Kioupkiolis, A., Nikisianis, N. and Siomos, T. (2017) 'Populism, anti-populism and crisis', *Contemporary Political Theory*, 17 (1), pp. 4–27.

Tormey, S. (2015) *The end of representative politics*. Cambridge: Polity Press.

Tormey, S. (2024) 'Populisation: populism – temporary dysfunction or modernity's revenge?', in Knott, A. (ed.) *Populism and time: temporalities of a disruptive politics*. Edinburgh: Edinburgh University Press, chapter 5, this volume, pp. 107–25.

Weyland, K. (1999) 'Neoliberal populism in Latin America and Eastern Europe', *Comparative Politics*, 31 (4), pp. 379–401.

Weyland, K. (2001) 'Clarifying a contested concept: populism in the study of Latin American politics', *Comparative Politics*, 34 (1), pp. 1–22.

Weyland, K. (2017) 'Populism: a political-strategic approach', in Rovira Kaltwasser, C., Taggart, P., Ochoa Espejo, P. and Ostiguy, P. (eds) *The Oxford handbook of populism*. Oxford: Oxford University Press, pp. 48–72.

Wodak, R. (2015) *The politics of fear: the shameless normalization of far-right discourse*. London: Sage.

Wodak, R. and Meyer, M. (2015) (3rd edn) *Methods of critical discourse studies*. London: Sage.

# Index

abolitionists, 209, 211
Aboy, G., 78
Acción Democrática (AD), 175, 179
Ackermann, B., 80
administration, 9, 45, 241
agency, 6, 13, 43, 133, 152, 155, 164
Aizpuru, M. S., 198
alchemy, 6
Alemán, J., 190
Alfaro, E., 198
Alfonsin, R., 176
Allende, S., 198
Amaru, T., 198
Amazon, 229
American revolution, 44, 133
Anastasiou, M., 17
Anaximander, 83
*ancient régime*, 46
Andrade, D., 217
anger, 5
antagonism, 14, 18, 45, 130–2,
    142–3, 150–1, 159, 169–70,
    172–4, 181–2, 184, 188, 190,
    193, 197–9, 201, 208, 212–14,
    217–18, 222–3, 225, 227–8,
    230–1, 243
anti-authoritarian, 53
anti-capitalist, 92, 189

anti-constitutionalism, 220
anti-corruption, 223
anti-democratic, 30, 52, 55, 56,
    60–1, 63, 71, 121, 141, 222,
    224
anti-dictatorship, 181
anti-elitism, 112, 170, 210, 218,
    230
anti-Enlightenment, 30
anti-establishment, 121
Antifa, 148
anti-government, 151, 183
anti-institutional, 179, 198
anti-left, 223
anti-liberal, 141
anti-populism, 14, 19, 31, 61, 239,
    241, 245
anti-socialist, 149
anti-system, 176
Arab revolutions 2011, 192
Aras, A., 228
Ardern, J., 52
Arditi, B., 97, 191–2
Arendt, H., 11, 154
Argentina, 29, 31–2, 172, 175–7,
    181, 193–6, 200–1, 212, 242
    debt crisis, 194–5
Aristotle, 54, 152

Athens, 29
austerity, 111, 121, 176, 195, 215
Australia, 111
Austria, 112
authoritarian, 29–30, 33–4, 52–5, 57, 61, 64, 70–1, 117, 119, 121, 170–1, 174, 178, 190–1, 207, 209, 211, 221, 226, 231
autocracy, 36
Azurduy, J., 198

Bachelet, M., 181–2
Badiou, A., 192
Bang, H., 120
Banzer, H., 176
Barcelona, 193
Barros, M., and Martínez, N., 190
beginnings, 20; *see also* origins, 27
Belgrano, M., 198
*Bell, The*, 35
Bellamy, E., 235–6
Benjamin, W., 95
Berlin Wall, 9, 192
Berlusconi, S., 171
Bertomeu, J. F. G., and Saffron, M. P., 226
Biden, J., 122
Biglieri, P., 190
Biglieri, P., and Cadahia, L., 190–1
Biglieri, P., and Perelló, G., 18, 97, 190–1
Black Lives Matter, 148
Blair, T., 12
Blengino, L., 191
Blyth, M., 111
Bødker, H., and Anderson, C., 128
Bolivar, S., 198
Bolivarian, 18, 198
Bolivarian Alternative for the Americas (ALBA), 201

Bolivia, 172, 175–7, 179, 183, 194, 199–201, 213, 225
   Constitution of the Pluri-National State 2009, 225
   Pluri-National Constitutional Court, 225
Bolshevik, 94
   Bolshevik (October) revolution, 34, 82
Bolsonaro, J., 171, 207, 209, 217, 220–3, 226, 228–31, 241
Bolsonarism, 221, 223
Bonapartism, 189
Boric, G., 181
Borriello, A., and Jäger, A., 45
Boulangism, 46
bourgeois, 95, 115, 217
Brasilia, 222
Brazil, 19, 53, 177, 180–1, 196, 207–10, 212–16, 218, 221–3, 227, 229–31, 242
   Chamber of Deputies, 228
   Communist Party, 211, 226
   Constitutional Charter 1824, 209
   Federal Police, 219
   Federal Supreme Court (STF), 182, 219–22, 227–9
   Fourth Regional Appellate Court, 219
   National Association of Federal Prosecutors, 228
   National Congress, 200, 216, 220, 222, 227–9
   'Old Republic' 1889–1930, 209
   Planalto Palace, 222
   Prosecutor General, 228
   Public Prosecutor's Office, 219, 228
   Republican Constitution 1891, 209–10

1930 Revolution, 215, 226
1934 Constitution, 210, 226
1937 Constitution, 210, 226–7
1967 Constitution, 211
1969 Constitutional Amendment, 211
1988 Constitution, 211, 220, 227–9, 231
Brexit, 31, 53, 108, 118, 122
Brown, W., 192
Bucaram, A., 176
Buenos Aires, 29, 33, 196, 201
Bustinduy, P., and Lago, J., 92

*cabecita negra*, 33
Cano, G., 81
Canovan, M., 8, 12, 41–4, 57, 128, 173, 193
capitalism, 31, 46, 115, 135, 149, 153, 157, 159–61, 189, 213
  advanced capitalism, 16, 108
  capitalist modernity, 108
  financial capitalism, 160
  industrial capitalism, 209
  monopoly capitalism, 235
Capitol, 52
Caracazo, 176, 194
Castillo, P., 178
Casullo, M. E., 18, 242
Catholic, 96, 182
Ceia, E. M., 19
centrist, 63
chain of equivalence, 152, 196–7, 241; *see also* logic of equivalence
Chartism, 44, 46–7
Chávez, H., 31, 169, 172, 175, 179–80, 183, 193–4, 198, 213, 242
  Chavism, 181, 197

Chazel and Fernández Vázquez, 77–8, 93
Chernyshevsky, N., 35, 40
Chesterton, G. K., 42
Chile, 177, 180–1
China, 173, 177
Christian Democrats, 181
Christian socialist, 40
*chronos*, 91
Chun, W., 161
citizens, 76, 110, 112, 117, 119–20, 151, 156, 158–9, 162, 200, 211, 214, 224
Civil War, 38, 94
class, 42, 77–8, 80, 109–10, 115, 130, 137, 172, 189, 196
  class conflict, 11
  class consciousness, 11
  class inequality, 148
Cold War, 30, 34, 189
Collor de Mello, F., 209, 216, 222–3, 226–7, 229–31
Colombian Plan, 195
colonial, 209
colonial state, 199
Comité de Oranización Política Electoral Independiente (COPEI), 175, 179
communism, 27, 29–30, 33, 94, 97, 114, 149
Community of Latin American and Caribbean States (CELAC), 201
comparative politics, 1
Concertación de Partidos por la Democracia, 180–1
Congress, 184
conservative, 29, 43, 58–60, 64, 75, 111, 142, 149, 192, 198, 209–10, 219, 221, 223, 225, 241

Conservative Party, The, 31
Constituent Assembly, 209, 211, 226, 228
constitution, 19, 198–9, 207, 209, 211, 219, 221–2, 225, 226, 228, 231
   constitutional democracy, 208
   constitutionalism, 207–8, 223, 227, 229–31
construction of the people, 40–1, 53, 77, 151, 159, 163, 201, 239, 241
*Contemporary, The*, 35
context, 19
contingency, 11–12
Convertibility Law 1991, 194
Corbyn, J., 97, 108, 118
   Corbynism, 53
Coronel, V., and Cadahia, L., 191, 199
Correa, R., 169, 172, 175–6, 179–80, 182–3, 193, 195, 213, 242
Couldry, N., 155
Couldry, N., and Hepp, A., 155
counter-hegemony, 76, 149, 162, 191, 199
coup d'état, 32, 173, 175–6, 180, 194, 220, 226
   military coup, 211
COVID-19, 117, 119, 171, 221
crisis, 8, 13, 16, 18, 39, 53, 65, 90, 108–14, 117, 119–20, 123, 128–9, 131, 148, 169, 172–4, 176–9, 182–4, 207–8, 211–12, 214–16, 218–19, 223, 225, 229–31, 238, 240, 242–4
   organic crisis, 76
   regime crisis, 76

Critical Discourse Analysis (CDA), 240
Cuban revolution 1959, 210
Cunha, E., 220
cyclical approach, 235, 237–43

Dardenism, 196
*decamisados*, 33
De Cleen, B., 191
decolonial theory, 18
'deep state', 116
De Ípola, E., 189
De la Rua, F., 176, 195
democracy, 14, 15, 20, 29, 30, 33–4, 40, 46, 52–8, 60–2, 64–71, 76, 92, 94, 113, 120, 134–5, 137, 140–3, 155, 157, 159, 162–3, 171, 173–4, 202, 207, 209, 211, 214, 224–6, 241, 243
   democratic illiberalism, 107
   democratic revolution, 58, 131
   democratic theory, 15
   *demos*, 107
Democrat Party, 39
Denmark, 79
de-proletarianization, 155
Derrida, J., 14, 67, 79, 92, 97, 192
De San Martín, J., 198
Deuze, M., 155
developmentalism, 3, 217, 235, 245
Devenney, M., 191
diachrony, 17, 126–8, 130, 135, 143
dictatorship, 3, 94, 173, 210–11
   military dictatorship, 3, 32, 175, 216, 218, 227, 243
dislocation, 135, 137, 139, 142, 189, 193, 196
Di Tella, T., 189, 245
dollarisation, 179
Dorrego, M., 198

Draghi, M., 122
Duterte, R., 31

Ecuador, 172, 175–7, 179, 183, 194–5, 199, 201, 213
Eisenhower, D., 116
electoral democracy, 32
elite/s, 17, 41, 44, 61–2, 107, 109–10, 117–22, 150–2, 158–9, 173, 183, 194–5, 207, 209–15, 217, 221, 223–4, 228, 230, 239
  cultural elite, 179
  economic elite, 176, 210–12, 215, 218
  European/EU elite, 31
  political elite, 31
  power elite, the, 116
Ellul, J., 153
Ely, C., 34
emancipation, 15, 191
Emancipation Act 1861, 28, 35
emotions, 5
empty signifier, 95, 140
'the end of history', 9, 149, 192
English Civil War, 44
Enlightenment, 30, 33
Erdogan, R. T., 31
Errejón, I., 76–8, 80, 89–91, 93
eruption, 5–6
Essex School, 107, 113, 190–1, 240
establishment, the, 10, 12, 14, 16, 38–9, 41, 109–10, 129, 132, 239, 241, 243
Europe, 4, 131, 235, 243–4
  Eastern Europe, 192
  European Union, 173
  European Parliament, 75, 77
  Nazi Europe, 193
  Western Europe, 4, 190, 243
experts, 17, 114, 120

explosion, 6
extremism, 61
event, 108

Facebook, 119, 160–2
Farage, N., 31, 110
fascism, 27, 30, 33, 53, 60–1, 71, 95, 137, 189–90
  postfascism, 30
Fassin, E., 190
feminist, 62, 190
  feminist populism, 190
feudalism, 35, 115–16
Figner, V., 36
finance, 38, 173; *see also* banking
  financial crisis, 221
  1929 Financial Crisis, 212, 215
Finchelstein, F., 27–34, 47
First World War, 94
Fixed Point Pact, 194
*Fort Apache*, 76
Fortuyn, P., 111
Foucault, M., 116, 240
France, 53, 122
Franco, F., 94
Frankfurt School, 97
Franzé, J., 78, 94
Freeden, M., 29
French revolution, 44–6, 54, 58, 82, 192
Frente Amplio, 180–2
Fujimori, A., 178, 213
*Futurama*, 159

Gaitán, J. E., 34
Gallie, W. E., 43
García, A., 178
gender, 130
general will, the, 43
Germani, G., 189, 245

Germany, 82, 112, 122, 189
  German, 85
Global Financial Crisis 2008, 111, 121, 148, 178
globalisation, 1, 12, 16, 109, 111–12, 114, 117–18, 137, 153, 237
Global North, 18–19, 160, 193, 199, 243–4
Goethe, J. W., 83
Goodhart, D., 111
Goodwyn, L., 40
Goulart, J., 211, 227
governmentality, 116
Gramsci, A., 13, 76, 78, 89, 92, 240
  Neo-Gramscian, 88
Grattan, L., 39–40, 239
Greece, 5, 111
  Ancient Greek, 9, 88
Gross Domestic Product (GDP), 177–8
*Guardian, The*, 55, 61
Guevara, E. C., 198
Gunnarsson-Payne, J., and Korolczuk, E., 190
Gutiérrez, C. L., 176, 179, 195

Hall, S., 243
Hamlet, 14, 75, 79
Hanson, P., 31
Heath, D., 160
Hegel, G., 10, 14, 79, 89
  Hegelian, 11, 14, 82
hegemonic, 58, 151, 153, 158–9, 162–3, 176–8, 188, 196, 240
  hegemonic formation, 8, 240–2, 244
  hegemonic framework, 13–14, 39
Heidegger, M., 2, 7–9, 16, 80, 84–90, 92–4
Henley, J., 55

Heraclitus, 84, 89
Herzen, A., 35–6, 40
heterogeneity, 78
history, 2–3, 20, 81–7, 89, 126, 130, 132, 135, 140, 153–5, 197, 207, 211, 222, 225, 229–31, 235, 243, 245
  historians, 42, 123
  historiography, 27, 35, 198
Hobbes, T., 43
Hobsbawm, E., 29
Hofstadter, R., 116, 189
Hong Kong, 53, 119
Humala, O., 178
Hungary, 171
Husserl, E., 9, 94, 193–4

Ibarra, J. M. B., 34
ideational, 35
identity, 109, 112, 129, 131–2, 138–41, 143, 150, 152, 154, 163, 172, 190, 197, 201, 213–14
ideology, 9, 30, 37–8, 40, 60, 62, 77–8, 80, 92, 107, 114–15, 118–19, 134, 141–2, 158, 170, 177, 214, 222, 225, 229, 231, 235–6
  thin-centred ideology, 35, 241
Iglesias, P., 76–8, 80, 89–91, 93–5
illiberal, 207, 224
illiberal democracy, 59
indigenous, 195, 198–9, 201, 225, 229
*Indignados*, 75–6, 89, 94–5, 119; *see also* 15M
individual, the, 42
  individualisation, 237
  individuation, 154
Industrial Revolution, 17

industrialisation, 28, 153, 210, 212, 215
Indymedia, 118
inflation, 4
Information Age, 155–6, 159
insecurity, 6
instability, 6
institutions, 6, 19, 43, 68–9, 76, 91, 112, 122, 128, 131, 149–52, 157, 170, 182, 184, 189, 191, 198–201, 207–8, 214–15, 218, 223–8, 231
institutionalisation, 18, 80, 139–40, 143, 181–2, 200–1, 216
intellectuals, 35
International Monetary Fund, IMF, 173, 195
international relations, 1
Internet, 17, 160–1
Internet Society, The, 160
Ionescu, G., and Gellner, E., 4, 54
Ireland, 123
Israel, 52
Italian city-states, 44
Italy, 52, 111, 189
Italy's Democratic Party, 53
*Izquierda Anticapilista* (Anticapitalist Left), 76–7, 80, 89, 91
*Izquierda Unida* (United Left), 77, 93

Jacobin, 192
Jay, M., 192
Johnson, B., 118, 121
Judis, J., 31
June Journeys, 219–20, 228

*Kairós*, 91
Kast, F., 181
Katari, T., 198

Kazin, M., 40
Keynesianism, 243
Kierkegaard, S., 90
Kioupkiolis, A., 76, 78
Kirchner, C. F., 169, 172, 175–6, 180–2, 193, 243
Kirchner, N., 169, 172, 175–6, 180, 182, 193, 195
Kirchners, 34, 176, 197, 242
Knott, A., 90
Kristeva, J., 192
Kukszinky, P. P., 178

Labour Party, 31
Lacan, J., 79
Laclau, E., 9, 14, 15, 41–2, 44–6, 53, 56–8, 76–9, 93–4, 130, 134, 140, 149–52, 159, 163–4, 170, 191, 193–4, 196, 214, 217, 222–4, 230, 240–2, 244–5
Laclau, E., and Mouffe, C., 15–16, 46, 57–9, 62–4, 66, 70, 129–30, 159, 188
*La France Insoumise* (France Unbound), 97
Lahtinen, M., 11–12
Lancaster School, 240
Land and Freedom, 35–6
Latin America, 3, 16, 18–19, 76, 97, 111, 170, 188–91, 193–4, 197–8, 201, 212–15, 226, 229–30, 235, 242, 244
*La Tuerka* (The Screw), 76
Lefort, C., 65–6, 69–70
left(-wing), 53, 56–61, 63, 91, 93–5, 111, 121, 169, 182, 184, 189–90, 192, 195–6, 217–19
left and right, 13, 52, 56, 61, 70–1, 112, 118
Lenin, V., 90, 94

Le Pen, J.-M., 5
Le Pen, M., 31, 110, 121
Le Pens, 111
Levinas, E., 67
LGBTI+, 201
liberal, 29, 32–35, 53, 58–61, 63–4, 70, 121, 137, 142, 149, 151, 189, 198, 209–10, 218, 227, 241
liberal democracy, 16, 27, 29, 34, 57–8, 108, 121–2, 160, 224, 228
   liberal constitutionalism, 208, 224, 229
   liberal democratic, 59–61, 63–4, 70–1, 120, 160, 213, 230
   liberal democratic constitutionalism, 19, 208, 222, 224, 227, 230
liberal-left, 55
libertarian, 162
Linz, J., 54
Lockean individualism, 41
*Looking Backward, 2000–1887*, 235
*L'Ordine Nuovo*, 78
Lugo, F., 169, 172, 178, 180, 182
Lula (Luiz Inácio Lula di Silva), 53, 171, 181–2, 208–9, 216, 218–22, 226–31, 242–3
   Lulism, 218
Lyotard, J.-F., 114

Machiavelli, N., 2, 7, 10–11, 14
Macri, M., 176
Macron, E., 118
Maduro, N., 171
Mahaud, J., 176
Managua, 193
Marchart, O., 190–1
Marcuse, H., 116

Marramao, G., 191
Marx, K., 10–11, 89, 95, 114–15, 135
   Marx, K., and Engels, F., 35, 88
Marxism, 10–11, 13, 15, 97, 192
Marxist, 14, 40, 69, 78, 89, 91, 149, 173, 196
masses, the, 170–1, 199, 212–16, 218, 223, 225
Mazzolini, S., 191
Mazzolini, S., and Borriello, A., 78, 90
media theory, 20
mediatisation, 121
Mélenchon, J.-L., 112
Meloni, G., 111, 121
Mendonça, A., 228
Menem, C., 176
*Mensalão*, 217
Merkel, A., 122
*mestizos*, 198
metaphor, 2
#Me Too, 148
Mexico, 213
middle class, 33, 76, 78–9, 115–16, 151, 177, 210, 219, 221, 223, 225
military industrial complex, 116
Mill, J. S., 65
minorities, 32
mobilisation, 4, 18, 32, 44, 78, 110, 113, 150, 169–70, 172–4, 180–4, 193, 199, 221
modernisation, 3, 189, 235, 245
modernity, 2, 9–10, 16, 46, 79, 109, 114, 116, 120, 126–7, 130–2, 135, 137–9, 153, 157–8
   late modernity, 16, 123, 138, 237
Moffitt, B., 1, 6, 47
monarchy, 65–6, 91, 95, 209

monopoly, 39
  monopoly capital, 41
Morales, E., 34, 169, 172, 175–6, 179–80, 182–3, 193, 195–6, 213, 225, 242
More, T., 88
Moreno, M., 198
Moro, S., 219–20
Moscow, 35
Mouffe, C., 53, 56, 58, 118, 190, 241
Movimiento al Socialismo (MAS), 175–6
Movimiento Nacionalista Revolucionario (MNR), 179
Mudde, C., 13, 35, 54–5, 60, 241
  Mudde, C., and Kaltwasser, C. R., 13, 59, 239
Mulattos, 198
Müller, J.-W., 54, 59
Mumford, L., 153
Murmis, M., and Porantiero, J., 189
*muzhik*, 36, 40
Myspace, 160

Napoleon, 90
*narodniki*, 28, 34–8, 40, 46
National Front, 5, 53; see also Rassemblement National, 31
nationalism, 132, 140, 148, 191, 210, 221, 236, 244
nativism, 112
necessity, 11–12
neoliberal, 3, 58, 60, 71, 149, 158–61, 163, 179, 182, 188, 190, 192, 194–6, 200, 212–13, 215–17, 220–3, 227
  neoliberal financialised globalisation, 243–4
neopopulism, 3, 209, 213, 215–16, 222, 230, 242

New Deal, 31
New Zealand, 52
Nicaragua, 52
Nietzsche, F., 16, 75, 80–5, 87, 89, 94, 114
Nijensohn, M., 190
non-democratic, 56, 61
non-populism, 169, 176–7, 182, 241–4
Nordic, 112
Norris, P., 111
nostalgia, 20
  nostalgic, 87, 96

Oakeshott, M., 193
*obshchestvo*, 37
Ocasio-Cortez, A., 13
Occupy, 5, 13, 31, 119, 148
Oedipus, 79
oligarchy, 32, 94, 191, 195–6, 198, 200–1, 209, 215–16
*On Populist Reason*, 45, 244
ontology, 2, 19, 27, 34, 40, 44–7, 65, 79–80, 84–5, 87, 107–9, 123, 126, 130–1, 135–6, 142, 191, 237
Operation Car Wash, 217, 219–21, 231
opportunism, 20
  opportunist, 87, 96–7
Orbán, V., 171
overdetermination, 134, 139

Pachakutik Movement, 195
Panizza, F., 78
Paraguay, 172, 175, 177–9
Paris, 69, 193
Partido Trabalhista (PT), 180, 217, 219, 221, 223, 228; *see also* Workers Party

peasant, 35–8, 195, 198, 200
Pedro I, 209
Pegida, 33
People's Party, The, 13, 28, 31, 34, 38–40, 46, 235–6
peopling, 40, 239, 241
Pérez Liñán, A., 174
Perón, E., 33
Perón, J., 3, 29, 31, 176, 198, 212
  Peronism, 33–4, 175–6, 189, 191, 197–8, 200, 243
Peru, 177–8, 213
Petrograd, 193
Philippines, 52
philosophy, 20
'the pink tide', 3, 18, 97, 213, 242, 244
Plato, 54, 65, 77
Plaza de Mayo, 201
Plaza Grande del Palacio de Carondelet, 201
plebeian, 43–6, 79
pluralism, 227
  pluralisation, 15
Podemos, 5, 16, 31, 34, 75–80, 88, 90–7, 112, 118, 188
  Unidos Podemos, 93
'the political', 9, 15–17, 28, 42, 45–6, 97–8, 129, 150, 154, 160, 163, 241–2
political class, 152
political science, 20, 107, 113, 123, 188
  comparative political science, 113
political theory, 20, 42, 87, 97, 123, 188
Popular Democratic Movement, 195
populism, 1–6, 8–10, 12, 14–20, 27–35, 37–42, 44–7, 53–6, 59, 61–4, 67, 70, 79, 88, 90, 93, 97–8, 107–13, 119–23, 126–33, 135, 138–43, 149–52, 159–60, 164, 169–74, 177, 181–2, 184, 188–91, 193, 196–9, 201–2, 208–9, 212–15, 217–18, 220–3, 225, 229–30, 235–7, 239–45
  authoritarian populism, 207, 221, 229, 231, 243
  classical populism, 196–7, 200–1, 207, 209, 212–13, 215
  ethno-national populism, 199
  European populism, 4, 20, 169
  Latin American populism, 3, 17, 20, 33, 189, 196
  left populism, 4, 16, 34, 56, 112, 118, 152, 159, 163, 172, 174–5, 177, 179–82, 190–1, 212–13, 218, 221, 240–1
  mass populism, 210
  'perma-populism', 243
  populisation, 17, 123, 235, 237, 242–4
  populism proper, 29–30
  populism studies, 41, 52–6, 59–61, 64–5, 70, 107–8, 113, 126–7, 169, 188, 208, 236, 241–4
  populisms in power, 18, 47
  populist authoritarian democracy, 29
  populist constitutionalism, 19, 207–8, 222–4, 226–31
  populist feminism, 190
  'the populist hype', 4–5, 27, 236, 243–4
  populist movements, 44
  populist myth, 172–3
  populist times, 52–3
  pre-populism, 29
  proto-populism, 29–30
  right populism, 54, 152, 163, 181,

191, 212, 216, 222, 240
  South American populism, 12
  transnational populism, 191, 201
  US populism, 13, 20
*populares*, 43
*populus*, 43–4, 131
Porta Caballé, A., 16
Porantiero, J., 189
Portugal, 209
postdemocracy, 117
Poster, M., 156
post-Fordist, 115
post-foundationalism, 15, 136, 162
post-industrialism, 128
post-Marxist, 126, 129–32, 134–5, 149
postmaterialist, 128
postmodern, 114, 149, 244
postnational, 1
post-politics, 149, 199, 241
post-truth, 141
Prague, 193
precariat, 116
premodern, 10, 136
Prestes Column, 196
proletariat, 11, 95, 217
  proletarianisation, 156, 160
Proust, M., 88
pseudo-people, 54

Quadros, J., 210–11
Quilombo of Palmares, 212
Quito, 195, 201

race, 130
radical democracy, 78, 149
  radical and plural democracy, 59
Rajoy, M., 75
Rancière, J., 2, 7–10, 15, 30, 42, 53, 67–70, 150

Ranger, J., 17
reactivation, 9, 96, 193
Reagan, R., 243
rebellion, 40
recession, 6; *see also* economic downturn, 4
re-democratisation, 210–11, 221–2
regime, 29, 33, 47, 57–61, 63, 68, 71, 107–9, 113, 173–4
Renaissance, 82
Rendueles, C., and Sola, J., 78
representative democracy, 32, 54, 65, 110, 120, 131, 188, 207
republic, 91, 95, 131, 211
republicanism, 190
Republican Party, 39
resilience, 18, 20, 169–74, 177–8, 180, 182, 184, 237, 242
revolution, 38, 59, 63, 82, 95, 97, 109, 131, 134, 140, 192–3, 195, 196
  Arab revolution, 192
  Mexican revolution, 196
  velvet revolution, 192
right(-wing), 53, 59, 61, 63, 121, 190, 219
  far right, 123, 143, 148–9, 230
  nativist right, 118
  neoliberal right, 162
  new right, 60
Riha, R., 192
Rinesi, E., and Muraca, M., 191
Robespierre, M., 65
Rodríguez López, E., 79
Roman republic, 42–5
romanticism, 88
Rosa, B., 17, 157–8
Rosanvallon, P., 42
Rossi, M. J., 191
Rousseau, J.–J., 43

Rousseff, D., 181–2, 208–9, 218–23, 226–31
rule of law, 29
rupture, 18, 20, 68–9, 78, 109–10, 116, 189, 197, 199, 201–2, 223
Russia, 35–8, 52, 119

St Petersburg, 35
Saint-Simon, H., 45, 241
Salinas de Gortari, C., 213
Sánchez de Losada, G., 176
Sanders, B., 13, 97
Sandino, A., 198
São Paolo, 181
Scandinavia, 123
Schmitt, C., 57
Schürmann, R., 86
Second Republic, 94
Second World war, 12, 29
sedimentation, 9, 96, 193
sedition, 182
Senate, 43
separation of powers, 29
sexuality, 137
Sferco, S., 191
Shakespeare, W., 75, 79
Silva, M. G., 218
Simondon, G., 154
Skinner, Q., 11
slaves, 198
social contract, 43
Social Darwinism, 41
social democracy, 33, 53, 58–9, 71, 94, 111, 243
socialism, 3, 29, 35–8, 63–4, 79, 148, 189, 192, 213, 241
Socialist Party, 181
Socialist Revolutionaries, 35
social media, 17, 113, 119, 123, 136, 148–9, 160–3

sociology, 20, 113
South America, 29, 169, 171–5, 177–8, 180–2, 184, 243
Soviet Union, 9, 35, 192
Spain, 5, 16, 75, 79, 91, 95–7, 111, 119
Spire, A., 192
Srnicek, N., 161
Standing, G., 116
Stavrakakis, Y., 190, 192
Steigler, B., 17, 153–5, 157
Structural Adjustment Programmes, 3
*Sumak Kawsay*, 199
Šumič, J., 192
Sweden, 52
  Sweden Democrats, 53
synchrony, 17, 126–30, 133
Syriza, 5, 31, 34, 112, 118

Tahrir Square, 119
Tea Party, The, 13
*techne*, 152
technics, 152–5, 158, 164
technocracy, 108, 149, 181, 184
technology, 16–17, 20, 38–9, 114–15, 126, 132–3, 135–6, 138–43, 149, 152–7, 160, 162
  technology studies, 20
technospheric, 17, 149, 152, 159–61, 163
teleology, 34
Temer, M., 220
terrorism, 37
Thatcher, M., 12, 118, 162, 243
Third Way, The, 118, 149
tidal, 3
time, 1–2
Toledo, A., 178
Tomsa, D., 173

Tormey, S., 16, 237–9, 242–3
totalitarian, 61, 63–6, 116, 192–3
transnational, 112, 143
Traverso, E., 192
Tribune of the Plebs, 43, 46
Trotskyist Marxism, 77
Trump, D., 5, 13, 31, 108, 110–11, 118, 121, 171
  Trumpism, 53
Twitter, 119
*Two Treatises of Government*, 35

Ukraine, 52, 119
*Uncle Tom's Cabin*, 235
undemocratic, 56–7, 61, 179
Union of South American Nations (UNASUR), 201
UKIP, 31
UK politics, 31
United States, 5, 13, 38, 52, 160, 195, 235
Urbán, M., 77
urbanisation, 28, 212, 215
Uruguay, 180–1
utopia, 20
  utopian, 87, 96
  utopian socialism, 88

Vargas, G.D., 3, 34, 207, 209–12, 215, 218, 222–3, 226–7, 230–1
  Varguism, 196, 215, 218, 227

Vázquez, T., 181
Venezuela, 171–2, 175, 177, 179, 193, 198, 213
Vilas, C. M., 190
Vistalegre, 77, 89, 91, 93
VOX, 95

Washington, 109
Washington Consensus, The, 3
wave, 4
Web 2.0, 160
Wellman, B., and Haythornwaite, C., 160
Westminster, 109, 120
Weyland, K., 170
Wilders, G., 111
will of all, the, 43
women's suffrage, 200
Woodford, C., 15
working class, 115, 140, 151, 189, 198, 200, 210, 212, 215–18, 223, 225, 235
  manual working class, 41
Wright Mills, C., 115

xenophobic, 191

YouTube, 160

Zapata, E., 198
Zemmour, E., 111, 121
Žižek, S., 89, 95, 189